HOW WE KEPT THE FLAG FLYING

HOW WE KEPT THE FLAG FLYING

THE STORY OF THE SIEGE OF LADYSMITH

By

DONALD MACDONALD

*The 'Melbourne Argus'
War Correspondent*

ILLUSTRATED

LONDON
WARD, LOCK & CO., LIMITED
NEW YORK AND MELBOURNE
1900

Published by Covos Books, 1999
87A Without Street, PO Box 6996, Weltevreden Park 1715,
Roodepoort, South Africa.

First published by Ward, Lock & Co., Limited. 1900

ISBN 0-620-22342-7

Cover design by Andy Taoushiani.
Cover copyright Covos Books cc.

Design and origination by Pointset 2000 (Pty) Ltd,
Randburg, South Africa.

Printed and bound by Color Graphic, KwaZulu-Natal,
South Africa.

A Covos Books' Anglo-Boer War Centenary Reprint
Series Edition.

ABOUT THE BOOK

How We Kept The Flag Flying is the exciting account of the Siege of Ladysmith.

It is eminently readable, intensely human, and is written with the journalist's eye for history in the making.

The author was in Ladysmith for the entire siege and witnessed first-hand the pathos and humour of a siege situation, cataloguing the effects of continual bombardment and ever-decreasing rations, coupled with the onset of the debilitating enteric fever.

He witnessed the battles and the hand-to-hand combat, personally accompanying many of the raiding parties.

This is not the official or military account of the event, but, instead, an unbiased observation by a man whose craft it was to report on the unfolding events of the world.

Although first published a century ago, the book is written with gripping immediacy and incisive insight.

It is a book for historians, collectors and first-time readers of the event. There are many in South Africa, Britain, Australia, New Zealand, Canada and Europe who, through those who went before them, are connected to these momentous events, which helped forge the course of history on this great continent.

How We Kept The Flag Flying is the first in a series of reprints published by Covos Books which celebrate the centenary years of the Anglo-Boer War.

Yours truly, Donald Macdonald

ABOUT THE AUTHOR

Donald Macdonald was born in Melbourne, Australia on 6 June 1859 and started his working life as a pupil-teacher, at the age of 17, before joining the *Corowa Free Press* and then, in 1881, the *Melbourne Argus*. He was nature writer and cricket commentator for both the *Argus* and the *Australasian*.

A selection of his nature writings was published as *Gum Boughs and Wattle Bloom* in 1887.

He was war correspondent to the *Argus* during the Anglo-Boer War. His book, *How We Kept The Flag Flying*, published in 1900, was born from his experiences during the siege of Ladysmith.

He went on to establish a weekly column in the *Argus* called "Nature Notes and Queries". It was extended to "Notes for Boys" in 1909 and led to the *Bush Boy's Book* in 1911, enlarged in four more editions from 1927 to 1933. Other writings included *At the End of the Moonpath* (1922), a nature book for children.

He died on 23 November 1932. A fountain, designed by Stanley Hammond, was erected in Macdonald Park, Beaumaris, in his memory.

AUTHOR'S NOTE

In this book I have attempted no specialist's description of the siege and battles of Ladysmith, but have given just the everyday impressions and sensations of an observer to whom war, with all its thrilling incidents and vivid volour, was a new and strange experience. It is not so much a history of the siege as a story of the siege written while the events were fresh in the mind. In a calm retrospective view much might be added, much omitted, but the complete military history of Ladysmith may be left to the historian and the expert. Without being consciously in error, I have sought to give the reader some idea of the moods and colour of the time. In the multiplicity of names there may be some confusion; thus I have spoken of the fight at Rietfontein as Tinta Inyoni, and of Wagon Hill as Cæsar's Hill, since local opinion always differed as to which was correct. With a full appreciation of the patriotism and pride of race which has made Australasia a fighting unit in the British Empire, I dedicate this book to my fellow-countrymen who took part in the South African Campaign

DONALD MACDONALD.

Melbourne, Aug. 6, 1900.

CONTENTS

PAGE

CHAPTER 1

NEWS OF BATTLE

The first news – The Boer invasion – Fight at Dundee –
Storming the heights – British artillery   1

CHAPTER 2

AFTER THE FIGHT

At Elands Laagte – The cavalry work – The wounded on
the field – The Boer losses – An international concert   7

CHAPTER 3

TO THE FRONT

By rail to Ladysmith – A natural citadel – The fight at Tinta
Inyoni – Shelling the Boers – Gloucesters in a hot corner –
Hospital work – Yule's retreat – The Fighting "Dubs" –
An Irishman's story   12

CHAPTER 4

THE BOERS CLOSING IN

The rush from Ladysmith – The *Powerful* guns – Long Tom o'
Pepworth's Hill – The ring closing – The river caves –
Echoes of fight   25

CHAPTER 5

ISOLATION OF LADYSMITH

The wires cut – Heavy cannon fire – Shell on the nerves – Testing
the investment – Early casualties – The luck of the
garrison – Realities of siege – The neutral camp   33

Contents

CHAPTER 6

BIRTHDAY CELEBRATIONS

The agreeable censor – The birthday salute – Shelling the town –
Fighting shadows – The plan that failed –
An inconclusive fight   43

CHAPTER 7

SIEGE IMPRESSIONS

The General's promise – A narrow escape – Spasmodic fire –
A reconnaissance – Settling Down – A night
bombardment   51

CHAPTER 8

THE LUCK CHANGES

A disastrous shell – Rumours of sorties – The silent guns – "The
March of the Cameron Men" – A doctor's tragic death – A midnight
scare – Football under fire – The passion for sport   58

CHAPTER 9

THE VAGARIES OF SHELL

Some narrow escapes – Firing on the Red Cross – The rival "snipers"
– The first woman wounded – A plucky spy –
The Liverpools suffer   69

CHAPTER 10

LAST DAYS OF NOVEMBER

An influx of blacks – More guns in action – Hints of hunger –
The intelligent horse – Foppish Boers – Casualties   79

CHAPTER 11

DAYS OF GLOOM

A siege menu – News from Mooi river – Hope deferred – Ungrateful
athletes – A disastrous day – For "Auld Lang
Syne" – A "die-hard" volunteer   87

Contents

CHAPTER 12

A NIGHT OF SORTIE

News of Buller – Mysterious preparations – Biltong – *The Ladysmith Lyre* – A dash for Long Tom – Blowing up a gun – Exultant volunteers   97

CHAPTER 13

A SURPRISE ON SURPRISE HILL

A night raid – Dilatory Hussars – A plucky Australian – A Boer letter – Physiology of funk – The rush on Surprise Hill – Deadly bayonet Work – A resentful enemy   109

CHAPTER 14

BLACK MONDAY IN LADYSMITH

Hope deferred – The distant guns – Enteric fever – A gloomy garrison – Bad news from the Tugela – The bombardment increases – A shell amongst the Carbineers   122

CHAPTER 15

WAR WITHOUT GLAMOUR

The Ladysmith oven – Dodging the shells – Burials after dark – Flies and mosquitoes – Our estimate of the Boer – Sickness and wounds – A threat of assault   130

CHAPTER 16

CHRISTMAS IN LADYSMITH

"A Merry Christmas" – The waits – A Christmas text – A Boer joke – Dead on the veldt – Hospital scenes – New Year greetings – Remarkable wounds – Commandeering supplies   138

CHAPTER 17

A DESPERATE ASSAULT

The Boers come on – The rush on Cæsar's Hill – Bravery of the Imperial Light Horse – The Manchesters' resistance – A stubborn enemy – The inopportune thunderstorm – Charge of the Devons – A costly fight   151

Contents

CHAPTER 18

AFTER THE BATTLE

The Gordon's loss – Incidents of the fight – A field of the dead – Greathead of the Guides – The Boer loss – Father and son – A stubborn foe – Why the attack failed   170

CHAPTER 19

THE GUNS ON THE TUGELA

Distant shell fire – Lyddite on the hills – The garrison underground – The town signals – Half rations   188

CHAPTER 20

IMPRESSIONS OF BATTLE

The folly of inaction – The first battle – A nasty few minutes – The impressive sequel – Conduct of the enemy – The lonely dead – Confusion of fight – How historians disagree – Night and the bayonet   194

CHAPTER 21

A TIME OF STAGNATION

Another disappointment – Reduced rations – A distant view – The Boer trek – Camps re-established – Signs of disaster – An exhausted garrison   209

CHAPTER 22

THE HORSE-MEAT ERA

Eating horse-meat – A black depression – The rush for rations – An expected assault – Bracing up the town – A faltering foe   217

CHAPTER 23

THE SIEGE ROUTINE

Tobacco famine – Commissariat trials – Cupboard love – Siege whist – The hundred days – A cricket message – Usury in trade – A contrast – Siege prices   225

Contents

CHAPTER 24

A TIME OF ANXIETY

Bird-seed porridge – The garrison meat bill – Preparing a welcome –
The Cossack post – A black night – The bridge builders –
Methodical Dutch gunnery   237

CHAPTER 25

NEARING THE END

A brave young surgeon – The rinkalse – Sir George White
and the garrison – Guns on the Tugela – "All going well" –
Quarter rations – Correspondents' luck   250

CHAPTER 26

THE END OF THE SIEGE

The great trek – How I saw it – A silver snake – A remarkable
retreat – Shelling Long Tom – Fine artillery work – Buller's
cavalry in sight – The rush to meet them – "Thank God we
kept the flag flying" – The fighting chiefs –
The fate of the flag   257

CHAPTER 27

AFTER THE RELIEF

A dead Boer – The toys of Umbulwana – Harassing the
rear-guard – A deserted camp – Mistaken for Boers –
A sailor's welcome   272

CHAPTER 28

ON TUGELA HEIGHTS

In the Dutch trenches – The Union Jack – Boer gun positions –
Where lyddite fell – A natural citadel – Gunner and priest –
A brave pair – An Englishman's experience – Good-bye
to Ladysmith   279

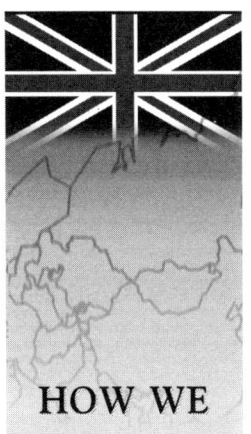

HOW WE KEPT THE FLAG FLYING

NEWS OF BATTLE

*The first news – The Boer invasion – Fight at Dundee –
Storming the heights – British artillery*

WHEN the S.S. *Australasian* left Albany and struck across the Indian Ocean, which is so rapidly becoming a great English lake, war had not been declared. A re-statement of peace terms was being sought, and for over a fortnight we on board speculated on the chances of peace and war. With head winds and seas for the greater part of the trip, the pace was slow, and instead of landing, as anticipated, on Wednesday, October 18, it was not until the following Saturday at noon that the high blue bluffs to the south of Durban entrance loomed up out of the thick grey haze, and we waited off the entrance with a tropical rain falling in cataracts. Those three lost days made a vast difference to some of us. On that day the second battle between the British and Boers had been fought at Elands Laagte; on the previous day a brilliant victory had been won by the Imperial troops at Dundee, a name rich in historic traditions to many who fought there. Durban was in a tumult of excitement, for the volunteers of the loyal little colony of Natal had borne themselves splendidly in the first deathgrip with the Boers, and in forty-eight short hours had built an obelisk in their history. The town teemed with refugees from the Transvaal and closer home. The Union steamer that dropped anchor alongside us in the Mozambique current was packed with the panic-stricken from Delagoa Bay, and steam tenders, black with passengers, were pouring their living freights into the big white Donald Currie liner that lay close by – all off for Cape Town or England.

These things told their own story long before the *Australasian* had dropped anchor, and we waited keenly expectant as a man-of-war's boat from H.M.S. *Tartar*, with a spruce, business-like lieutenant in the bows, came alongside on the look-out for contraband of war. "What's the news?" was shouted impatiently from the deck of the *Australasian*; "has there been any fighting?" The mystery of uncommunicativeness had fallen upon her Majesty's service, and the spruce flag-lieutenant said – nothing. A kindly purser put us out of misery with a bare hint that the Boers had been beaten near Glencoe on the previous day, and there was cheering, broken at intervals, when the crowd on one boat sang "Soldiers of the Queen," and it was caught up and echoed from another. It was sweet tidings, with a dash of bitter in it, for I had just missed it. Oriental-looking Durban, with its hosts of Hindoos and its hundreds of rickshaws, drawn by big Zulu boys – who were perhaps fighting the British themselves when last the town saw such excitement – was trying its best to meet the strain. The Johannesburg millionaires had first pick of the hotels, and the unfortunate traveller was lucky if he could get a chair for the night, not to mention such a luxury as a shake-down. When a town of 8 000 people suddenly takes in 17 000 extra there must be a crush.

It was known that the Boers had invaded Natal in three columns, the main column, under General Joubert himself, coming by Laing's Nek. Joubert's last message to the burghers had ended with the words, "I want you to be prepared for the worst," and at Dundee and Elands Laagte the worst was waiting for them in disaster and death. Though there were many complaints from refugees of injury and insult, this generally occurred with small parties of Boers, who were out of hand for the time, and General Joubert, in reproving some of his men for looting, said – "I will not allow robbery or plunder, and forbid any injury to be done to any private person."

One mistake of the British forces in the earlier wars with the Boers was not repeated this campaign. As the Boers advanced and the pickets and vedettes came into touch and exchanged shots they found no rooi batjes. The red coats, which blazed so vividly of old under the African sun, and made such a splendid target for sharpshooters, had disappeared. Whether English or African, volunteer or regular, the whole of the Imperial troops were in their favourite fighting khaki, the corps distinguished only by the smallest badges.

When Sir George White passed through with his Staff, all wore the familiar Stanley cap, and thus only were they distinguishable from the rest of the fighting force. Sir George White's eye brightened when he saw the Gordons, for years ago, when he was winning the V.C., his Afghan and Mutiny medals, and his Candahar star, he was for a time in command of them. Speaking of the Gordons, it is worth noting that very many of the men in South Africa took part in that famous rush on the heights of Dargai, made memorable amongst other things for the slogan of Piper Findlater –

> "When one with his legs shot under,
> Sat down 'mid the fire and thunder,
> And still, to the world's wide wonder,
> 'The Cock of the North' he played."

One thing noticeable in these highly-trained Indian troops was their fine mobility. Little time any of them wasted in Durban.

As the transports came down buoyantly on the Madagascar current, they were rushed alongside the wharves – the armoured trains were in waiting, and the style in which the chargers of the Lancers, Hussars, and Dragoons were swung from ship to truck was a perfect triumph in military transport.

At Dundee the Boers had advanced, halted – some say irresolute in their movements, and wishing for touch of the other columns, others that they merely wished to rest their horses after the forced march – and retreated, but before daybreak on Friday morning they backed up their threat of driving the British into the Indian Ocean with a decisive movement. Before dawn a picket heard men approaching quietly. They listened, found that they were talking Dutch, then challenged, and fired. A bare-headed vedette, who had lost his helmet in the brief exchange of bullets, rode in with the intelligence into the streets of Dundee, and the trumpets blared the assembly. The clatter of his horse's hoofs in the early morning, and the impetuous haste of the rider, telling that his mission was one of importance – the first note in the coming struggle for supremacy in South Africa, the revival of the old feud of the days of Blake and Van Tromp.

The Boers came on with the daylight in strong force, and the first intimation the British had of it was the whiz of shells from the Creuzot and Krupp field guns. From the first their fire work was erratic, and when it came to the artillery duel there was but one in it. It was not the armament, but the man behind the gun. Talana Hill, from which the Boers opened, is a kopje half-a-mile or so to the west of the town of Dundee – for there was something of a new Scotland about this place, with its Bannockburn and Craigieburn farms lying in the hollow. The Boers fired right over the town of Dundee, to pitch their shells into Glencoe camp beyond it, but their range-finding was bad at first. They picked up the range as the light improved, and several shells burst in a clear space in the centre of the camp, while another passed on the ricochet just over the horse-lines of the Natal Carbineers. Then the artillery duel blazed, and the people of

Dundee stood dazed in their own streets as the storm of iron passed overhead, battery answering battery from ridge to ridge, while the whirr of shell was varied by the burr of quail startled from cover by this tremendous din, the echoes of which lingered amongst the ridges.

In a few minutes the greatest battle in South African history was in progress, and the deadliness of the Imperial field guns was at once evident. The Boer artillerymen were silhouetted on the ridge against the bright sky-line. Soon their movements were more brisk, and little white puffs of smoke amongst them showed where the British shells were bursting. Nothing could withstand this deadly accuracy. The clamour of guns on Dundee ridge died down to a splutter, then to single shots, and the Boer artillery was silenced. They had had their answer. They had boasted of their artillery, and had bombarded the veldt sometimes short of the enemy's position, sometimes far beyond it, often wide, but seldom on it. The only Boer shell which really got close to the British battery after they opened, passed a little overhead. A body of Boer infantry tried to creep up on the right under shelter of some native kraals, but one of the batteries concentrated on the spot, and the enemy were driven back. Soon it was evident that the Boer infantry would make their stand on the summit of Talana Hill, and under cover of a tremendous artillery fire pushed to close range. Preparation was made for the crisis of the fight – the storming of the mountain.

It looked a desperate enterprise, for though a long plantation covered the approach for some time, the ground beyond was open and clear. General Penn Symons, the British commander, rode up under cover of the plantation, and gave directions for the final attack. It was there he fell mortally wounded by a shot through the stomach.

A mass of Boer infantry suddenly concentrated on the right of Talana, but as the mass came together the British shells were bursting amongst them again, and the terrible shrapnel drove them back. So well had the khaki blended with the surroundings that the British lines appeared to be painfully sparse, and to carry the crest in face of the Mausers of the ever-gathering clusters of Boer riflemen looked sheer suicide. About 600 yards from the top of the hill a stone wall ran parallel with the Boer position, and this was the first British objective. Under its cover they halted momentarily, while ever and again the Boer riflemen rushed to the crest of the hill, only to be driven back.

It is doubtful whether the best-trained European troops could, with more of heroism, have withstood the torrent of splintering shell that fell upon them. Hour after hour it had found them, till the sweat of the British gunners sizzled on their own gunbarrels, and still the Boers had to be beaten. Hurled back by the artillery, they rushed up to the crest to pour upon the advancing line of infantry the rifle fire in which they still believed themselves unequalled, while the Dublins and the Royal Irish answered with volleys that floated back across the open in a single crash, and must have been terribly demoralizing. There discipline and training told. The fall of many men in succession is bad enough, but when they go down in clusters no nerves can stand the strain. Behind the British fighting line was here and there a patch of brown, showing a khaki-clad soldier lying still.

For over six hours they had been fighting fiercely – the end seemed yet far off. The change came with a sudden forward dash of the 69th Battery. Like a flash they had limbered up, and galloping to short range, were in action again before the Boers on the hill-top seemed to realize the nature of the movement. The effect was instantaneous – the Boer exchanges slackened, and, noting the effect, the 13th was also brought up to short range. Silence fell upon them soon for want of a target, but sill the snappish bark of the Maxims served by the Dublins kept on. The last effort by the Boers was on the extreme left, where a group of them made a rush forward to a kopje. The shells of the 13th burst among them once again, and after eight hours' valiant fighting, British soldiers had won the first great battle of the campaign.

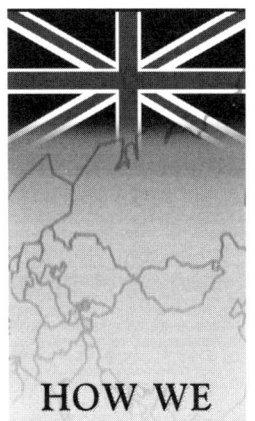

HOW WE KEPT THE FLAG FLYING

AFTER THE FIGHT

At Elands Laagte – The cavalry work – The wounded on the field – The Boer losses – An international concert.

AS this book is chiefly the story of a siege, I shall dwell but lightly upon a few incidents of the second fight at Elands Laagte, for the battle has been described in detail by many eye-witnesses, more skilled in war and its detail than an Australian novice, whose experiences of fighting had hitherto been confined to such a small bush affair as the destruction of the Kelly gang of bushrangers, or a second-hand recital of the revolt of the Ballarat miners at Eureka.

All night the wounded at Elands Laagte lay upon the field, for the last charge of the Lancers through the demoralized Boer ranks took place in actual darkness – so bad was the light, indeed, that one body of Boers mistook the cavalry for their own men, and the deadly lances were within forty yards of them before they realized their danger.

While to some extent indifferent to bullet wounds, the Boers have a deadly horror of steel – especially of the lance. Some of them fell upon their knees with uplifted hands, praying for mercy. "I have five children," screamed one of them. "For God's sake, spare me." The Lancer raised his point and passed on, but on turning saw the man he had spared in the act of reaching for a Mauser rifle. He turned back, ran him first through the muscle of the arm, as he sought to shield himself, and then through the body. "At the last moment, I tried to let off one poor devil who was white with fear," said a Lancer, "but my horse knew his business too well, and the lance-point found." One of the lance thrusts, after passing through the body of a Boer, pinned him to his own horse's neck.

Most of the British wounded were brought in during the night, but some of the Gordons, who had fallen just as they were charging home, had been overlooked. They lay along the rocky ridge, with the rain beating upon them, realizing to the full the horrors of war.

Boers brought in by the British ambulance expected to be treated fairly, but were for the most part astonished at the solicitude of their captors. Occasionally they presumed upon it, and at Ladysmith Camp some of the slightly wounded had to be brought to their senses at times at the point of the bayonet. One man from Johannesburg, who had been shot in the stomach, though in agony from his wounds, and drenched with the night rain, pleaded piteously that the ambulance men should not kill him. The poor fellow never realized how mistaken were his notions of British clemency, for he died on his stretcher while being carried into the hospital. Count Zepplein, a German whose father distinguished himself greatly in the Franco-German war, was found to be past all aid, for he had been shot in the head, and the bullet wound exposed the brain.

The dead remained upon the field until Monday, and the story of the fight with the advance of the different regiments of British infantry was sadly told by the bodies, some lying face down, as though peacefully asleep, others tortured and stiffened into strange attitudes, all gruesomely flat and shrunken, amongst the rocks. Near the crest of the hill, and close to the Boer position, the green kilts and brown jackets of the Gordons were lying thickly. Three officers and twenty-two men were buried there, and furthest into the medley of broken guns, dead Boers, and mangled horses, which marked their last stand, lay the body of Major Denne, a big, handsome fellow, who was shot through the body. As the Highlanders approached within fifty yards, the excited Boers stood up, and some even rushed forward to meet them, but the instant the Gordons brought their bayonets to the charge a panic seized the burghers, and they fled. Only a few dead Boers had the mark of the bayonet on them, but further on, where the Lancers came in on their flank, more had died from the thrust than the bullet. Many of them had loaded revolvers, but were so panic-stricken that they made no use of them, and sought only to dodge the lance-points. By Monday the Kaffir bands, whose kraals are scattered all over the veldt, had been looting the dead, and Mr. Brooks, a road superintendent, who with his Kaffir boys buried fifty-six Boers and forty-four British, found the bodies stripped of everything. The Kaffirs had hesitated in some cases about touching the British dead, though they had cut Major Denne's stars from his shoulders.

He must have been the last man killed before the enemy broke and fled, for none lay nearer the breastworks. With the suicidal chivalry which marked the British officers throughout the fight, he led on his men, disdaining cover, and this policy, brave though it may be, led to the loss of many gallant men in giving the Boers fair targets for their matchless marksmanship. No corps in the British camp at Ladysmith was so bitter against the enemy as the Gordons. It was evident even when they were bringing in the prisoners. One Pretorian sought to carry it off with a bragging air as they came into Ladysmith, but a big Highlander, with a flitch of bacon under his arm - a queer mixture of the fighter and forager – turned abruptly and struck him backhanded across the face, with a curt "Shet yer moo." The Boer shrunk up and was silent.

At the point stormed by the Highlanders most of the Boers were shot either through the chest or the lower part of the body, for even in that hurricane of death these well-disciplined fighters had kept the points of their rifles low. Their fighting was superb, and the Boers admitted it.

The compliment is the more genuine in that the quality of mercy is nŏt being strained by the Gordons. "I pit me bayonet through one big red-headed chap," said nuggety little Malcolm, of Perthshire, "an' I had to pit my foot ta his chest to poo' it oot." Nor were the Dublin Fusiliers over-nice with the enemy. Two of them at Dundee found a young Boer lying partly under an old man, who was dead, with a little heap of Mauser shells beside him. "What's the matthor wid ye?" said a big fellow. "I'm shot here," said the burgher, pointing to his right thigh. They searched for the bullet wound and found none. "Why, blasht ye, it's only shammin' ye are," said the Irishman, as he laid him out on the veldt with a heavy right-hander on the chin.

The tenacity of the Boers in adhering to denials of any great loss was illustrated while Mr. Brooks was still engaged in his sad mortuary task. He met a Dutch doctor on the field, and told him he had just buried twenty-two of his men in one grave and twenty-four in another, and offered to show him the spot. "You have made a mistake," was the reply; "these were not our dead, they were English. We had very few men killed." "He was the first man," said the impulsive Brooks, "who did not try to hit me when I called him a liar." Just then a Kaffir boy came up with ten dead Boers in his wagon. The doctor was obliged to admit that these were burghers, but he was not at all anxious to have proofs as to the identity of the others, by having any of the bodies raised from their shallow graves, though none the less anxious to obtain a description of the dead. As the burial party passed along the ridge Mauser rifles were lying everywhere, and the bolts were taken from them and thrown into the river.

A party of twenty-five, in galloping away for their lives, got separated from the commando and were met by Dr. Rupert Hornabrook, of Adelaide, who told them that the British had won the fight, and that they must accompany him as captives to Elands Laagte railway station which they did. The medical profession has already won much honour in the campaign. A week before, Dr. Buntine, of Maritzburg, was out with the Carbineers, who had a brush with the Boers, during which Lieutenant Gallwey, son of the Chief Justice of Natal, was taken prisoner. As the Carbineers retreated one of the trooper's horses fell, partly stunning him. Dr. Buntine, who is a Victorian, rode back under fire, and helped him to safety.

That racial hatred had not died with the second generation of burghers was shown by the fact that most of the Boers who fell at Elands Laagte were young men. The only white-haired man buried was the father of W. Blignaut, a champion South African athlete. The Boers declared that it was the riff-raff of their commandos – the larrikins of Pretoria and Johannesburg – who first broke and fled as the British infantry charged up the ridge, but once they began to run it soon became a rout.

On the eve of Elands Laagte, some of the Boers spent a merry evening with a number of Englishmen at the railway station. The first seen of them was a patrol of about forty, under Field-Cornet Pienaar, who seized the station and captured a mixed train that was just coming in. They behaved very decently afterwards. While waiting for General Kock, the field-cornet suggested that they might as well have a concert, and he asked an Englishman named Ganthorpe to play and sing – both Dutch and English joining in the chorus of "They All Take After Me." "It's a funny world," said the field-cornet. "Here are the Dutch and English at war, and we're all enjoying ourselves together."

On Friday night there were about 1 500 Boers at Elands Laagte, and early on Saturday morning the British made their appearance, and one of the first men killed was the sentimental field-cornet of the international concert. A shower of Lee-Metford bullets suddenly rattled upon the station buildings, and a party of Boers who were in barrack there rushed out. The field-cornet turned to see whence the shots came, and at that moment a bullet passed through his head.

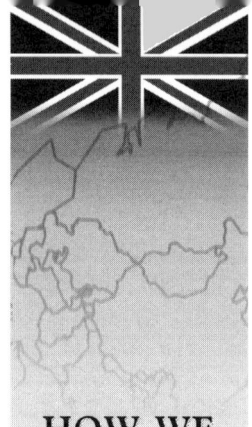

HOW WE KEPT THE FLAG FLYING

CHAPTER 3

TO THE FRONT

By rail to Ladysmith – A natural citadel – The fight at Tinta Inyoni – Shelling the Boers – Gloucesters in a hot corner – Hospital work – Yule's retreat – The Fighting "Dubs" – An Irishman's story.

WHILE casual and somewhat frenzied accounts of that brilliant little fight at Elands Laagte (pronounced Elandslockty) were still coming into Durban, I caught the evening mail train on Monday, and started for the front. Martial law had just been proclaimed in Durban, the military authorities had seized the South African Bank, and the town was simmering with excitement. One could not even buy a Webley revolver without going through a long licensing ceremony before a magistrate, so that in the event of the weapon being found either in the possession of a Zulu boy, a Kaffir, or a Boer the ownership could be traced. Up a narrow-gauge line with sharp curves, on to cool hills covered with the broad wind-frayed fronds of miles of plantains and bananas, broken by occasional patches of mealies, pine-apples, and paw-paws, the Kaffir mail climbed slowly. The quaint little

Mozambique monkeys darted through the low oak-like trees, and bigger apes scampered scolding to the shelter of rocky ledges.

Every country has its characteristic odour, and that of the colony of Natal, and especially the far-out towns, is as distinctive, as indescribable, as penetrative, but barely so pleasant, as the characteristic scent of old Murray pine. It began at Durban; it lasted to Ladysmith. The ordinary seats in the Natal trains were converted into sleeping cars by the addition of a rug and pillow. There was not much sleeping though. At every station the excitement burned. Towards morning one was awakened by a storm of groans, a shout of "Ha, you German dogs," and we were in a siding to make way for a special with one hundred and ninety-six Boer prisoners on their way to the Maritzburg Gaol. The captives were either asleep or pretended sleep, and beyond an occasional sickly smile, took no notice of the hooting.

Just at daybreak the train ran into Ladysmith, a scattered town, enclosed in an amphitheatre of rocky hills.

One had hardly set foot on the platform at Ladysmith in the grey of the early morning, before he found that something special was pending. All through the British lines there was a stir. The army mule, in teams of ten, and driven with wonderful skill – and a long whip – by shouting Cape boys, was everywhere mixed up with long trains of long-horned, black, scraggy bullocks clogging the streets. To reduce this chaos to order was the work of the Army Transport Corps – a flesh-wearing, brain-racking problem in organization. This army train seemed to loosen itself to disorder in the early morning, the strange shouting of the Cape boys, Kaffirs, Zulus, and Indians making it a scene utterly opposed to all preconceived notions of a British column waking up to duty – and possibly to death. Later it formed itself slowly into a train, and went through a gap in the hills, out over the rolling veldt – a train miles long it seemed, and so unwieldy that one could understand the ease with which a routed enemy's baggage may be cut off and captured by cavalry.

This stir was the visible sign of probable conflict, and it was not without reason that it was being sent out this burning hot morning. The Boers routed at Elands Laagte on Saturday had reappeared in greater strength, having been reinforced by another commando at a point at least seven miles nearer Ladysmith. Rietfontein, a farm owned by Mr. Pepworth, a member of the Natal Parliament, had been seized and looted by them on the previous evening. Early that morning an Afrikander lying hid in a reedy spruit had watched one of the Boer commandos taking strong position on the crest of a round scrub-capped hill. As they would have to come into the open approaching Ladysmith, there was little fear of the Boers leaving this position, but the necessity of stirring them up arose from the fact that their left was in touch of the road between Ladysmith and Dundee, along which Yule's column was retreating.

Horses were at a premium, though Boer mounts and Basuto ponies were obtainable in Ladysmith on the morning after Elands Laagte at prices ranging from a sovereign to a box of cigarettes. For one brief half-hour I was flattered by the hope of getting a pony, owned by a missing officer of Hussars, one of the finest polo-players in the British army, but another officer had first call, and he called. There was nothing for it, therefore, but to try Australian legs over the rocky South African veldt on a day that made marching to flaccid muscles anything but a luxury. Earlier in the morning one heard that the fight pending would be greater even than Dundee or Elands Laagte, for the Boers were in greater strength and a stronger position. But Sir George White had concluded that beyond shaking the abundant self-confidence of the Boer, giving him another taste of his doom, and weakening his contempt for British soldiers, there was nothing to be gained in driving them from positions which the victors were not desirous to hold, and which could be reoccupied by the enemy on the following day.

Elands Laagte was a brilliant fight. Even people on the scene had hardly realized how brilliant, but the position was won only to be abandoned, and where was the good of repeating the assault? Unless the Boers came out into the open they were only to have another taste of artillery. Sir George White, having found by reconnaissance that the enemy had taken possession of two green hills, or kopjes, commanding the road, determined to dislodge them. The enemy's position as it faced us, consisted of a series of five hills. On the extreme right was a grassy hill, without scrub, its flat top inclining slightly towards the British lines, and known as Tinta Inyoni. Next to it, and further away, was a lower hill, gently rounded, while in the foreground was a little hill, not more than a hundred feet high, and directly behind it a tableland mountain, the crown of which was fringed round with thick scrub, like a monkish tonsure. It was a tremendously strong position, which could only be carried with great loss of life on the part of the assaulting column. Between it, and separated by a deep gully, was another high and long hill, end on to us. The British advance was over a slightly rolling grassy veldt, and everything in front looked peaceful and pastoral – not a man in sight upon any of the hills, though a farmer lying in shelter that morning had watched one body of the enemy, and by counting one hundred men and guessing the others in groups of about the same size, had calculated that there were 1100 riflemen in this one position.

Their front covered several miles, for it is an old fighting plan with the Boers to extend thus, and it had the great advantage, from their point of view, that, even if driven out, it was utterly impossible for cavalry to outflank and punish them with the lance, as at Elands Laagte. The course, dry grass crackled with the rustle of hay under the feet of the British infantry, and had something of the scent of a newly-reaped wheat-field. Occasionally from a reedy watercourse a little brown buck, not much larger than a hare, bounded out – three low bounds and then a high one – while small black birds, with long streaming tails, like a bird of paradise, rose, complaining, in front of the column. The scarlet Natal lily spotted the hill-sides, the bright chalice of the flower a refuge for scores of golden-green beetles. Underfoot large brown spiders were rolling small balls of earth, reminding one something of the circus acrobat and his globe-walking. All the highlands in front of us, from the green hills of the foreground upon which the British assault was directed, to the towering and distant Drachenbergs, were convulsed and torn in every conceivable outline, reminding one of the serrated ruggedness of the Grampians of the Western district, but of nothing else in Australia. Nowhere one of our own conical peaks, or nicely-rounded and timbered ranges: nowhere any of that beautiful blue haze that so softens our mountain distances.

Suddenly from the green hill on the right, geographically described as "two miles south of Modder's Spruit," came a spluttering crackle of Mausers, but nowhere a sign of smoke. The 19th Hussars, who were feeling the way, were within the danger zone, and for the first time I saw the British soldier under fire. Immediately upon the heels of the rifle fire came the bursts of white smoke along the high central ridge, showing the position of the Boer artillery, and in a few minutes puffs of smoke around about the Hussars and the artillery showed where their shells were bursting. They picked up the range quickly, and the accuracy of their shrapnel fire declared at once that the Free Staters were better gunners than those of the Transvaal who fought at Dundee.

The British artillery swung their guns into action with the splendid promptitude of the highly-trained Indian troops, but before they could do so three or four of the gun horses were hit, and a couple of gunners wounded. One thick-set Tommy, as he ran past with a couple of brass-capped shells, cried out, "This is the medicine for 'em, Beecham's pills – a 'ole box-full given away," and he affectionately kissed the shell, which the next instant was bursting over the heads of the crouching Boers on the hill-top. As he ran from the limber with the next charge he suddenly said "Oh!" and fell – the red, white, and blue shell he carried rolling away down the slope – the one spot of colour in the green landscape. The gunner was dead with a Mauser bullet through his mouth. A few of the earlier shots struck before exploding, and threw up columns of red dust, but once the range was picked up the fire was deadly. All along the crown of the hill the white puffs showed more thickly, the explosive in the shells making a much denser cloud of smoke than the cordite at the gun's muzzle – a yellowish haze, through which the spirts of flame after a moment showed.

In about twenty minutes the Boer guns slackened, and then the fighting line of the infantry was brought up, and for a time their volley fire was the dominant note of the fight, though the men themselves, especially when prone, could be scarcely seen against the brown veldt. One or two of the wounded whom I saw here had been simply raked by the bullet as they were lying down. One poor fellow of the Devons came strolling out of the din, both hands held helplessly before him, and the front of his brown tunic smeared with blood from the neck down. I asked him where he was hit, and he held out his hands with a Mauser bullet-hole through each palm. "One were damn bad," he said, "but it were dog's luck to ha' both hit." There was very little crying out from the wounded, some of whom as they dropped gave a sudden gasping respiration, and that was all. Wonderful things happen in battle. Excited men are hit, and, quite unconscious of it, go on fighting. One incident of this fight was too surprising for fiction – it could only happen in fact. A private of the Natal Mounted Rifles had his horse shot, and the rider cried out, "I'm hit." "Nonsense, man, it's only your horse," said a comrade, and the man, accepting the assurance, went on fighting. He returned to camp with his corps, strolled about the town in the evening, suffered a good deal during the night from what he called spasms, and only next morning found that a Mauser bullet had gone clean through his body. Then he collapsed, and was taken to the hospital.

Occasionally the spitting whistle of a Mauser bullet came to us over the fighting line, but the real ordeal to nerves for the first time strung to the sounds of battle was the whiz of the sharp-edged splinters of shrapnel. One shell burst close to a group of mounted war correspondents, whose horses at once lost all sense of self-respect and plunged wildly. The confusion was emphasized by the fact that the field batteries at the same instant came tearing round to a new range. One correspondent was dismounted, and as he ran to get out of the way he slipped and fell. It looked as though nothing short of a miracle could save him from being crushed to death, but the R.A. are wonderful drivers, and when the guns passed he was safe. *Mental Note.* – If one finds oneself suddenly in the way of a galloping battery, the better plan is to stand still, and trust to the drivers.

From the accuracy with which the first of the Boer shells was planted there is very little doubt that, anticipating an attack that day, they had, either during the night or in the early dawn, carefully measured the ground, and fixed definite range points. Heavy casualties in the Gloucester regiment were due to their literally marching into a death-trap – an accident that in broken country so well known to the enemy is likely to be only too frequently repeated before the close of the war, and as a matter of history was sadly repeated in the case of the Gloucesters at Nicholson's Nek. It was after the Boer artillery had been silenced, and while the Royal Artillery field guns were shelling the face of Tinta Inyoni mountain, to cover the British infantry approach, that a company of the Gloucesters, in fighting formation, marched up a steep hill, from which it was thought they would have an advantageous position for rifle fire on the retiring enemy. Suddenly a strong body of Boers, who had been hidden behind the crest of the ridge, fired a slaughtering volley at not more than two hundred yards, and thirty men of the Gloucesters fell either dead or wounded. That one volley accounted mainly for the six men killed and sixty wounded, which was the sad official record of the brave Gloucester boys, saddest of all being the death of their commanding officer, Colonel Edward Percival Wilford.

The loss of the Boers in killed, if not in wounded, was certainly heavier than ours, for they went down chiefly to shrapnel, which wreaks havoc on the human frame harder to heal than the little punctures of the Mauser. So strong was their position at the point where the Gloucesters were ambushed, that Sir George White sent the Liverpools and King's Royal Rifles with the Natal Mounted Rifles to outflank and carry it, and they did it under a heavy fire.

It was about noon when the Boers began to give way on the coveted position next the road, and most of them on their left were screened in their retirement by intervening high ground, but in the centre there was a perfectly open flat. The British shells had fired the grass on the right, and the flames were creeping in between the Boer advanced lines and their base, two of the hills being already burned black. Suddenly, from a little hill that seemed quite incapable of sheltering so many men, about one hundred mounted Boers, the last of the advanced lines, went scampering back to safety. Puffs of white smoke suddenly appeared here and there amongst the galloping horses, showing where the R.A. were planting their shrapnel, timed to the bursting with perfect accuracy. It was a moving target, but they were on it all the time.

The last act in the fight was the long-range shelling of the Boer position, and though a great many of them must have been killed, both then and during the earlier fight, it was impossible to calculate their losses, and Tommy Atkins's estimate of the enemy's loss is ever sanguine as sanguinary. Having accomplished the object upon which they set out, to facilitate the junction of the two columns, the British force retired to Ladysmith. No conception of war is complete until one has watched its painful sequel – the bringing in of the wounded and the burial of the dead. The central British field hospital was the Town-hall, Ladysmith, where the Red Cross, the emblem of all that is beautiful and beneficent in warfare, floated from the tower. All round there was the reek of iodoform, and as the first of the wounded were brought in one heard the groans of a Boer, who had had three shots in the thigh, and was having the bullets extracted. There was no other sound as the sisters and white-aproned dressers moved from bed to bed. The wounded were brought in dhoolies or stretchers, hooded over with green canvas, to keep off sun and rain, and suspended from a bamboo pole carried on the shoulders of four black bearers, who, taking short, quick steps, did their work with wonderful gentleness, and scarcely any oscillation of the cot. As the wounded arrived a dapper, thick-set surgeon lifted the hood of each dhoolie, with a cheery, "Well, my lad, what's the matter with you?" Some explained, others feebly pointed to the locality of the wound, or the card attached by the field ambulance men. One had a bullet through the middle of the foot, and he and others lightly wounded waited their turn, or were carried away to the pavilion hospitals, while the more serious cases were taken first.

One lingered longest at the Boer hospital, where amongst the eighty wounded, who occupied a line of tents, one got a good idea of the Boer soldier, three wagon-loads of whom, wounded at Elands Laagte, had been coolly sent in to Ladysmith for treatment. The Boer professes a contempt for the British soldier, but has the greatest possible faith in the British surgeon. His ambulance, like most of his army appliances, were commandeered, and two of these were the delivery vans of business firms in Johannesburg. A noticeable point was that a great many of the Boers wounded at Elands Laagte had been shot through the left arm, presumably while they were in the act of aiming. Save in that nearly all wore cord riding breeches, broad felt hats, and black or brown leggings, there was no uniformity in cut or colour. Some few had soiled hat-bands, the original colour of which was barely determinable, and this seemed to be the only corps or regimental badge. "How are they treating you?" I asked one young fellow who strolled down to the church gate, where a sentry of the Manchester regiment kept guard. "Oh, pretty well, considering everything," he answered in perfect English, and from the freedom with which they chatted with the visiting officers, few of them had need of the official language of the South African Republic to make themselves understood. Most of them were young fellows, and, save for the wounds, a very slight stretch of the imagination was required to fancy them a camp of Australian shearers waiting for a shed.

There, as at Dundee and Elands Laagte, the Boers fought bravely, and the retirement of the Dundee column strengthened them in the assurance with which they set out, of dancing in Maritzburg in a few days. It was a remarkable retreat, though the marching was, the Fusiliers say, less difficult than in the Soudan. There they knew exactly were they would find the foe, and here they looked for him in every spruit and kopje, for they were passing through a country infested with the enemy. Once a body of them were sighted marching down a valley, and apparently unconscious of the proximity of the British column. The field guns were promptly taken up a ridge, and, burning with a desire to be at them again, the light-hearted gunners waited for them to come and be killed. Probably their scouts caught a glimpse of the column, for greatly to the disappointment of the Royal Artillery, nothing more was seen of them.

I shall never forget the appearance of that column as it came into Ladysmith – the gallant Fusiliers, conspicuous by the square green badges on their helmets, having the place of honour as rear-guard. The khaki had changed in colour from a yellowish-brown to dirty red, and upon officers and men alike were brown blotches of mud, where they had thrown themselves upon the miry ground whenever the whistle sounded for the brief five minutes' rest. "Good luck to you, boys. We're glad to see you safe back," shouted the crowds on the path-ways, and at intervals cheers were given for the fighting Fusiliers. "I suppose you can do without work for a day or two," I said to one stalwart, who, with a click of the brogue, answered, "Shoore, we're as fit as fiddles, and whin we get about three pints o' beer in us we're ready to go out again to-morrow." There was no difficulty about the first pint, and though, from the point of view of the moralist and teetotaller, it may be a saddening admission, yet the fact is borne in upon one every day, that next to the British flag and the honour of his corps, the thing that stands highest in the estimation of Tommy Atkins is beer. You may praise him, and cheer him, but if you wish to find your way straight into his good graces, make it beer.

The more one heard of Dundee the more fully he realized the gallant part played by the Dublin Fusiliers. They went into action at short notice, some of them having gone out for running exercise a few minutes before the fight began. As they lay in the shelter of the plantation the General said, "That hill must be taken." "The Fusiliers will do it, sir," said Captain Connors, and the Fusiliers did it grandly. A little knot of men got ahead of the main line, racing for first with the Royal Irish, and had they lived to reach the ridge, there must have been Victoria Crosses for some of the Fusiliers. But all save one man, who owed his life, perhaps, to the fact that he missed his foothold and fell, died near the summit. Captain Connors fell as he was leading his men up a slope, so sharp that they had at times to hold on to the grass tussocks. "Go on, boys," he said, "I'll see you to-morrow." And he will see them, perhaps, on that to-morrow when the Dublins answer the bugle-call for the last parade, for the brave Irish captain died with a bullet through his body on the man-sown slope of Talana.

A funny account of a tragic affair is that afforded by a little Irish private of the Fusiliers, authenticated by his captain, who laughs every time the incident is mentioned. "I kem up to a house," he said, with a broad smile on his brown, corrugated face, "and there was a Boer back to me, wid his rifle pushed through a hole in the stone wall. I brang me rifle to the ready and sez, 'Hello, me man,' and the sick luk uv him ud make an army mule laf. 'Dhrop it,' I sez, 'and turn out your pockets, or I'll blow a hole a-through you.' Gar, an' he dhropped it quick, and the little wee shee slide thing wid the ind o' the bullets pushed into it. 'I've got more cartridges in me overcoat,' he sez; 'wait an' I'll get it.' 'Nivvor mind yer overcoat,' I saz, 'but come wid me,' an' I gev him over to the corporal, an' tuk his horse to ride, an' there was the captain behoind me, laughin' fit to split. I wint into the house, an' there was the owner sittin' quiet, radin' the paper, an' not knowin' there was a sojer near him. 'How dar ye come into my house?' he sez. 'Nivver moind argyin',' I sez, and I wint rumagin' about, pokin' a clane handkerchief into the sleeve o' me tunic, an' fittin' on the pick o' three waterproof coats. Whereivvor I wint he kem walkin' behind sayin', 'Oh, there's nothin' there; there's nothin' there at all.' 'Will you go out the door,' I sez, losin' me temper, 'or will you go in bits up the chimbly?' Anyways I had no luck. I thried three overcoats for nothin', and wan o' the Lancers got a hatful o' money in the only wan he went troo. Don't be talkin' about overcoats." It is a pity to have to tell the sequel. The desire for loot was so strong upon the bold Fusilier that next day he was found in an officer's tent, whisky, it was believed, being the object of the raid, and "clink" the sequel.

A few days later came the sad news of the death of Major-General Penn Symons, shot through the stomach at Dundee. It was wired through in sympathetic terms by General Joubert, who closed, however, with a note from the string upon which the Boer perpetually harps: "It is a pity so brave a soldier should have lost his life in an ungodly war promoted by capitalists." General Symons was shot just after leaving the cover of a plantation, when riding with Colonel Dartnell and his staff. He made no attempt to conceal his position, for wherever he rode on the field he was followed by his orderly, carrying a lance and red pennant, and as most of the better class of Boers had good field-glasses, there would be no difficulty in picking him out. Just as he was being carried off the field, he passed a line of infantry, and said, "Go on, my lads; you are fine fellows, all of you;" then to an officer, "Tell General Yule of my wound. Say that it is but slight, and I shall be out again in a day or two." He had declared on seeing the precipitous slope of the Boers' position just before the fight began, "We shall show them now that British soldiers can scale a mountain as steep as Majuba in face of the fiercest Boer fire."

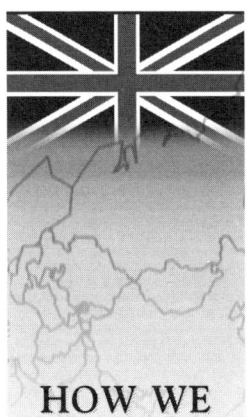

HOW WE KEPT THE FLAG FLYING

CHAPTER 4

THE BOERS CLOSING IN

The rush from Ladysmith – The Powerful guns – Long Tom o' Pepworth's Hill – The ring closing – The river caves – Echoes of fight.

THE engagement of October 30 had, from the military point of view, one good effect on Ladysmith. It cleared the town of its human refuse – the mass of Hindoos and unattached Kaffirs who form such a very large share in the population of Natal, and will one day, I have no doubt, furnish it with its great social and political problem. The Asiatic was prominent in this railway rush. He carried with him as much of this world's goods as he could bundle together. He was wildly excited, and the more congested the crowd the more he chattered, and the faster he ran. There were three trains – the carriages filled with white women and children, the open trucks packed thickly with Kaffirs and Hindoos. White men who wished to go, and in many cases were ordered to go, stood back in despair or shame from this shrieking horde, steaming in the hot, thunderous Natal night, for they felt their manhood would have been smirched by flight in such company. The native police rounded up the blacks like sheep, and packed them as sheep are rarely packed, prodding them on with their knobkerries, while the seething mass inside protested in vain. It was a strange sight – on a smaller scale resembling the flight from Johannesburg, where, I am told, some of the miners behaved in a way that will make them a by-word and a shame on the Rand for many a long year to come. They forced themselves into the trucks set apart for women, trampled upon them, thought of nothing but the safety of their own miserable skins, and for such human garbage were brave men in British uniforms wasting their lives by the kloofs and kopjes of Natal. It was a novel sight, and yet a noble one, to see English officers giving drink from their own flasks to some of these miserable refugees at Ladysmith station, who were first dripping in the tropical heat of the oven-like town, then drenched with night rains on the colder uplands. Coming back from all this scare and clamour, I passed a little dhoolie-bearer, resting on the kerb and absorbed in playing an English marching air, "The Lincolnshire Poacher," on a mouth harmonicon – calmly self-confident in his association with the soldiers of the Queen, lifted by the magic of discipline and duty from a craven to a man. The white man sometimes does much for the black when he admits him to a companionship of arms, and when the dhoolie-bearer trots after British regiments into the front of fire, the black man does something in return for the white. During the quiet of Tuesday and the armistice of Wednesday the scare grew instead of subsiding. Rumours clashed and congested. The Boers were mounting guns upon many commanding points; the town would be at their mercy. It was noticed that officers were sending their wives and families down to Maritzburg; an excusable precaution after all, for no woman except those brave army nurses should have been left in the town; but it gave fresh impulse to the rush, and on Wednesday night there was again a trying scene at the railway station. Many women were carried in on stretchers, utterly collapsed under the strain, often screaming hysterically. Too often men showed an utter want of thought or sympathy in talking of the possibilities in the presence of woman. These were usually the men who wanted the Boer position stormed at once, and wondered why the Devons were not allowed to do it when they volunteered. In some cases husbands were begging their wives to go, and the wives just as stoutly refusing. "I'll stay by you, whatever comes," I heard one old lady say to her entreating husband, "and God's will be done." Few were so bravely confident, and until the trains of refugees had started on their uncertain journey, with a pilot engine ahead, and all chance of leaving for that day had gone, the scene was on a lesser scale than the one of Waterloo described in *Childe Harold's Pilgrimage*. Those who had been most contemptuous of the Boer a month ago now most feared him. In the town on Wednesday night few people had much to say. They sat in little knots, for the most part gloomily reflective.

Two more guns from the *Powerful* were being hurriedly placed in position and ballasted with 10 in. shot. The Boers, who seemed familiar with our every move, and had no doubt many spies in the town, sent in to say that if lyddite were used there would be reprisals, and the town would be shelled. On our side it was rumoured that if the enemy refrained from pitching shells into the town, and fought a fair artillery duel, the terrific lyddite would not be fired. The whole country around looked so calm and peaceful before sundown on Wednesday, November 1, that it was difficult to believe that war was only in suspense. Our Naval Reserve were dragging a 4.7 in. Armstrong to a convenient hillock for mounting, and the Boers were steadily bracing up their dreaded Long Tom with further earthworks. They imagined that a little tree to the right the gun helped our range-fingers, so it was cut away, but the mound of earth made a target quite conspicuous enough. At daybreak on the morning of Thursday, November 2, the thunder of the guns began. As I dressed hurriedly and ran to the crest of the hill outside the town to watch the big gun duel, a mass of splintered shell came hurtling over the camp and took the leg off an unfortunate

Kaffir who was standing in the main street. Yet the Boers were not really shelling the town, and even then, after two days of the bombardment, I doubt whether they had really tried to plant a single shell amongst the private houses. Before I had reached the crest of the ridge a large portion of the base of a

"Ware 'Long Tom'!"

shell fell within a few yards of me. It was really being fired at our 4.7 in. on the opposite slope, but the ground there was so stony that plugged shell, instead of burying itself as in the soft alluvial by the river side, broke into splinters that searched the whole face of the hill, and glancing obliquely off the rocks were very dangerous. It was difficult to find cover from such a fire – as difficult almost as with the shrapnel bursting overhead, where the best shelter is a cleft between two rocks, just wide enough for one to tuck himself in. There was no need of instructions to lie close, for one becomes particular both as to his precautions and his company under fire. I heard one officer fuming because Steevens, of the *Daily Mail*, was riding a dapple grey stallion, very showy and handsome to look at, but a conspicuous mark. A considerate Tommy kindly suggested that my own blue shirt was not exactly the approved fighting colour. The Boers adepts as they are at taking and keeping cover, had a great many grey horses, and sometimes at a distance it was hard to believe that one was not watching Kaffir cattle – owing to the prevalence of the greys, to which Colonel Price so much objects.

Our fellows had nothing but the best of Thursday morning's duel. The Boers had their Long Tom; we the 4.7 in. and the two long-range naval 12-pounders that harassed them so much on Monday. The Boers ignored the smaller guns, and concentrated their fire on our largest. The object of the 12-pounders seemed to be to pitch their shells short and rattle the enemy's gunners with the forward rake of their shell, when the larger gun went pounding straight at it. The firing on both sides was first-rate, the line of the shots being splendid, but the nicest calculation in elevation was required, for anything low flew off the face of the hill, while a shell the slightest bit high went down the receding slope behind and burst far in the rear. In this they had the best of us, for while our over-pitched shells were lost, theirs became a menace to the town. Several shells burst right round our 4.7 in., and three of the naval men were badly hit, two being carried off with shattered legs, while a third was mortally hit in the groin. It seemed to me that they were contemptuous at times in exposing themselves, for if they were nearly finished loading, they went on with the work, even though the shell from the enemy's gun was then in air coming for them. The Boers were more careful, though there was dare-devilry on both sides. Once I saw through the glass five Boers in their shirt-sleeves step from cover, and with their hands on their hips watch their shot, but the instant the spirt of flame came from our gun they disappeared like rabbits in a burrow. Counting quickly one could get to twenty from the time the flash of their Long Tom was seen until the shell reached us. By breakfast-time they had temporarily silenced our best gun, and they wound up with three shells on the outskirts of the town, where the squat green tents of the volunteer brigade made a tempting mark. Fortunately the shells burrowed there, and did little damage.

Before noon on Thursday there was the roar of cannon on three sides of the town. North-west of us was Pepworth's Hill, where Long Tom held sway; north-east of us, and four miles away, was Umbulwana – a somewhat reduced Mount Macedon – to the top of which the Boers had, in the teeth of incredible difficulties, dragged a gun. It was a splendid position for shelling both the camp and the town, and from there they opened on us about noon on Thursday. It may seem strange that Sir George White had left such commanding positions to the enemy, but with his lesser force it was quite impossible to occupy them in strength, and lightly held they were certain to be isolated. The trouble was that the mobile Boers moved about so rapidly that many points were threatened in quick succession, and the defensive ring required to be as compact as possible.

Early in the forenoon of Thursday the cannonade to southward became so heavy that it looked as though a serious attack were being made from that direction. Riding out, I found that a body of volunteer mounted rifles had marked down a party of Boers quietly breakfasting in a hollow, and, creeping up, had poured a destructive volley into them. Once again the Boer proved that he is rarely a craven. This party, instead of scattering, ran to their field guns, and got them into action so quickly that the volunteers had to retire, and lose no time about it. For some time from opposing ridges they kept up a duel with our guns, but no great damage was done. I saw one Lancer lying on the veldt with a Mauser bullet through the back of his head, and his horse grazing near. He was both alive and lively, and the astonishing thing is the little harm done by a Mauser or Lee-Metford bullet in the upper part of a man's body, unless it happens to touch one or two really vital points. I was under cover that morning with an R.A. gunner, who looked the picture of health and vigour. Yet at Elands Laagte a Mauser bullet had gone into the left of the heart, and passed out under his shoulder-blade. He was barely fit for duty, but had come out of hospital to get off the sick ration.

To southward of the town the Klip river ran close under the hills, and there, in the soft banks, hundreds of the residents of Ladysmith had dug out caves – a splendid protection from shrapnel, unless fired directly from southward. With so many women and children, it looked at first like a large picnic party, save that every moment squadrons of Lancers, Hussars, and mounted infantry came down to water their horses under cover of dense milk-bloomed syringas. There were other sights and sounds offensive to the Peace Congress. Drivers of the R.A. galloped out with spare horses to supply the place of some of their gun team that had been hit, and – most lamentable proof of the horror and reality of war – a little party of infantry with arms reversed were marching out, and lying upon stretchers, wrapped in the British ensign, were two who would no more waken to the *réveillé*. They were shot through the stomach – where perforations are fatal – and had lingered on for days. "We have many cases of bullet wounds through the lungs," Dr. Hunter said to me. "There is a little hæmorrhage, but they soon begin to look all right again." One man brought in on Monday had eleven holes in him, five of them exit. Brave Lieutenant

Meiklejohn, of the Gordons, who won the Victoria Cross, was hit in six places. He had two shots through his body and three through his forearm, while the sixth took off one of his fingers. He was the first man up the heights of Dargai, and was well in front at Elands Laagte when he fell. Lightly built, and somewhat effeminate-looking, there was nothing of the bravo about him. But men fight in all shapes and sizes. Another of the Gordons who won distinction was Bugler May. There was a time in the hot fight when the Manchesters wavered – not for want of courage, but because some one had by mistake or through excitement sounded the retire, and Tommy Atkins, though he will go anywhere when well led, is not good at retiring. Bugler May saw them falter, so he blew their regimental call, then the "Forward," and finally the "Charge." "You are a brave lad," said the adjutant, who rode up and took his name.

If the Boer had all the worst of the artillery fire in the first fights, he paid us back in our own coin. From two points of the compass he was pitching shells, and one's nerves were always on the tension with the bursting of shrapnel. The outer camp lines or the masses of army stores near the railway station received most attention, and we were powerless to silence them. Most of our shells were grape or round leaden bullets; theirs, ring shell or plates of metal, thinly attached, and which flew apart on the explosion, the sharp edges making wounds of the most horrible nature. Sometimes when our shrapnel burst directly overhead, the Boer marksman died hardly knowing what hurt him.

Thus they found on Monday a rifleman lying in a little stone enclosure. The barrel of his Mauser was still thrust through the aperture he had made for it, and his cheek lay upon the breech, just as death had found him, ready for another shot. A lump of shrapnel, flying downward, had passed through his head. Most of the men mortally hit were found lying backward, sometimes only partly reclining, as though with the first shock of the bullet they had sat up suddenly and never stirred again.

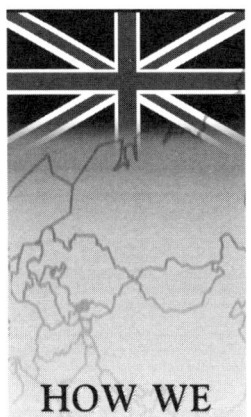

HOW WE KEPT THE FLAG FLYING

CHAPTER 5

ISOLATION OF LADYSMITH

The wires cut – Heavy cannon fire – Shell on the nerves – Testing the investment – Early casualties – The luck of the garrison – Realities of siege – The neutral camp.

ON November 3 our isolation became complete. The wires were cut on Wednesday morning. No train came through from Maritzburg on Thursday, and presumably the rail to southward was in the hands of the enemy. They had us under their guns then from three points, and nothing that we had been able to mount seemed fit to do more than temporarily silence them. On Friday they pitched many shells right into the heart of the town, with no other idea apparently than that of intimidating and injuring the townspeople, for our guns were not answering at the time. The big gun, a 6 in. Krupp, looked straight down the main street. The townspeople could stand at their doors and see the burst of smoke and flame from its muzzle, then wait anxiously for the scream of the shell and the explosion, the dust from which soon rose high over the tops of the houses. Their second gun was so perfectly hidden that few knew its exact location, though its tune was as familiar as the National Anthem. The third gun was to the north-west at Surprise Hill.

To southward of us they had not then placed a gun to do any mischief, but some of the heaviest fighting had taken place in that direction. Although many shells fell in the heart of the town during the early part of the week, it could not be said that the Staats Artillery – who manage the big Boer guns – were actually shelling a town filled with women, children, hospitals, and wounded, but on Friday there could no longer be any doubt of it. From midday until dark – when the fire invariably ceased – they came in at irregular intervals. One of the first pitched just outside the Royal, the largest hotel, while the dining-room was full. It exploded in a cottage usually occupied by Mr. Pearse, the Morning Post correspondent, carried out the side of the house, and blew everything to fragments. Splinters of shell flew upward through the windows of the dining-room, which was filled with shattered glass and dust, yet not a man was hurt. This was generally assumed to be a Transvaal welcome to Dr. Jim and some of the Rhodesia people. It was probably known to the Boers also that scores of British officers were accustomed to lunch at the Royal, and they nearly got a bagful. Several houses were destroyed by shell during the afternoon, a number of people wounded, yet not one life lost. It made one wonder whether the destruction wrought by our field guns was, after all, as great as they said, even admitting that our shrapnel was so much better timed than theirs.

The extraordinary mastery which their guns had secured over us was evidenced when there was a sudden hurried movement of our cavalry, mounted infantry, and flying artillery to southward, to meet a threatened attack of Free State Boers. As our troops hurried out the three guns were shelling them at long range, right over their own camp and town. Fortunately a high ridge close to the road protected them from the two most dangerous guns, while the sweep of the third did not enable it to come nearer than within fifty yards of the column. Our men absolutely marched out through an avenue of bursting shells, which did them no damage.

Although our common sense told us that the Mauser bullet was really the more searching and the more sudden, though infinitely the more polite messenger of the two, there were not ten per cent. of the men in Ladysmith who would not prefer to sit under Mauser rather than shell fire. On the first day, when the shells were few in number, people laughed – a mechanical, crackling laugh, like the rustle of dry straw, but still a laugh. On the second day there was rather less laughter, and more of smothered swearing. On the third day there was an impressive silence, people answering curtly when spoken to, every one thinking a good deal. It was not a friendly act then to throw an empty bottle or a can amongst the rocks close to where a man stood. He was too proud to make any protests, but still his nerves betrayed him. On the fourth day men had a hunted look, and I never fully realized what a hunted look meant until the bombardment of Ladysmith. Most men were morose. It was not so much the Krupp shell that worried them as the waiting for it. The most courteous man in the world became short-tempered then. On the sixth day he was savage, and asked people whether the British soldier had deteriorated, that he didn't go out in the dark and take that cursed Krupp gun? There were thousands anxious to go, but it would have been a bloody struggle in the night, and the loss of life from the Krupp did not yet justify such heroic action. Heart's-blood is an expensive tonic for shattered nerves. The women, whom one greatly pities, began to have those crows' feet at the corner of the eyes which usually come with old age, and when a fork fell on the floor at luncheon they started and gasped. People were trying themselves pretty highly then.

Our war balloon was twice struck. The Boers had realized the futility of shooting at it with artillery when high in the air. So they got the exact position, and poured in their shell as it descended. In return a shell from one of our naval guns fell right on the Krupp, apparently killing or wounding nearly every man working it. Instantly their white flag was hoisted, and while they were carrying away their men, we fired no more. It was a doubtful use of the flag, especially as they took advantage of it to get the gun into action again, and the flag had barely disappeared when the flame was again bursting from its muzzle. We had losses at our guns. Poor Lieutenant Egerton, of the *Powerful*, a gallant young sailor, would persist in standing to his gun on the exposed ridge, though his men were ordered to the shelter-trench whenever the Krupp's smoke was seen. Finally came a shell which, passing through the sand-bags, literally burst at his feet, carrying away both his legs, and though amputation was tried, they could not save him. With Major Taunton and Lieutenant Knapp, of the Carbineers, who were killed in yesterday's fight, he was buried to-day, their only wreaths the little mountain marguerites growing on the rocky hills where they fell. I saw two of the volunteers turn to help a mate who had fallen, when the rattle of the Mausers was like a mowing-machine in the November hayfields, and strangely both of them were hit through the upper part of the left arm. On another occasion a half-dozen Imperial Light Horse patrols simply trotted on to a flat swept by both the rifle and artillery fire of the enemy. We who saw their peril a mile away could do nothing to warn them. The Boers, with that consummate patience which marks them, waited till they were fairly in the open, then the hail of nickel and splinter fell upon them. In a few seconds three of them were wounded, one horse was killed, and another was shot through the upper lip with a splinter of shell. Our cavalry and mounted infantry were continually falling into such death-traps. Sometimes they were drawn on in a running fight with the idea that they were being opposed by something like their own number, and getting the best of it. Then of a sudden they found the rocks in front of them literally swarming with the enemy, and had to beat a retreat, with the Boers just pumping rifle bullets into the dust of the flying squadron. The enemy can lie as low as quail in summer time, and rise with equal suddenness.

Sometimes there was fighting going on all around Ladysmith, the fire covering a circle of about twenty-five miles. They threatened everywhere, yet so far had not come on in force. We drove them back at every point, yet as soon as we retired to camp they re-occupied their ground. Yesterday, when they were retreating from the ridges under stress of our artillery fire at nearly four thousand yards, they reminded me of the big apes one sees bounding away from the train on the ridges above the Berea of Durban. I use the simile without contempt – our men in dodging amongst the rocks, no doubt presented to the Boers exactly the same impression. When men are in riding breeches and short tunics they look long-limbed and short-bodied. We fought on somewhat novel lines at Besters. Under cover of our field guns, the 5th Dragoons, 5th Lancers, and 18th and 19th Hussars were rushed up under shelter of the kopjes in the hope of cutting off the enemy, but though the move often promised to be successful, the Boers were too cute to be cornered. The burgher who had seen his mate run through with a lance, the while he clutched with both hands – a death-grip – at its shaft, saw something that would last him through the campaign. He spread the story in the commandoes, and none of them wanted those big Australian horses – which in substance overshadow alike the thoroughbreds of the English officers and the spare, gaunt Basutos of the Boers – thundering amongst them again. We must have had half-a-dozen batteries in action, and the most deadly, as usual, was the 42nd, the gunners of which did tremendous work at Dundee, and claim to be second to no field battery in the world. The volunteers had an hour's solid fighting on our left flank, and Captain Arnott, one of their most popular officers, was shot through the body just as he was urging his men to take every advantage of cover, and at the same time exposing himself. There were some unpleasantly narrow escapes from instant death. Lieutenant Brabant, a volunteer officer, was shot through both cheeks as he was giving orders, yet the Mauser bullet missed his teeth. A trooper named Norman M'Leod had his tunic torn from his back by a large splinter of shell, which just cut a slight furrow across his spine. I can understand now how utterly puzzled the Americans must have been by the hidden fire of the smokeless Mausers from the tree-tops of San Juan. I could see the Boer bullets clipping up the dust all round our men; yet, in constant searching with the glass, failed exactly to locate them. There was no a whiff of smoke anywhere. Nor is it possible, except in absolutely open country, to estimate the loss on either side in these running fights. In the dust one hears the faint call of a wounded man amongst the rocks, but he can best estimate the casualties by watching the movements of the ambulance wagons.

Day by day we marvelled more at our immunity from hurt, though the luck might turn at any moment. Hair-breadth escapes we had by the score, but in proportion to the weight of iron thrown upon us our losses were absurd. Most of the inhabitants of the much-battered town went their way confident that they would die in time of old age and general debility. With good shrapnel the place might have been at once a hell, a hospital, and a charnel-house any time these first ten days. It was on November 4 that the Ladysmith population began for the first time seriously to accept the possibility that the Boers might take the town, or at any rate so batter it to pieces that the ruins would be scarcely worth claiming. A meeting of the local council was hurriedly held, and Sir George White was urged to communicate with General Joubert, asking that the wounded in the hospitals, the women and children, as well as civilians generally, should be allowed to leave the town. The General sent on the message with some reluctance, and Joubert, who was found seated under the shade of an ox wagon smoking, promptly replied that he would allow neither man, woman, nor child to go southward by train.

They might, if they pleased, form a non-combatants' camp some five miles out, for all who had not taken up arms against the South African Republic. A meeting of the townspeople was held to consider the proposal, and, as often happens, one eloquent man carried all before him. It was Archdeacon Barker, a tall, white-haired clergyman, with something of the erect carriage of the soldier in spite of his years. "Our woman and children shall not go out under a white flag," he said. "They shall stay with the men under the Union Jack, and those who would do them harm may come to them at their peril." There was cheering – cheers for the Queen, for Sir George White, for the army, and for Archdeacon Barker – and there was no more talk that night of white flags or of running away.

But when the cannonade grew fiercer they went out, not women and children only, but men too, though scores of brave women declined to stir. The field hospitals were removed, for the condition of wounded men in that part of the town, where the shells always fell thickest, was not an enviable one. They were taken some miles out, to a spot selected as neutral ground, and there Boer and Briton often met in harmony, for the enemy frequently sent in for medicines and surgical equipments, and were never disappointed. When Major Taunton fell dead, Dr. Hornabrook, of Adelaide, sat down beside the body to bring it in later, as he had brought in the body of another plucky young volunteer, Lieutenant Clapham, from the summit of Umbulwana. The Boer riflemen took the ridge fifty yards above him, and he watched them as they literally threw clips of bullets into the magazines, and pumped them after our galloping troopers, who had been taken by surprise and heavily outnumbered. In the heat of the firing one man called to him from the ridge, "I say, are you shooting down there?" "No," said the doctor; "I've nothing to shoot with." "That's all right, old chap," said the Boer apologetically. After the firing ceased they came down to him, and chatted about the war and the incidents of the day. "What a fool he was to stand up," one of them said, pointing to the body of Major Taunton. Many of them confessed that they were already very tired of fighting, and whatever the spirit in which these Roundheads of the veldt had shouldered their rifles and gone abroad to war, they had no delusions as to the end. "We'll be beaten," said one of them; "no doubt about it, but before we have our last kick we'll blow Johannesburg to bits." As the dusk came on one of them said, "Don't you think you'd better go now? Some of our pickets may be firing on you in the bad light, and you can't blame them."

Another remarkable sight seen that week was the loosing upon us of a horde of starving Indian coolies, and their women and children, fugitives from Dundee, whom the Boers would no longer feed. Percy Greathead, of Johannesburg, and others of the Guides, were chosen for the work, in that, besides knowing the locality, they have the gift of tongues, most of them speaking not merely Dutch and English, but Kaffir also. When they went out to take over his horde of miserable wretches from the Dutch envoys, they saw a pitiable spectacle. Children that had been born by the wayside, and were but a few hours old, were being carried along by their fainting mothers until our military authorities, listening in horror to the story told by the Guides, sent ambulances to bring them in. The Guides had another surprise that day. They spoke to the Boers in Dutch, and were surprised when one of them replied, "Can't you fellows speak English? Only one of the three of us knows Dutch, and he isn't very good at it." So they talked in English, and it was found that of those three Boers two were Irish, the one a burgher of some years, the other only six months out, while the third was a Frenchman. Be not self-righteous, though, ye Scots and English. I know of one Boer who sent a message to the colonel of the Light Horse asking to be favoured with a description of the uniform of his corps, as he wished to pay them particular attention. His name was M'Nab, which I take to be rather more Scottish than Dutch. Tom Loxton and Greathead, of the Guides, had a long talk with the young Irishman I have mentioned, who already regretted joining the Boers. "Why do you fire on our ambulance?" Loxton asked. The Irishman denied they had ever done so. "Why, you've done it three times to-day," Loxton declared. "Well, the truth is," said the other, "that our fellows believe that a great many of their wounded were killed by the Lancers in the charge at Elands Laagte. We had a lot of men killed there." Then he added, significantly, "Don't let the others know I told you."

The Boer guns were never silent on Monday, November 5, yet they did little mischief, save amongst the houses on the ridges to westward of the town, which were for the time being the habitation and playground of shrapnel and plugged shell. People suffered a good deal under the bombardment from hunger and thirst. Every shop was closed, every hotel kitchen demoralized, so that those who had not already attached themselves to a military mess took with them just what they could commandeer. In company with Messrs. Greenwood and Mitchell, two of the South African correspondents, I was the joint owner of a can of Californian pears and a bottle of German lager beer – but no corkscrew. However, a rusty screw and a bit of pliant wire made an admirable substitute, and after that day there was no suffering. People got used to it, and took regular meals. There was one admirable feature in the Boer methods of investment. When they sprang a fresh surprise upon us it was never more than two guns a day. Had they got all their guns in position first, and then suddenly commenced to bombard, it would have been distracting, perhaps deadly, but they began with one gun, and by the time a second was ready we were getting ourselves disciplined and had become expert in shell-dodging. Thus it went on, gun by gun, until they gradually completed the ring of fire to south and west, leaving fewer ridges behind which troops could shelter, and thus made ready for an appropriate Dutch celebration of the Prince of Wales's birthday. On the eve of it I saw some really fine artillery work. Coincidently with the placing of their second big gun on

Umbulwana, we got our second naval gun in action to the north-west, and the clever way in which the fire of that gun was masked for the whole of Tuesday forenoon was beyond praise. Using cordite, there was only the slightest whiff of light buff smoke hanging low about the grass, while both their big guns belched out a cloud of snow-white smoke, reminding one in bulk of the huge woolpacks that chase each other across our Australian skies on a windy spring day. Our gun never fired except in answer to Dutch Long Tom, and then fired instantly on his flash. It was so promptly done that our shells, driven with greater muzzle velocity, often exploded before theirs, yet we invariably fired at their flash. It was a sharp bit of artillery work, and Long Tom, feeling for this hidden enemy, sometimes dropped his shells into the town, sometimes amongst the ridges and it was well past mid-day before our gun was at last discovered. Then from three high points they turned on him angrily, and a hail of shells fell upon him. Indeed, it looked as though they had blotted him out, but we learned later that our gun had bucked from its bearings and reared straight up, so that it was some time before it was got into position again, This was our disadvantage. We were using naval guns, which had to be set in concrete; they had guns specially intended for redoubts, and which were readily placed in position. Before our left front gun came to grief on Tuesday, it had a single-handed duel with a big Boer gun mounted on the shoulder of Telegraph Hill, west from the town, in which the shooting was the finest I had yet seen. After a furious exchange the Dutch gun ceased fire, and it was some time later when it again opened by pitching shells into the remnants of the Gloucester camp.

The men came out, and strolled down to look at the visitor's marks. While they were gathered in a clump around the rent in the earth, a second shell burst right amongst the tents they had left. By such slight chances were men almost daily saved from certain death, and we appeared to have a monopoly of the good fortune.

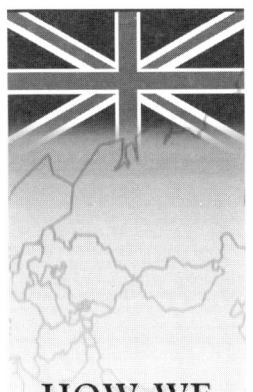

HOW WE KEPT THE FLAG FLYING

CHAPTER 6

BIRTHDAY CELEBRATIONS

The agreeable censor – The birthday salute – Shelling the town – Fighting shadows – The plan that failed – An inconclusive fight.

THE guide, philosopher, and perhaps one may say friend of war correspondents was the press censor – Major Altham of the Engineers, a man who combined the directness of the soldier with the literary sagacity of a sub-editor. He was absolutely merciless with his blue pencil, but accompanied the crucifixion of a cable despatch with such a pleasant and pointed fire of running comment that one could never be offended. There was such perfect candour in his comments, that even those who had argued most eloquently against the excision of some precious item of news came away bearing no ill-will towards the censor. He was most busy and most merciless in those few uncertain days when the Boers were closing about us, and the wire might be in their hands at any moment; still more merciless to the enterprising journalist who had arranged with a Kaffir to run the gauntlet of the Dutch sentries. The despatches were then likely to fall into the hands of the enemy, and they were not in cypher. One enjoyed the censor most when criticizing some other fellow's correspondence. Here is a transcript:–

Censor. – "Can't let you say this, you know."

Correspondent. – "Well, it's of interest to the public."

Censor. – "We're not considering the public, though; we're considering the enemy."

Correspondent. – (with a weary air). – "Oh, very well, strike it out."

Censor. – "And here again you say, 'Great satisfaction expressed here arrival General Buller. Feeling that siege will not long continue.' That's a reflection on our General. You don't mean to say that we're skulking behind rocks, and that General Buller has only to come here and personally drive the Boers away."

Correspondent. – "No; but he has an army corps with him."

Censor. – "Then why don't you say so? Hum! ha! What's this? Question of tactics. Where did you get your knowledge of military strategy?"

Correspondent (triumphantly). – "It's no so much a matter of strategy as of common sense."

Censor. – "Your conclusions in that vein, don't you know, are admirable, if the premises were correct, but unfortunately they're not. I suppose that doesn't matter though."

Correspondent (seeing an opening). – "I shall be very glad, major, if you will amend them where incorrect."

Censor. – "No doubt; but then, you see, I'm not acting as correspondent for your paper."

And so it went on day by day – some swearing, some surly and reflective, others laughing and accepting the inevitable.

At about dawn on the morning of the Prince of Wales's birthday I dreamed that some one was rolling an empty iron tank down a rocky hill, and awoke to find that the Boer guns were roaring outside, and Boer shells bursting over, around, and in the town. It began with daybreak and ceased with sundown. During that time it is estimated that nine hundred shells were fired, and that six hundred of them were Dutch. The estimate may be slightly exaggerated, but the proportion of Boer to British is about correct. And they came from every side. Early in the siege one could dodge shells with a fair degree of dexterity, for he knew exactly where the Boer guns were, but on the Prince's birthday it was different; they came from every side, and one never knew whether they were past him or still coming. Some burst in the streets, some in the houses, some overhead, yet – the marvel of it – no civilian was killed, and the casualties even amongst the soldiers who lined the ridges upon which the Dutch guns rained their shell were not large. A sergeant of the Liverpools, who would persist in exposing himself, though repeatedly warned, was literally torn to bits – and buried in a blanket. A man who stood near him was seriously hurt. Two others were killed by Mauser bullets, and the butcher's bill for the day on which the Dutch had set themselves to blow us to perdition was three killed and fifteen wounded. Rarely has there been such a rage of shell with such trifling loss, and the cost of it as an engine of destruction must have been enormous. Our guns, fewer in number, answered them all through the burning day, and our shooting from first to last was superb. There were short periods when the guns roared less furiously than usual, and the shells rioted less ominously overhead, and then many of the townsmen crept timidly from their tunnels and went about their business until a shell pitched close to them. "Is Jones's store open?" I heard one of them ask. "I fancy the door's locked," was the reply, "but you can go in at the window." He was right too for a shell from Long Tom had gone through the window and taken a considerable portion of the wall with it. But these were trifles. During that day the Boer artillery must have fired every available shell, for on Friday they were silent, and the contrast with the din of the day before was curious. One missed something. Just about noonday, when the bombardment had conveniently slackened, there was a ring of bugles through the heat, and then one heard the tune "God

Bless the Prince of Wales." Our guns thundered – twenty-one of them – in a Royal salute, and few Royal salutes have, I dare say, been fired with shell. Then the cheering rang from ridge to ridge and regiment to regiment, and once again the enemy must have wondered. Twice during that eventful day word went round that the Boers were coming in. They did in one instance, but soon went back again. It had been noticed from the balloon that in the early morning a number of the enemy – dismounted – always came in and lined a particular ridge, but rarely held it during the night. Under cover of darkness some of the Leicesters and Liverpools took possession of the hill, and when the Dutch came up our men poured several volleys into them before they got back to shelter again. It was a body of "Zarps" – as they are called from the initial letters of the South African Republican Police – and had only come down from Pretoria a few days before. Some of them got to the shelter of a donga, and lay there all day safe from rifle fire, but unable to get back to their lines until covered by darkness. Most of the fighting here was at long range – something like one thousand five hundred yards – where the shooting was done mainly by the crack shots, of which there are a few in every regiment, the Rifle Brigade, it is said, having the best. Now and again they bagged their man. The Manchesters were attacked at Cæsar's Hill, but persistent as the Boers were in worrying them, they neither pressed the attack home nor drew the Manchesters out.

The Boer losses must have been heavy, for at night we could see the lanterns of their ambulance men moving over the field, and during the greater part of Friday, when for a time rain and hail fell in tropical torrents, they were still moving about the veldt, flying the red cross. The Boer wounded, when able to do so, frequently signal to their ambulance by firing their rifles, and they could be heard at intervals all through the night. One of our shells burst near a party of Boers who were off-saddled, and their panic was unmistakable. Those who could do so ran, leaving horses and equipment behind them, and some of the saddles were brought into Ladysmith by the Kaffirs. Wonderfully keen-eyed these black Africans are. They invariably go out with the Guides and pickets to look for the enemy, and long before the sweeping glasses of the white men have helped them, the "Look, boss!" of the Kaffir tells that he has found the foe.

On Saturday afternoon, having lulled every one into expectation of a holiday, the Boer guns opened suddenly on the very centre of the town. There was no mistaking the wantonness of the move. Their ordnance was not turned against ours, or upon the hills under which our infantry lurked day by day – waiting. It was a deliberate attempt to do as much harm as possible amongst civilians, lulled to a false sense of security. Thick and fast the big one hundred-pounders fell upon us with a roar through air, and a thunderous explosion. At the Crown Hotel, while we sat at lunch, a huge slice of shell came crashing through the roof of the bar, another banged upon an iron building – yet every one finished his meal. A fortnight ago such a thing would have been impossible. People don't accustom themselves to shell fire all in a day. Sometimes I rubbed my eyes wondering whether I was dreaming, or watching one of Bland Holt's military dramas. And yet there was always at hand some proof of the awful possibilities in this shell fire. A mule was feeding in the lines, and suddenly its heels were in the air. Where is the wretched thing's head? Gone – blown literally to the four winds by a big shell, which took it ere it had yet exploded. Another mule was plunging entangled in heel and head ropes. Don't look – it has been disembowelled. Apart from the big guns, the desultory fighting outside kept one on the *qui vive* with death and suffering. So many men one knows by sight, or has heard of as brave soldiers, went out in the morning with no other purpose than a reconnaissance, and were brought in by the dhoolie-bearers. It was so with Colonel Gunning when he led his lads to victory. "One more effort, boys, and we are on them," and in that one more effort he sank down, and was dead ere "the boys" who followed could stoop to look in his face.

To the correspondent, lying inactive on the veldt, and watching through his glasses a regiment preparing for assault, there was a painful waiting for the first man to fall. If the soldier has all the danger, he has too all the stir of the battle, and giving back shot for shot; he has also that electric glow of comradeship which seems to run like a flame through the line when men prepare for battle. The minute they show themselves above the hill-cap a fierce crackle of rifles breaks, and each minute the crash of sound grows denser, until one wonders that men can live in it. And still they go on, and it might be a sham fight at Langwarrin, except that there is no spirting smoke, as from the Martinis. The sound may come from anywhere, the shots from spectres, for all that one sees of it. It is the day of the long-range rifle, and men fight far off and over wide distances, especially in Africa. Then the first man is on the grass, and some cord seems to snap within one – the first tension of waiting is over. Not a man watching but his heart is with that drab band of earth-stained, hard-swearing, beer-drinking British soldiers. Tommy is a hero then, and one has no thought, not even a little touch of sympathy left for the enemy. To see him dart away amongst the rocks or die in his trenches is a fierce satisfaction. It may be inhuman, savagery perhaps, but it is war.

Sometimes there is a brief minute's respite for the advancing line – a sheltering watercourse, as when "The Dubs" charged up the hill at Dundee. "Close up, men, and rest a minute," said Major English, "and then come on." "Maybe there are some in the timber to front of us, sor," said a rich Irish voice in the line. "So much the worse for them then," replied the officer. "Forward." They sprang from the donga after him, and that awful rattle of Mausers, stilled for the moment, broke again. One cannot help thinking that on the first few strides in the teeth of that shower of Mausers, men ask themselves, "Why am I soldiering? whatever brought me here to this hell?" "How did you feel?" I asked a young lieutenant of perhaps twenty-three. "In a miserable funk," he answered candidly, "but I knew I had to go through with it." That is the only grandeur in it – the stern repression of every natural human emotion and weakness; the full knowledge that it may mean death, but that he must go through with it. I shall never while I live cease to admire the soldier, and, above all, the British officer, though perhaps the officer is much the same all the world over. He has no rifle, no cover. With his useless sword in hand he strides bravely on, pointing the way, a conspicuous target for every sharpshooter on the ridge above him. It is the correct thing to do. It is the caste of the officer as compared with the man – and it is magnificent.

Watching a hard fight affects different men in different ways, though the same tone of awe and repression runs through every observation. On that Monday, when the Dutch turned their guns on Ladysmith, and we went out to a disastrous fight, I saw the British soldier retiring, and it was not a pleasant sight. He had not been beaten in fight or driven from his position. Two far-separated columns were to act in unison. An unforeseen mishap had given the one column over to destruction and capture near Nicholson's Nek. The second had been hidden for hours under shelter of the ridges, half-way to the Boer position, waiting for the signal that their comrades had turned the enemy's left ere they sprang forward to the assault, but the enveloping wing was at that instant fighting for life miles from where it should have been and there was nothing for the main force to do but come in out of the storm of shrapnel that was being thrown upon them, and from which even the fire of our own well-served field guns could not shelter them. They came in, swearing a good deal, caring little for formation, not running, but marching in clumps anyhow across an open flat, where Krupp and Mauser burst full upon them. "My God," said a man near me, in a voice which was absolutely one of agony, "they are walking right into it. Why don't they go round by the shelter of that ridge?" Tommy has the genius for assault, but not the stomach even for a tactical necessary retreat. If he got out of hand then for a moment it was not in panic, but in obstinacy. He walked sulkily straight into it. It was no one's fault – the plan was a good plan, but the uncontrollable and the unforeseen spoiled it. You may deem all this emotional – strained, hysterical, if you please – but it is actual war, and in it the everyday emotions have no place. Every chord in one's being throbs, every sense is thrilled, every emotion is highly wrought. One may be cool under perpetual bombardment, though even there "the night cometh when no man knoweth," but to the novice in war the actual movement of men against men is gigantic.

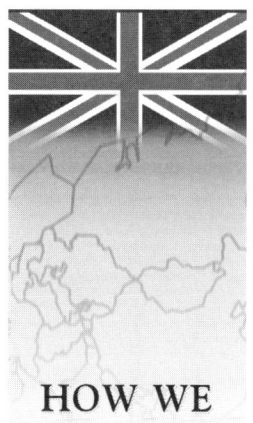

HOW WE KEPT THE FLAG FLYING

CHAPTER 7

SIEGE IMPRESSIONS

The General's promise – A narrow escape – Spasmodic fire – A reconnaissance – Settling down – A night bombardment.

ONE day, while we were spending a quiet afternoon with the Guides in their tunnel, the Commander-in-Chief, Sir George White, with Colonel Ian Hamilton, came down to look at it. The fame of that tunnel has spread through Ladysmith. It goes under the bank and out again, and has little side vaults where one might almost expect to find mummies or some of the relics of the catacombs. The officers laughed, and Sir George, on leaving, significantly observed, "It's a fine tunnel, but you won't need it long – there are three brigades coming." We would have wished to question him as to details, but generals commanding are not good under cross-examination

Every day the assemblage of civilians by the river tunnel became a more curious study. Single men with a strong sense of self-preservation might be seen hurrying down each morning with a well-filled hamper. One old lady I saw often, and she always brought down with her a green African parrot and a canary. Others sat back well in their tunnels, and with long hand-lines passed the time eel-fishing in the Klip river. On the fourteenth day of the siege the fire became more spasmodic. There was a particularly hot hour of it just before breakfast perhaps, and then a long and blissful quiet. The very worst shells next to shrapnel were those which pitched upon the macadamized road. Off that hard surface, as from the rocks on the ridges, they flew into a thousand splinters, and their onward sweep was awe-inspiring. One would have expected such an effect as a swivel punt gun fired into a flock of wild duck, but the immunity from injury continued. A picturesque ivy-wreathed building at one of the street corners was commandeered by some members of Sir George White's Staff, who had as visitors Dr. Jim, Colonel Rhodes, Lord Ava, and others. They had arranged to sit for a photograph before breakfast, and while they were absent a shell from Long Tom passed just below the foundations of the building, and burst in the cellar. The floor of the breakfast-room, where five minutes later they would have sat at table, was blown to fragments. Where there had been a room, there was a chasm choked with splintered timber. When an eminent divine of the town heard of it he said, "Good gracious! and Olive's violin is packed away in that cellar." Then, as an after-thought, "Was any one hurt?" They followed Colonel Rhodes around with sleuth-like persistency, and seemed determined to carry out that death sentence, passed a few years ago in Pretoria, on account of the Jameson raid. So it looked at first sight, when one remembered the family antecedents, but the range of the guns was too long for it to be anything more than coincidence. At lunch time, on the same day, a shell from Umbulwana came through the roof of the Royal Hotel, tore its way through Colonel Rhodes's bedroom and burst in the dining-room. Again the wreckage was something to remember, and again, as a matter of course, no one got a scratch. Not so with the Boers. They hoisted the white flag over their Umbulwana gun – and a wagon climbed the mountain to take away the wounded. The naval men claimed that theoretically both the big guns had surrendered to them in hoisting the white flag during the thickest fire – but the Boers still kept possession of them. One of the last buildings destroyed by the Dutch fire was their own Lutheran Church, but the Dopper Church – to which most of the Boers belong – escaped injury. Not so the other denominational buildings. The Roman Catholic convent and sanatorium, which had a commanding but exposed site, on the crown of the hill overlooking the town, and right in the rear of our naval guns, was shot through and through. Every wall had a shell-hole through it, and the devastation inside was terrific. Fortunately it was vacated early in the siege, the sisters going out to the neutral camp to nurse the wounded, when the convent was no longer required as a hospital. There was a chapel attached to the convent. One of the largest of the Dutch shells exploded just as it had pierced the outer wall, and raked the sanctuary from end to end. Scarcely a yard of wall or roof or floor that was not pierced with those diabolical splinters of metal that, fashioned like the teeth of a cog-wheel, flew to pieces on impact. And amid the ruin was a carving of the Saviour on the cross, a statue of the Virgin, a picture of the Crucifixion, with not a chip nor a stain on the marble, not a scratch on the gilding. It was all wonderful.

The forenoon of November 14 was a day which promised much, but in the end fizzled out rather tamely. On the night before, a veldt farmer, who had sought refuge in the town, got news from his Kaffirs that the Boers would attack that day; and when before breakfast they opened a heavy fire on the town, apparently as a screen to some ulterior purpose, it looked as though for once rumour and truth were identical terms. Some of our batteries had gone out at daybreak, and when early in the day they opened with crashing salvoes, and one heard in the clear morning air the man in the balloon call, "Fifty yards to the left," "A little short," and other such instructions to the gunners, it looked as though they were really coming in at last.

Nothing of the sort. Our guns had merely gone out to clear a few square miles of kopjes to south and westward, which had become a favourite hunting-ground of the Boer sharpshooter. I watched the operation with interest. First a shell short and low, then a couple high, and bursting on the further ridges; then, pip-pip-pip, the little balls of snow-white smoke showed all over the intervening ground, and broke and spread into a vaporous morning fog. Thus the programme was repeated over and over again, and for nearly three hours our roaring Armstrongs searched many square miles of country. The Boers never knew where to look for the shells, though, as usual, one had to guess at the execution. I lay alongside an officer of the Highlanders wounded through the left arm, but he steadied his deer-stalking glass on his knee, watched the guns, and with a characteristic Scottish economy of words, declared once that they were "very pretty." Our mounted infantry dodged around meantime as supports to the batteries, but never got a chance. When they were coming in, however, the big Boer guns opened on them with some very good shooting, three separate streams of fire being directed at them across the town. Not a man was touched. A member of the Natal Mounted Rifles as he rode in said to a comrade who had remained in camp, "You missed nothing. It was a wasted day. Let us go and have a sleep." He went to his tent, and as he slept a shell fell upon him and almost severed his head from his body. His friend, reading beside him, saw his legs draw up ever so slightly and that was all. The poor fellow never knew what hurt him, so benignantly and suddenly grim death came to him. He was the first man killed by a shell pitched at random into the town, and they had been shelling us for over a fortnight. The net result of this heavy three hours' artillery fire was nil. It may have shown them that we were alert – it did little more. The intention was, I imagine, to cut off and, if possible, capture a heavy Boer gun that was enfilading us. They were compelled to desert it for a time, but the minute our mounted infantry showed in sight, so fierce a fire of rifles rang along the Boer ridges that to have gone for the gun would have meant heavy loss. On our retirement they came back as usual to their old positions. One or two incidents showed the Boer fighter in a favourable light. One man rode quietly along the slope of the hill, fully exposed and with our shells bursting all around him. He never hurried, and all agreed that he was a brave man. Again, two Boers sat fully exposed on a rock, and never shifted from the shrapnel. Of course, they were seen so plainly only through the glass, and were not under rifle fire. Dr. Hornabrook and Dr. Platts had a narrow escape as they came in with an orderly riding close on their heels. A shell burst right between them, the smoke of it blotted them out, and those of the Staff who saw it said, "They must be killed." Yet when the smoke lifted they were riding quietly on, and not one of the three had a scratch. Indeed, all the fighting here strengthened one's conviction that the more perfect the appliances of war, the greater the range and accuracy of the rifle, the less deadly the fight – assuming always that both sides are about equally armed.

One thing in the African soldier that impressed me was the physique of the Afrikander volunteers. They are not only exceptionally tall men, but finely built, and the British soldier bears poor comparison with them. Mount them upon such horses as are ridden by heavy Dragoons and there would be giants soldiering in the land. Yet one of the best and biggest of these corps is known as the Imperial Light Horse. In a hand-to-hand rough-up on a dark night these fellows would be terrors – not perhaps with the bayonet, which they do not use, but certainly with the butt. I mentioned this in one of the volunteer camps, and pointed to a young giant of 6 ft. 4 in. as an illustration. He was an Australian, born in Castlemaine, an old Scotch College boy, who inquired affectionately after Dr. Morrison, and a brother of Miss Lillian Wheeler, the Australian actress. Another thing that appeals to an Australian is the superb driving of the Cape boys – generally half-castes, between Dutch and Kaffirs, or Hottentots. One man holds his team of ten hard-pulling, galloping mules together swinging round corners and down the rough military roads, while a second, standing on the wagon, wields a terrible whip, with which he can flick the leaders of the span just as surely and mercilessly as the polers. Sometimes when they appear to have the best of the driver, the other boy turns them with his whip. I have seen them in queer places, always in a hurry, but never a capsize. It is a different kind of driving from that of our Cabbage Tree Neds of the old coaching days, more rough-and-ready, perhaps, but all the same a masterly thing. The bullock teams are worked differently from ours, and the yoke – a strip of green hide round the neck – is even more barbarous. It was adopted in the old trekking days, when in crossing unknown and often unfordable rivers it was sometimes necessary to cut away the yoke hurriedly to save the whole span from drowning. They are driven by Kaffirs, who keep up a continuous yelling, and the leader is not a bullock, but a boy. The loads are small, and by comparison with our big shorthorns at least 50 per cent. of the power for each bullock is wasted.

The besieged residents of Ladysmith were so entirely satisfied that Boer artillerymen never worked at night, that they were considerably startled when awakened soon after midnight on November 15 by the roar of artillery. Running out in the rain, they could see the flash of the big guns on Pepworth's and Umbulwana, while in the quiet of the night the shells seemed to hiss closer than ever overhead. A score of theories were in circulation. They had evidently taken the precaution to train all their guns on the town every evening, for shells were whooping noisily in the street. We had been just as careful to train our guns on theirs before dark, for we answered their fire with remarkable promptitude, and our shells in the distance were an eruption of red flame. The facts apparently were that the Boers were paying us back for our Prince of Wales's birthday salute. On the stroke of twelve that morning a rocket soared as a signal, and they fired their salute at us as we had fired at them –

with plugged shell and shrapnel. If on our night alarm we had an unpleasant time turning out suddenly into the darkness, how much worse the wretched condition of the Boers standing guard on the exposed hills. Every one has heard of the mobility of the Dutchman, horse, rifle, and biltong, and he is ready for the veldt – to fight or march as occasion may require. It works admirably in fine weather. But think of the plight of those thousands of Boers with no tents, no other protection than waterproofs after forty-eight hours of the drenching grey, ceaseless rain we were then experiencing! His veldt-schoen – the soft, broad, brown leather boot he usually wears – help him in dry weather to spring from rock to rock like a mountain goat; help him to creep noiselessly where the clatter of "Tommy's" thick army book would betray him. When the rain comes the veldt-schoen are reduced to so much sodden pulp – as serviceable on the feet as a wet dishcloth. We under shelter, besieged though we were, could not but pity the poor wretches crouching under bush and wagon, making the most of every scrap of shelter on the bare pitiless veldt.

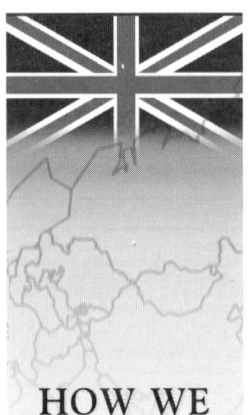

HOW WE KEPT THE FLAG FLYING

CHAPTER 8

THE LUCK CHANGES

A disastrous shell – Rumours of sorties – The silent guns – "The March of the Cameron Men" – A doctor's tragic death – A midnight scare – Football under fire – The passion for sport.

WITH the first shell fired at us on the morning of November 16 the luck changed. It was shrapnel, and burst straight over a group of men standing on the railway station. Seven men – four of them white and three coolies – were stricken down by it, one of them, a railway guard named Mason, being so fearfully mangled the he died an hour later, and before night he had been buried uncoffined like a soldier. The wounded were taken out to the neutral camp next day, and there we heard little more of them, for communication between the town and camp was slight. The rapidity with which men wounded by rifle bullets recover is marvellous. I heard some cheering one day as a man of the Natal Mounted Rifles rode into camp with a new sergeant's badge on his arm. He was Private Kirk, of the volunteers, when Dundee and Elands Laagte were fought, less than a month before, and was brought in fairly riddled with wounds. He was hit time after time, and went on fighting until the seventh bullet brought him down. Yet he was no sooner patched up and on his legs again than he was back to duty, promoted to the rank of sergeant in recognition of his bravery. He and many others of the volunteers were men absolutely without fear – some of them old Zulu and Basuto fighters, with the yellow and blue ribbon on their tunics. But in the volunteer casualties were some men really unfortunate. No man came into the field more determined to pay the debt he owed the Boer than Colonel Wools Sampson. He will be remembered as one of the two men who, after sentence had been passed for the Jameson Raid, declined either to pay the fine of £2000, or to give the promise as to neutrality in politics, which would have secured his release. It was not a question of cash, but of principle, so he served his term in Pretoria Gaol. Here, in his very first fight, he had his thighbone broken by a shot, and his one regret was that it might be his first and last chance to get even with the enemy. Many of those who impulsively joined the volunteers on the declaration of war quite failed to realize the extent of the task they were undertaking, but for the most part they went through with it like men.

The mystery of mysteries was to fathom Dutch designs in connection with Ladysmith. To reduce the town by famine looked hopeless, and the bolder course of assault they shrank from, as often as they appeared to have worked themselves up to the point of storming. Our shrapnel was, I think, the chief impediment to daylight attack, the bayonet a sufficient reason for not attempting it in the dark. There was one night – that of Wednesday, November 15 – when we hoped that inaction had ended, and the time had come to show the enemy we were not skulking. The whisper went round – as whispers will – that at midnight Umbulwana mountain would be rushed by two battalions of British infantry, and the Boer guns taken at the bayonet point. The night was favourable in one respect – black as ink, and raining as it might have rained when the first navigator, Noah, launched his craft. The spruits were running deep with flood waters, however, the banks and mountain slopes slippery as glass, and the rain so blinding that the attempt was abandoned. On the night before it might have been managed comfortably; on the night following the valley was flooded with a silvery moonlight that made a surprise attack impossible. The Boers would have picked off our men as easily as in daylight. Sometimes when they had a chance of picking off they made rather a mull of it, and war correspondents were greatly pleased when Major Henderson, of the Intelligence Office, benefited by their loose shooting, for he was the most tolerant of all the censors. The major, with some of the Guides and a small escort, were out on a private prowl, and decided to climb to the top of a kopje giving them a good view of the enemy's country. They left their horses at the foot of it, and started to climb, but had not got far when a volley was fired at them at a range of not more than four hundred yards. They ran to their horses, and all the way across the valley were fired upon, yet not a man or horse was hit. It was an exceptional bit of luck though, for the bullets were all around them. Had the Boer retained his traditional skill in marksmanship the first volley must have settled some of them. As the party tore up the opposite slope a young Hussar officer, lying on the crest, and taking stock of everything through his glass, asked, "Why don't you fellows get to cover?" "What the b-----s do you think we're doing!" was the unamiable response. On the 17th the enemy began to cultivate a nasty habit of throwing small shells into the street from nowhere in particular, and a gun which apparently made no report. There was a sudden rush of sound, like a locomotive throwing off steam, and people ducked in a vain endeavour to get out of the way of a shell that had already passed them. It was an alert and expeditious shell, which always beat the sound over the distance. With Long Tom – who threw his shell high, like a tennis-player tossing – you heard the report of the gun at the long range some two or three seconds sooner than the howl of the shell, while with the small, hard-hitting sort, that volley just over the net, there was no warning. The exclamations one heard were consequently unstudied, abrupt, and more in harmony with the impulses of the primitive man. Our own field guns, except for an occasional foray, had been spelling for the last fortnight, while the gun horses and ammunition mules, revelling in good living, had to be trotted in big circus-rings at dusk every evening to keep them fit for work which might come at any moment. The exercise was necessarily given late in the day, for the Staats artillerymen had a playful trick of dropping a shell into the ring if tried in daylight. The gun teams were always harnessed, ready to go anywhere at a moment's notice.

Horses and men had both waxed fat under bombardment, and the only signs of famine in the land were that the military authorities had put all the Kaffirs on a diet of mealie meal, and commandeered all the liquors in the hotels. Of necessity, therefore, the civil sojourner in Ladysmith had become temperate, and some became correspondingly sad. It was the most complete experiment in prohibition yet made in South Africa. Otherwise there was nothing to indicate a camp shut off from the world and threatened with destruction. There were no bands, of course, and no cheerful camp-fires, even on cold nights; for once, when the 5th Dragoons built one, it was too tempting a mark, and the shells came in and found them. But the tum-tum of the banjo and the drone of the accordion were heard on all sides, save out on the ridges, where still great-coated figures, rigid with cold and drenched with wet, were staring always out through the darkness, listening for the quiet tread of the Boer veldt-schoen, and hearing from their own camp below like a wail in the distance the strains of "The Old Folks at Home." Under such circumstances there is more music and meaning than one usually finds in

"There's where my heart is turning ever,
There's where the old folks stay."

Rudyard Kipling, as usual, was the first to see it. The banjo is king out here. Where the fore-loper leads the banjo follows; it is the music of the veldt, of the transport riders, the Rand miners, and the heretofore unenlisted legion who volunteered against the Boer. An incident, in which some discovered also an omen, occurred one day. Some soldiers were gathered in the bar of the Crown Hotel listening to a musical-box playing "The March of the Cameron Men," when a shell burst just inside the slates. There was a rush in to the open, the bar-room was filled with dust and pungent shell-smoke, but through it they could still hear "The March of the Cameron Men."

Just about dusk on the evening of the 18th, the mysterious gun, which no one heard, sent two shells hissing into the town, both evidently aimed at the Royal Hotel. Dr. Starke, a visitor from Torquay, England, was standing near the door, talking to Mr. M'Hugh, of the *Daily Telegraph*, and they turned as the first shell struck the pavement on the opposite side of the street. Within a few seconds another came through the roof, passed through two bedrooms, and went out at the front door, taking poor Dr. Starke just above the knees as he stood sideways. One leg was cut clean off, the other frightfully shattered down to the foot. "Catch me," he moaned as he fell forward on his face, his blood absolutely splashing over M'Hugh's hands and arms. The correspondent escaped without a scratch, though two others who stood by – one of them a soldier - were hit. Dr. Starke's tragical experience was an illustration of the futility of trying to avoid shells. He was quite a familiar figure in town, and each morning was to be seen, a tall man in a long overcoat, walking placidly down to the river with an angler's basket slung upon his shoulders. In this he carried his luncheon, and his anxiety to get out of danger led to a good deal of banter. He had just returned from the river-bank. "Well, doctor," said a friend, "got back from your daily picnic?" and before the poor fellow could answer he was cut down. He had had bad luck from the beginning. Unknown to many in the town – and present merely with

Death of Doctor Starke

a tourist's curiosity to witness great events, and a desire to be of use in ambulance work – he was arrested early in the siege on suspicion of being a spy, but several of the correspondents were able to vouch for his *bona fides*. He died on the operating-table an hour after being hit. There were circumstances in the case which made a deep impression. Dr. Starke was a widower, who had left daughters in England, a quiet, quaint man, who went about sometimes with a butterfly-net, sometimes with a fishing-rod; a man of queer little fads and fancies, who could not move in a community without exciting notice, but always genial and popular. We buried the poor fellow on Sunday afternoon in the little cemetery, where new graves were becoming painfully plentiful. A week before his death the doctor had found a cat mewing pitifully at a deserted home, and made friends with it. He took it every day with him to the river-bank, and had it in his arms when he was killed.

In the shock that follows upon a tragedy such as this there are bitter things said between clenched teeth. " 'E's a Devonshire man," said one of the Devon regiment, "an' I'm Devonshire mesen.' Whoy doan't they let us taake yon gun?" As casualties from shell fire became more frequent, the exodus to the neutral camp – or Fort Funk, as those who stayed in town scornfully termed it – grew greater. As an artilleryman the Boer became more boorish every day. He knew that the town was under martial law, that the streets were cleared at eleven o'clock, and that an hour later the residents were in bed. So exactly at midnight on Saturday a salvo of shells came bellowing into the thick of us, and if big shells are awesome in daylight, they are simply demoniacal in the stillness of the night. For twenty minutes, perhaps, they showered upon us, then, as our guns answered them on the flash, they ceased fire as suddenly as they had begun. It was simply an exhibition of pure devilry, and in that light an entire success. Men in their pyjamas thronged the streets, woman half-clad, and almost speechless in terror, fled to the shelter of sand-bagged cellars and barricades. Fathers were hurrying their families away to the tunnels on the riverbank, where without wraps they crouched shivering until the morning. Having done as much mischief as possible, without hitting anything or any one, the enemy stopped firing, and went home to keep the Sabbath. That became the characteristic of the bombardment – surprise firing in unexpected hours and from unlooked-for places.

A curious fatality seemed to have followed the leaders of columns in the Natal campaign. First Colonel Moller, of the Hussars, had command of the advanced column. He was cut off from his regiment with twenty or so of his men, surrounded in a farmhouse, bombarded with field guns, and took the less unpleasant course in the option of death or surrender. Colonel Gunning, of the King's Royals, succeeded him, and was killed at the head of his regiment. Death, too, deprived of his command that grand soldier whom all the army loved, Major-General Penn Symons. He was succeeded by Major-General Yule, who, just before leaving Dundee, had a shell from Long Tom burst under his horse's nose. Some say he was struck by a splinter in the face, others that the mortification of leaving his tents and baggage behind, coupled with the responsibilities of the forced march, broke him down. Anyhow, it was quiet, slow-speaking Major Murray, and Colonel Dartnell, of the Natal Police, who brought the column through. Then Colonel Carleton took a column to Nicholson's Nek, for a flank movement, fell into the hands of the enemy, and became a prisoner of war at Pretoria. Rather a rapid series of misfortunes for a week's campaigning, even though every day almost had its fight.

By Sunday, November 19, and after three weeks' siege, the position had become almost intolerable. Funerals were more frequent in the afternoon, and as no one could make the plainest deal coffin at less than £10, the dead were usually buried in a brown Kaffir blanket. There were deaths from enteric fever as well as shell, and the grim skeleton stalked so often in the half-deserted streets that many began to lose their fortitude and patience. On this particular Sunday there was an ominous preparation on both sides that caused all to look forward with anxiety to the next few days. After the surprise salvo of Saturday night, there was the usual cessation of hostilities for the next twenty-four hours, and in the Dutch lines that early morning worship which impressed Sir George Colley when, peeping over the rim of Majuba Hill one Sunday morning, he saw the Boer wagons and laagers suddenly lit up on Laing's Nek, and heard, in the clear morning air, the voices of the burghers raised in prayer. All Saturday the Boers had been at work mounting new guns, and Umbulwana promised to be more truculent than ever. A visit to the higher points in the ringed ridge encircling the town, and an endeavour to locate the Boer artillery by the line of flight for their shells, with which we were now pretty familiar, left the impression that some fifteen guns, of varying calibre – from one hundred-pounders downwards – had been place in position. Just think of it, and say whether the unprogressive Boer had not surprised us as much to-day as in years past, by doing the very thing which those who know him best always predicted he would not do. These siege guns that shut us in were bought to hold the "bottle-neck" on the Transvaal border. What Englishman ever dreamed that they would be brought down here into the heart of hostile Natal, to hold thousands of the best of Britain's soldiers, themselves well equipped with siege guns and flying batteries, inactive almost week after week? On Sunday there was in Ladysmith the double and contradictory note – the concentration of dhoolies, promising outward and aggressive action; the other indicating more burrowing, a determination to sit faster than ever – a resignation to shell fire. On Sunday afternoon the engineer officers were round about the more exposed volunteer camps, and as soon as darkness covered the operation, big fatigue parties, with pick and shovel, were at work, and shelter-trenches were being dug by the Carbineers, the Imperial Light Horse, and the Natal Mounted Infantry. It encouraged little expectation of early

The Luck Changes

relief, and held out little promise of sorties and cutting-out expeditions.

It was the digging of new shelter-trenches after three weeks' siege that bred new anxiety in Ladysmith, and we, who had dodged from post to pillar for twenty days, taking shelter where we could find it from the thickest of the shell storm and chancing it for the rest, thought the time had come for cave-building, so on Sunday night we set to work. The walls were of baled hay, four trusses thick, the roof girders were railway sleepers, the roof another layer of hay, three trusses deep. With its springiness and its density we concluded that we were bomb-proof to anything except Long Tom o' Pepworth's, whose weight coming from such an elevation would probably reduce everything to squash, so that instead of being shot we might be ingloriously smothered. It was recognized that precautions against the occasional shell were useless; but in a heavy bombardment such as that of the Prince of Wales's birthday, or during these night salvoes, when with the sudden awakening, the rawness of the chill air, the silence which intensifies the roar of the shell, and the quick transfer from it may be soft dreams to hard realities, the ordeal becomes rather more difficult to bear – the possibilities the more discomforting. Yet, to our surprise, the forenoon of Monday, the 20th, found everything mysteriously, inexplicably quiet. What could mean? Were the Boers determined still to waste the time so much more precious to them than to us? The explanation given was an armistice. General Joubert having, it was said, all his guns ready, sent in demanding the surrender of Ladysmith, and gave Sir George White a few hours to think over the matter. It needed serious consideration, but the British Commander-in-Chief was a man of quick thought and made up his mind in half-a-minute. Failing surrender, Joubert threatened to lay the town in ruins, and the owners of the prospective ruins waited with what patience they could command the fulfilment of the threat. Meantime the Carbineers were playing the Imperial Light Horse at cricket – in accordance with the traditions of other campaigns, for whenever British armies are in a really serious fix they bluff it on the national affection for sport. On Friday the Gordons played the Light Horse Association at football, and during the game the envious Boer artillery dropped a shell on the playground. Under cover of the smoke the Gordons sneaked a goal, and the point as to whether such a contingency is covered by the rules of the game was remitted to English sporting authorities. Military sports were arranged to last for three days. For that period we were safe. No earthly power could prevent a British people carrying a sports meeting to the bitter end.

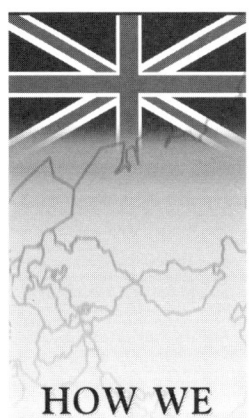

HOW WE KEPT THE FLAG FLYING

CHAPTER 9

THE VAGARIES OF SHELL

Some narrow escapes – Firing on the Red Cross – The rival "snipers" – The first woman wounded – A plucky spy – The Liverpools suffer.

THE theories of truce and armistice framed to account for the inaction of the Boers during the forenoon of November 20 were shattered when, early in the afternoon, the enemy opened fire on the town. The Dutch artillery evidently sought to drop shells from their biggest gun at intervals of about one hundred yards all along the main street, and the accuracy of their fire was admirable, for when the shells did not actually drop on the road – making a terrific crash on the hard metal – they were very near it. One of the shells went through the roof of the Church of England, and blew the porch down as it passed out. Another shattered the rail upon which Mr. Oddy, a Yorkshireman, was sitting, going literally within inches of him. Personally, I was close enough to one to suffer slightly from the concussion, although escaping splinters. This one struck the roadway under a large syringa tree, and the explosion seemed to be mainly upward, for the splinters tore a hole straight up through the tree, bringing down a shower of branches. However close a shell might come to a crowd, there was always a rush for the fragments as trophies.

A new note in the crashing of the Boer guns was discernible that day, indicating a fresh gun in position. We recognized it at once, for we knew the bark of all the others so well that it was impossible for a stranger to join the chorus without betrayal. The Carbineers got the first shell, and exercised the discoverer's right of naming it "Jangling Jane." Almost every night the Boers had us out of bed and on the night of the 21st they gave us two hours of it. As a spectacle a bombardment improves at night, whatever other disadvantages it may have. The fiery track of the shell can be followed, and the explosion of the larger ones lights up the whole town for the moment. But people bustled unceremoniously out of bed to seek some safer shelter, grow morose and irritable when the thing is continued night after night, and are not in the mood to enjoy fireworks. It was noticeable that the firing of the Boers was never long continued. It was furious for a while, whether at night or day, but the instant our guns began to answer they ceased firing, and we were always agreeable to let it stand at that.

On the 22nd we had the rarest of indulgences – a quiet night, and the explanation was that Sir George White had informed General Joubert, that if the night shelling were repeated, his answer and next remonstrance would be lyddite in such a form that the Boers would have no difficulty in understanding it. They have a horror of the new explosive, and are as yet apparently unaware that it had several times been fired at them. They made up for it on Monday with a succession of bombs from their two largest guns, aimed apparently at the Town-hall, which stood up a tempting mark in the centre of the town. It had a square tower, with a clock in it, and from the flagstaff the red cross was hanging loosely in the stifling air. It was a deliberate, but may have been a resentful, fire at the Geneva flag – resentful in that the refuge of a neutral hospital being available, the Boers thought the red cross was being used only for the protection of the building. A number of the wounded almost convalescent were still in hospital there, and the very fact of their electing to stay may have been taken by the enemy's gunners as a reflection upon their artillery work. At any rate, after four or five shells had passed close to the tower, one from Umbulwana came through the roof of the town clerk's room, and carried out one of the solid stone walls. The room was at once ravaged and emptied, everything light being blown through the windows into the street. No single shell that had been fired during the siege wrought quite so much havoc as this one. Three wounded men were sheltering under the wall, entirely satisfied as to the safety of their position, when the mass of masonry – cubes of basalt 18 in. square – fell upon them. One man was lightly cut on the side of the face, another on the knee; the third, who sat on a chair immediately under the rent, had a miraculous escape. The legs of the chair were cut from under him; the mess-tin, from which he was breakfasting, was punctured; the man himself had not a scratch, and lost nothing but his appetite. An Indian dhoolie-bearer, standing a little way off, was killed. On the pavement in front was a great red splash – no, not blood – but copying ink, a stone bottle of which had been blown through a window.

We replied to their fire with a couple of rounds, when, with their matchless impudence, up went the white flag over their gun on Umbulwana. There were gunners there who wished, like Nelson, they could have pleaded a blind eye, and overlooked the flag. But Englishmen differ from Boers in that they have a soldier's record to maintain, so, though the white flag may have been just a bit of insolent humbug, they bowed to it, and were silent.

One day I watched the King's Royals sniping on the western ridges, and the lessons given by the Afridis have made some of our shots as adept in this art as the best of the old game-stalking Boers. Early in the morning the Royals had pushed out a half-dozen of their crack shots to a hillock a quarter of a mile in advance of the main position, and covered by the rifle fire of the regiment from all risk of attack. Peeping over the stony cap one saw on the left a large farmhouse, the headquarters of one of the Boer commandoes. It was a wooden house; so one of the Royals would take position, and having ascertained the range to a nicety, plug bullet after bullet into it. The angry occupants swarmed out at intervals like ants from a hill, and then the other five marksmen began the sniping. For a couple of hours the Boers were puzzled as to the whereabouts of these mysterious marksmen, for the smokeless powder did not betray them. Sometimes the Dutchmen got behind their barricades and began searching the hills about for the hidden foe, then the Royals would glide carefully feet foremost from the little boulders behind which they had crouched to rest, stretch themselves, and clean out their rifles. And while they did it a few others wormed themselves snakelike to the top of the ridge, and went on with the sniping. "I bagged two on 'em," said a Cockney shot – who reminded me of Learoyd of *Soldiers Three* – as he let the plummet of his pull-through slip down the barrel. The puzzled Boers brought along a Maxim to root out the wasps who so annoyed them; but, under fire, the Royals went on with the game as coolly as in the forenoon. Their tactics were slightly altered. One of them would push the barrel of his rifle very slowly past the base of his shelter stone, slip a brown night-cap on his head, then slowly push his helmet over the top of the stone, and wait for some one to fire at it.

The day had been one of hairbreadth escapes. A shell entered a room in which a little child was sleeping, and blew one of the walls of the bedroom out. In the midst of the dust and smoke the parents heard the cry of the little one, and rushing to the room found her absolutely unhurt, while not more than twenty yards away a fragment of the same shell absolutely disembowelled a man of the Natal Police. It was one of the most shocking sights I have seen during the siege. At the same house later in the evening two Englishmen called to congratulate the parents of the narrow escape of the child. They were being shown the little one's pet rabbits, when another splinter of shell passed within a couple of feet of them and clove one of the rabbits in twain. A thoughtful Tommy took it to his tent for a stew. These things sound extravagant, and like siege tales, which are not always reliable, but I speak of what I have seen.

I was in the lines of the Natal Mounted Rifles during the afternoon, and as we discussed the perils of the day, and made comparisons of what we had heard of other sieges, a man lying on the floor of the tent said, "This must be a good deal worse than the siege of Widdin. I see by this book that the Russians pitched shells into Widdin for two months, and had a nasty trick of sending in about twenty every night, yet the casualties were only twelve killed and twenty-seven wounded." I glanced at the book, and saw that he was quoting from an Australian work, Dr. Charles Ryan's *Under the Red Crescent*. One man was having a quiet bath on his own verandah, when a shell struck a tree, cannoned off the side of the house without exploding, and rolling like a hoop along the verandah, upset the bath-tub and its occupant without injuring either. The rooms I occupied with other correspondents were struck by three separate splinters of shell, the largest of which was ominously suggestive of Judgment Day. A South African journalist, who had been as much under fire since Dundee as any man outside the ranks, only lost his nerve when he threw himself down suddenly to avoid a roaring one hundred-pounder, and slightly sprained his shoulder in doing so. The largest of the splinters scalped part of the eaves, glanced off, and struck a wall under which a young fellow was crouching. He picked it up, burned his fingers, and dropped it again.

From the bottom of his heart one pitied the women who stayed in Ladysmith, especially those who had young children. They had an absolutely hunted look in their eyes, and their faces were more drawn and haggard with each succeeding day of suspense and anxiety. Many of them aged prematurely before the siege was over, and the worst is, that even when occupying the best shelter available, much persuasion was required to prevent them rushing into the open air whenever a shell burst close to their hiding-place. It was then, too, that men complained most bitterly of the humiliation of British soldiers sitting down placidly to be shelled by an enemy whom they hold in professed contempt. It may be that the issues at stake were too momentous for a commander-in-chief to permit himself to be swayed by the impulses of ordinary humanity, and that the inevitable end was being neared the more rapidly, and with less waste of human life than by the bolder and bloodier method of a bayonet charge after dark.

The 22nd and 23rd of November were tissue-wearing, nerve-shattering days in Ladysmith. On the night of the 22nd we had heaven's artillery and the Boers' at the same moment, and in the darkness the two combined made a paralyzing din. The night-shooting had done very little damage, though occasional horses were hit. On Friday the first woman was wounded in the siege of Ladysmith. One of the heaviest of the Boer shells struck the thick rubble wall of a cottage in which Mr. Davis, the school-master, lived. It made a huge gap in the wall, and burst as it passed through into the bedroom. Mrs. Davis, who was crouching at the foot of the bed, came staggering out through the rent wall, with both hands to her face and bleeding. She had been grazed by two splinters of shell along the temple and between the chin and mouth – and once again there had been a miraculous escape from death. How even a mouse could have come alive from a room not one foot of which was without its rent was a mystery. It was not well to accept implicitly stories of narrow escapes told by the persons concerned, for some men have at siege times a vivid imagination, but of those well authenticated, one of the most remarkable was that of a Natal Mounted Rifleman. He was lying in his tent, stretched himself wearily, and turned over. In the instant that he did so a shell struck the spot he had just vacated, buried itself, and burst. The tent was blown from its fastenings, the pillow on which his head rested, together with his clothes, were tossed into the air, so that his comrades had a fearful glimpse of what they believed to be a body without arms or legs. Then they ran to the spot, and saw the rifleman sitting up, white, but absolutely unharmed, though a splinter had torn his cartridge-bag from his waist-belt. Less fortunate the poor military cook, who, as he bent over his pots, was taken by a shell in the very middle of the back.

On Friday, the 24th, it was rumoured that there was a Boer spy in Ladysmith – a man named Oscar Meyer. They were on the look-out for him, and he knew it. He went to our horse-lines, picked out a horse and saddle, and quietly rode out of town. As he wore the khaki dress and blue and white puggaree of the Guides, no one suspected him, but his risk was greatest when he reached our furthest outpost. Riding boldly up when challenged, he exclaimed in perfect English that he was one of the Guides, and had been sent out to reconnoitre. "Where's your pass?" the sentry asked. "Confound that pass!" said the spy in well-affected annoyance. "I'm always losing it. It must be in one of my pockets though." He went through the pretence of searching for it, and all the while an apparently restless horse was taking him further away from the sentry. Then suddenly he jammed in his spurs, bent low over his horse's withers, and galloped away at full speed over the veldt straight to the Boer lines. The audacity of the act fairly dazed the sentry. He was so puzzled and uncertain that he never even thought of firing, possibly because no one ordered him to fire, though had the positions been reversed the Boer would not have waited for orders, and for a thousand yards that plucky horseman would have run the gauntlet of the Mausers. One could hardly regret a brave man's escape, even though the circumstances were humiliating.

On the same day a large mob of the town cattle were grazing just outside our outposts, and within the protection of their rifles. The herd gradually moved further out, since the grass, cleared of stock for a month past, was better there. Suddenly the Dutch artillery away on the right began firing shells into the valley between the cattle and our lines. It looked at first such an aimless fire, but it had its purpose – a rather neat one, too. The bursting shells drove the cattle further out, and when the design was seen it was too late to frustrate it. Six Boers galloped down from the ridge, and started to drive off the stock, and instantly a number of our cavalry dashed out to recover them, but from a force of hidden riflemen they were met by a fire so hot that they came back at full gallop, losing two horses. The Boers had foreseen everything. No doubt they had had covetous eyes on the cattle for some time, though there could have been no pre-arranged plan. The cue came from their own guns on the right, nearly three miles away, and, with the matchless resource that characterizes them, they played up to it instantly. Such men are not baulked by any rule of three.

There was one corner of Ladysmith defences which, escaping the general line of shell fire, occasionally received special attention from the Boer gunners. The inner ring of hills came round the town like a horseshoe, with its ends pointing due east, and at the northern end, full under the fire of both Pepworth's and Umbulwana, was a post held by the Liverpool regiment. For a long time it was blessed with a rare immunity from casualties considering its exposed situation, but early on the morning of the 23rd our field guns were sent there to shell some of the Boer batteries to eastward, and very smart work they made of it. They crept round quietly, before daybreak, under cover of the horseshoe; then, dashing into the open, poured in their shrapnel. The enemy had four field guns there, and at no time during the campaign had I seen such a marked difference between Dutch and English shooting. The Boers fired perhaps forty rounds in all before they were silenced, while from the first our guns were simply finding them at every shot. One saw a clump of unmounted men rush wildly across an open space to the shelter of broken ground – then the shrapnel burst in front of them, and they ran madly back again. They were in a maze of fire, and once again the impression given in the distance was that of a lot of big apes scampering to their rock holes. No better proof of deadly shooting was needed, for when the Boer runs it is a pretty sure sign that Death, and not merely Danger, is driving him on. Otherwise, he lies as close as a rock-rabbit, especially if the position be a favourable one for his rifle fire.

The enemy may have thought that the Liverpools, who hold the ridge, were responsible for this early morning salute, and they had not long to wait for their revenge. The next evening, just before sundown, they suddenly opened with several guns on the Liverpool's post, and, in a few minutes, eleven shells were dropped into the camp – one with disastrous effect. The men had dug a large shelter-trench, and covered it with a broad tent for the sake of the shade. The big shell came through the top of the tent, and burst in the hole, killing two of the men outright, and wounding eleven others. Every one knew at once that a calamity had occurred, for close upon the explosion of the shell came one united groan of agony, then a deadly silence. One of the wounded only survived a few hours. By Monday, six were dead – a terrible record for this single shell. Our guns opened with an indignant burst, and quickly silenced the Boer fire; but the mischief had been done. One of our shells blew up the breastwork of their largest gun on Umbulwana, but, although this had happened several times during the siege, the stoppage was never more than temporary, and as soon as our guns ceased fire, the Boers were busy building up their walls again.

It was near the Liverpool's camp, and while the firing was hottest, one day that another honour was added to the many the medical staff have already scored in the Natal campaign. A sergeant-major of the infantry fell badly wounded, and with his legs shot under by a shell. Surgeon-major Jones saw him fall, and coolly walked out through a hail of fire to where the wounded man was lying. He got him to the shelter of a rock, but the poor fellow was so badly hit that he died while the doctor was applying a tourniquet to stop the flow of blood. Having failed in his brave, humane mission, the doctor came back, still under fire. There is more of the heroic in this calm, cold-blooded disregard of death and stern recognition of duty than in half the great deeds which in the stir of action win the Victoria Cross. That night the town rang with the brave surgeon's feat, and the Boers, I feel perfectly sure, were glad they missed him when they knew the facts. Let it not be supposed, though, that when in action a man becomes conspicuous by any act of gallantry, either Boer or Briton makes it light for him. For the time being he is the centre of attraction. The sharpshooters unconsciously pick him out, as a sportsman would a black or yellow rabbit in a drove of browns, without any conscious effort of will. Indeed, the sharpshooter feels his skill in marksmanship challenged by the audacity of the deed, and it is afterwards only, when he has time for reflection and can give free rein to his more generous impulses, that he says in all sincerity, "I'm glad he got away! he is a brave fellow." A soldier can pay his enemy no greater compliment. Such deeds are fortunately not often overlooked by those whose duty it is to note them officially, but it seemed to me more than once during this campaign that the courtesies of war were incomplete without some means by which either side could, when it thought fit, express its admiration for an adversary. That would be the very essence of chivalry, for surely no honour which the soldier can win would be greater than the voluntary attestation of a generous foe.

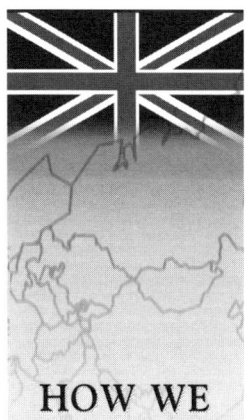

HOW WE KEPT THE FLAG FLYING

CHAPTER 10

LAST DAYS OF NOVEMBER

*An influx of blacks – More guns in action – Hints of hunger –
The intelligent horse – Foppish Boers – Casualties.*

THE Boer was always bringing off surprises. Even if absolutely idle for a day, he picked for his idleness the day upon which much was expected of him. Thus on Saturday, November 25, we had all agreed that he would prepare for the sanctity of his Sabbath by a particularly devilish bombardment of Ladysmith. Yet the hours slipped away, and not a shell came into the town from his big guns, though the lighter ordnance was never long silent. On both sides there were troops constantly in motion, and in the hollows of the hills they occasionally came into view of the field guns, when the temptation to throw a shell at a fair target was too overpowering to be resisted. The side fired at invariably retorted with a couple of rounds at the gun which had taken the initiative, and so there was generally a shell moving somewhere in the vicinity.

The only people who appeared to be particularly busy on this Saturday were the military messengers bearing white flags between the opposing lines. The Dutch were anxious to hand over to our care some 250 coolie refugees, who had probably got through all the fatigue work just then required of them in the Boer camp, and were a drag on the biltong department. Sir George White was at first firm in refusing the favour, pointing out to Commandant Schalk Berger that he must not regard Ladysmith as the headquarters of the British forces, and that any refugees he wished to pass on must be sent south to Estcourt. Considerations both of health and of food made it undesirable that Ladysmith should be made a tip for the waste humanity of Natal; but eventually humanity prevailed, and we took them in.

In the early morning sounds which announce a new day's bombardment, there was always a certain amount of repetition. One heard afar the boom of the gun, followed by the humming of the shell. Then a peacock in the town screamed shrilly in the still morning air as the shell exploded, and there was instantly a clatter of Kaffir and coolie tongues, followed by the bray of army mules, jealous that anything should challenge their capacity for discord. Next came a terrific, ear-splitting crash, apparently right over the town, though really on the ridges half-a-mile away, and as surely as there was a white man near he remarked, "That's one of ours." Latterly, Long Tom had been more intermittent in his fire, and decidedly more erratic, encouraging the impression that he had been time-served, and would be of little more use to any one. With our 6 in. guns the armourer begins to pay attention to the rifling when 100 rounds have been fired, and another jacket is usually fitted to the shell, in addition to the soft copper band which takes the rifling. The Boers had no such contrivance, judging from the whole shells we picked up, and as the big fellow had certainly not fired less that 250 rounds during the campaign – exclusive of his work in driving General Yule's column out of Dundee – his life, we thought, must be very near its end. They put another gun up on an adjacent ridge – one of the unobtrusive sort, which the bluejackets have named "Silent Sue." This made about twenty-five guns of all calibres which the Boers had mounted for the subjection of Ladysmith and its garrison. Yet, in spite of all this direful throwing and threatening of shells, the town continued frivolous, and voetsak – Dutch for "clear out" – is not yet the word in Ladysmith. On Sunday, the 26th, it used its Sabbath leisure to run off the final events in the Imperial Light Horse sports, and to play a cricket match between the local team and the Gordon Highlanders. Although the Boers are so strict in Sunday observance, their religious feelings must not be trifled with, so, when a group of Mohammedan coolies went impudently out on the exposed river-flat on Sunday morning and started to dig a trench, the Boers, after watching them for a time, gave them a sharp moral Christian lesson. A shell dropped almost into the trench, and five others kicked up the dust round about before the agitated coolies, who scattered like plover, got to the shelter of the river-bank.

A survey of the defences of Ladysmith as they stood then and as they were a month before, showed how greatly the position had been strengthened. When Tinta Inyoni was fought, and the Boers had their first distant view of the town, little stone breastworks, rarely three feet in height, crested the hills, each giving shelter, perhaps, to a corporal's guard. During this month the entrenching tools had never been idle; every breastwork, thrown together as a mere temporary shelter, had been broadened and built up into a redoubt impervious either to bullet or shrapnel. The navals made the mistake of assuming at the outset that one bag's length of earth would be a sufficient protection, but the shell that killed their brave Lieutenant Egerton bored its way through that thickness of belting before bursting at the officer's feet. Now the hill forts stood up red and conspicuous by the hundred, and the Kaffirs called them Nkonjanas, after a kind of swallow, which builds mud nests on the rocks. Every possibility – except always the main one – had, I think, been foreseen, and where roadways had been cleared up to the redoubts the paths were whitened, so that in the event of a hurried rush of reinforcements becoming necessary on a dark night, there was no danger of men missing the way. Riding round the defences, one noticed in the fire-zone between our lines and the Boers an occasional conspicuous white stone. They were not geological curiosities, but carefully marked ranges, known to the men who held the fort on that particular section.

On Sunday, November 26, we knew that our own commandant, if not the enemy, had fixed a definite limit to the siege. The horses were already on short rations, and fodder was becoming so scarce that grass-hay, originally intended for bedding, was being cut into chaff. Of meat, flour, and meal we had abundance, but the stock of tea, coffee, and cocoa would not last long; and in the substitution of innocuous ginger-beer for that other beer which his soul loveth, Tommy Atkins was already experiencing all the hardships of siege. For a fortnight it had been an intensely sober camp, but not a bit better-tempered on that account. After Tommy has broken out himself for a day he is more tolerant of the eccentricities of his horse, and a horse on active service is the curse of life. In saying so, I may forfeit the respect of many Australians – the Man from Snowy River and the rest – who have ridden and sung of the horse until it has become by sheer force of imagination the noblest creature of them all. A month amongst the horse-lines has convinced me that a horse is just a marvel of stupidity, and whether you heel-rope him, knee-halter him, side-line him, or fetter him with ordinary hobbles, his capacity for getting himself injured is enormous. All the night through he rears, kicks, squeals, plunges, and generally worries himself and his owner to death, instead of going to sleep decently and making the best of it. Ordinarily the man owns the horse, but on active service the horse owns the man – body and soul. The little Indian donkeys, which carry water-barrels afield pannier-fashion, are clever on their feet, intelligent, even more adaptable to circumstances than a dog, yet they figure as the emblem of stupidity, while the horse is exalted. When an ammunition mule finds himself entangled in the harness, he hops along on three legs until his driver is pleased to release him, while a horse under like circumstances conducts himself as a raving maniac, turning handsprings and back somersaults, and doing his best to tie the whole team into a knot. All a matter of spirit, protests your horse-lover. Maybe, but coupled with his suicidal freaks in camp it would be described in any other animal than a horse as sheer stupidity. With all their bountiful lack of intelligence, though I was sorry to see seventy of the worst scarecrows in camp led out for execution on Monday morning, for we could no longer afford to waste even straw-chaff and mouldy mealies upon anything out of condition. On the same morning the Boer gunners disposed of a few of considerably greater value. So the people of Ladysmith reluctantly made up their minds to endure yet more shelling and stewing, more thirst, and more flies, which had become a plague and a horror in the town. They smothered themselves to death in your food, drowned themselves in your tea, even as you raised it to you lips, until your soul revolted at food, and your waistcoat got more slack and baggy with each succeeding day.

It was November 28, and exactly a month had gone by since the Boers at ten minutes past five on a Monday morning fired their first shell into Ladysmith. Berger – whose Christian name and surname are always used as one, making Schalkberger – had followed his usual policy, a hot burst of fire in the forenoon, then an occasional gun through the day, as some careless corps of ours gave the Dutchman his opportunity. The Boers shoot as they trek, generally early and late in the day, and unless there was some pressing need, were silent during the hottest hours. A month under shell fire without a scratch is calculated, you may think, to make men indifferent. Not a bit of it. The actual number of deaths was not great, but every man went out of a morning with a feeling that it might be his turn, and experience had convinced him, too, that ordinary precautions were useless. Death came impartially. Sometimes a man rode gaily into his shell, at others he stood still and patiently waited for it. The best thing was to follow one's inclinations, and take one's chance on the law of averages; but every one was more or less harassed, even if advantaged by narrow escapes. That morning we narrowly missed another stampede on a large scale. The volunteers, in watering their horses, were instructed to turn them loose for the sake of a run, and the horses, feeling their oats, at once bolted. There was considerable trouble in rounding them up again, as the Boers, with their usual 'cuteness, were quick to aid the confusion with shell fire. Later in the day we returned the compliment by shelling a train of Boer wagons, which were moving from our southern flank in the direction of the railway. An opening in the hill exposed the road at one point, showing, perhaps, a length of nine wagons, and passing through this I counted not less than one hundred and sixty. They had no sooner got through, and were apparently safely screened, than with a high elevation, we began pitching shells on top of them. It was purely speculative shooting, but its effectiveness was proved when, a few minutes later, the long train hurried through the gap again, returning whence it came. In one thing the captain of H.M.S. *Powerful* had placed us under lasting obligations. We asked for a particular gun; he sent two, which, in his opinion, would better suit the circumstances, and, with our small armament, these swivel guns proved invaluable.

The Boer is a strange mixture of Christian fervour and pure brutality. On the one day he is a stern Sabbatarian; on the next he will relax sufficiently to schambok an offending Kaffir to death without a qualm. As a fighter, he prefers to see the back rather than the face of his enemy. On three separate occasions during this siege, I have seen British troops drive the Boer from his chosen positions, have heard the command to retire given, and invariably disobeyed at first, for Tommy's invariable rule is to sit down when he is first ordered to retire, and on the repetition of the command to retire slowly, the while swearing. Twice the position had been almost won, and the Boer rifle fire had thinned, but no sooner were British backs turned to them again than the Dutchmen swarmed to their old position with the fury of bees from an upset hive, and their rifle fire is never so destructive as then.

Some of the Boer officers were evidently anxious to make a good impression when they met members of our Staff, to discuss some point which had arisen during the siege. Germans were almost invariably entrusted with the task. On Saturday a big handsome chap, believed to be Erasmus, commandant of the Staats Artillery, was one of the envoys, and his collar and cuffs shone with a spotless lustre that quite put our officers in the shade. A younger man, who accompanied him, was spruce and foppish, but one little detail noted by the eye of an adjutant gave all the splendour away. The youngster was wearing women's boots.

I am not at all anxious to make these daily notes of a great siege a mere catalogue of horrors, but a death from shell fire which took place one day was so fascinatingly horrible that, even at the risk of being "bluggy", I must mention it. A coolie was bending over his pot of dall when a 15 lb. shell struck him fairly in the centre of the face. His head was not shattered – the forehead, chin, and ears were intact and perfect – but there was nothing but a clean-cut hole in between. He just raised his hands a foot or so, and was dead.

The unexpected always happens in war – it happened yesterday. A mounted rifleman sat quietly on his horse under a ridge, absolutely sheltered from every Boer position. Theoretically, it was impossible to reach him with a bullet, but suddenly he exclaimed "Ah!" and reeled in his saddle. They opened his shirt, and found the tiny familiar puncture of the Mauser. The only possible explanation was that a dropping shot, fired at random, perhaps two thousand five hundred yards away, had just cleared the top of the ridge, and, by a bitter freak of fate, had found that one man dozing in his saddle. On the following day another dozing rifleman, lying at the foot of a tree in the volunteer camp, woke suddenly to the fact that half his own rifle barrel and the upper part of the tree had disappeared before a shell. "These Boers are getting very careless with their shooting," the sufferer said. "If they don't mind they'll be hitting some one."

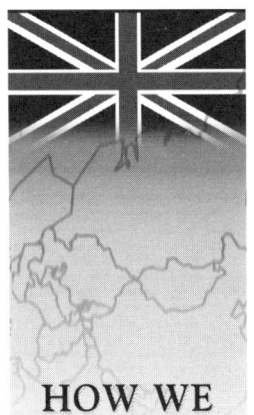

HOW WE KEPT THE FLAG FLYING

CHAPTER 11

DAYS OF GLOOM

*A siege menu – News from Mooi river – Hope deferred –
Ungrateful athletes – A disastrous day – For "Auld Lang Syne" –
A "die-hard" volunteer.*

SOME may be interested in knowing exactly how men live in siege time. Thus far no one had been reduced to horseflesh or rats, as was the case in Paris, the worst that had happened being biscuit and "bully beef". Some of the correspondents, myself amongst them, were so fortunate as to be refused accommodation at a leading hotel, which was already overcrowded. It was soon shot through with shells, and since closed, while a couple of poor fellows, who thought themselves fortunate in getting there, were in their graves, oblivious to shell and all earthly turmoil. We found at the little Crown a Lancashire host and hostess, and a table which was at once the pride and wonder of Ladysmith. How does this read for the third Sunday of an unlooked-for siege, with all supplies cut off?-

MENU. Dinner – Onion soup, breast of mutton and onion sauce, roast chicken, roast veal, roast leg of mutton, roast round of beef, potatoes, beans, apricot pie, currant sandwich, cheese, with a bottle of Barsac to wash it down. What though the Barsac be a Cape wine that would defy all the wine judges in Australia to class it, and the mutton invariably Angora goat, it was yet both passable wine and very excellent goat. Heaven send I may eat nothing less palatable. What wonder then that we favoured ones of the Crown could say, "Grieve not for us, dear friends; we are bearing up bravely. We are quite happy. A time of want may come, but we are quite ready for it." Yet with all the good living, it was singular coincidence that after a month of siege several of us went on the scales, and found that the loss in weight ranged from 14 lbs. to 21 lbs. per man. From this I infer that men do not readily fatten under shell fire, however tenderly treated.

A month had passed since the siege of Ladysmith was made complete by the cutting of rail and telegraph at half-past three on a Thursday afternoon. The relief which seemed on the point of being hourly given kept off strangely, and people in Ladysmith would accept the news of succour as authoritative only when they saw the troops marching through the town. Every one was in high spirits when, early in the week, the following bulletin was issued from headquarters:- "The enemy has been defeated at Mooi river by portion of the column advancing from the south for the relief of Ladysmith, and has retreated on the Tugela river. General Clery's force occupied Frere (about twenty-four miles away) on Monday, 26th inst." Every night thereafter was one of alarms and excursions. Troops were ordered to be ready to march with three days' rations; others were told early in the morning to get what sleep they could during the day – a sufficient hint that they might be wanted at night – yet before morning every such movement was countermanded, and the men went quietly back to bed again.

The Staff did not, of course, take war correspondents into their confidence as to their reasons for altering the plan of action, but it was assumed that the cloud message from Colenso had something to do with it, while a still more sensational reason for abandoning the *coup* was soon afloat. A man had been caught that same night in the very act of lamp-signalling our movements to the enemy. A change of sentries had just taken place, and the soldier fresh on duty is at the outset always more alert and suspicious than the tired-out sentinel he relieves. This man saw something suspicious on his front, so crept up, and having satisfied himself that a traitor was at work, shot him through the shoulder. That the message reached the enemy there could be little doubt, for early next morning our outposts saw the Boers in strong force leaving an ambush from which they would have had our troops at their mercy had the Light Horse tried to break through this pass to join General Clery.

The traitor turned out to be a Cape boy named Ventor, who had been attached as a mule-driver to the 10th Mounted Battery of artillery. The significance of the connection at once excited suspicion. It was the mules of the 10th Battery which stampeded at Nicholson's Nek when Colonel Carleton's column was cut off and the Gloucester regiment taken.

There were rumours that the balloon had sighted the advance guard of the relief column, eight miles to the south of Umbulwana, but one found it difficult to reconcile such a statement with the fact that the Boers still held all their gun positions. When on Saturday we could see them at work dismantling Long Tom on Pepworth's Hill, many declared, "This is the beginning of the end. They know our troops are moving up from Estcourt; they know that the two columns will effect a junction, and that it will then be too late to get their guns away, so they are taking time by the forelock." On Sunday we saw men busy excavating on the shoulder of Lombard's Kop, but never guessed that a new position was being made for Long Tom, and that, so far from preparing for flight, the Dutch were bringing down more guns from Pretoria, intent only upon making the bombardment of Ladysmith still more severe.

Racial hatred is a deeper thing in Africa than an outsider can realize. Let me give an example. On the night the Elands Laagte prisoners were sent away south, my friend Greenwood, of the *Johannesburg Star*, pointed out an athletic-looking Boer in one of the ambulance wagons, and said, "I'm blessed if it isn't Phil Blignaut. So he went out after all." This Boer, who was wounded in the shoulder, was on of the finest athletes in South Africa – a man in whom the sporting residents of Johannesburg had long taken an interest. Both at Grahamstown and Johannesburg he had twice won all the South African amateur championships from 880 yards down to 100 yards, and a finer all-round runner has seldom been seen in any country. His brother Piet – better known as P.J. Blignaut – was also a magnificent runner, and there was so little to choose between them that, some years ago, the people of Johannesburg subscribed the expenses for sending both of them to England to run for the amateur championships. Though they won scores of events in England, they were not successful in the championships. Quite lately a thousand pounds was again raised in Johannesburg by public subscription, and Phil Blignaut was sent home a second time, accompanied by Harry Morkel, a champion hurdle-racer, and Mike Griebenow, a cyclist.

All four of them were men who mixed much with the Uitlanders, showed little interest in political disturbances, and held that high place in public regard which successful athletes do in a sporting community. If any Dutchmen in the Transvaal could be well disposed to the Uitlander it should have been these men, yet three of the four – the two Blignauts and Griebenow – were amongst the first in the field, and Morkel was probably fighting for the Dutch also.

Phil Blignaut was shot through the shoulder and captured at Elands Laagte, his father was found amongst the dead on the same field, and his brother, Piet Blignaut, was shot under remarkable circumstances. He was lying wounded on the field as the Gordons drove home with the bayonet, turned on his side, drew his revolver, and fired at an officer of the Highlanders, who had just passed him. A private of the Gordons, who saw the act, put the nozzle of his Lee-Metford against Piet Blignaut's temple and blew out his brains. So died a great athlete, who, forgetting the many kindnesses shown him, had fought against the Uitlanders to the last with such animosity as might be expected from a dervish of Omdurman, but is, fortunately, rare in this war. On the other side there was no feeling. Amongst the Guides, who saw Phil Blignaut taken away a prisoner, were many of his warmest friends, and I heard nothing from them but expressions of regret. They were amazed that his brother should have fought so bitterly, but respected both men far more for fighting with their countrymen over a lost cause than if they had shirked it and stayed at home.

On the 30th the Boer gunners threw, perhaps, a hundred shells into the town, and the last round of the day proved most disastrous. Earlier in the week, as I have already stated, they shelled the Town-hall, which was still being used as a hospital, and struck it more than once. Sir George White, it is believed, wrote to General Berger, pointing out this flagrant violation of the usages of civilized war, and for a little time the protest was respected. On the 30th shots began to drop all round the hospital again, and the enemy's gunners were clearly experimenting for the range. One shell burst just in front of it, the next passed through the roof of the hospital, and exploded before reaching the floor. Many wounded were lying in the beds, and a poor fellow of the balloon section, who had only come into hospital that day suffering from sore eyes, was killed instantly. The outer casing of the canister shell struck full on the chest as he lay on his back, smashing it in. Nine other wounded men who were rapidly approaching convalescence were also hit, but none fatally, though the ordeal of probing, stitching, and dressing had to begin all over again. Nothing that had latterly occurred in connection with the siege excited so much anger and indignation. Men may lose their dearest chum in action, and call it the fortune of war, but there is something peculiarly pitiable in the condition of a hospital full of suffering men being shelled by an enemy. "It's pure brutality," I heard one of the Carbineers say, with clenched fists, "and may God Almighty help the first Boer who asks me for quarter."

The shell which did the damage was a 6 in. fired from Long Tom, in his new position on Lombard's Kop. To those unacquainted with ordnance it may be of interest to explain that during the siege of Ladysmith five types of shell were generally used by the Boers. One of them, common shell, more destructive to buildings than men, was of solid metal some 2 in. thick, having a central cavity of about the same diameter for the explosive. The outer shell of canister, specially designed to be destructive amongst large masses of men, is a thin skin of steel, the interior packed with a shrapnel of a special form. If you can imagine the hub of a bicycle cut into section, with the bearing balls adhering to its outer rim, you have a very fair representation, on a small scale, of the appearance of canister. The holder has, however, a great number of shallow sockets, in which the round leaden balls fit, and are held in place by some composition like resin. On the explosion of the shell every one of these balls detaches itself, and the area of destruction is very great, the wounds, however, being less horrible than from other shrapnel, save when – as in the case just mentioned – the jacket of the shell hits a man. A third type of shrapnel largely used by the Boers in their field-pieces and siege guns of lighter calibre is segment, or ring shell, the fragments of which I have described as somewhat resembling the cogs of a metal wheel, which had flown off under an extreme strain. Then there is the little Vickers-Maxim shell, only a pound in weight, and a slightly larger shell from a new French gun, which they brought into action late in the siege.

On December 1 we were again keenly on the lookout for the relieving column, for on the night before they had been signalling us from the south by flash-light, and from the Gordons' camp all the messages were taken without difficulty. Whether the enemy realized that their opportunities for shelling Ladysmith were nearing an end or not, they opened on us heavily early on Friday morning, picking the exposed southern end of the town, as usual, for the first few shells, and then searching it systematically from end to end. Before breakfast their shell fire had killed four men. Two of the Gordons were frightfully torn while standing in their own lines, and a Cape boy of the artillery had both legs shot from under him a few minutes later. At the other end of the town a trooper of the Natal Mounted Rifles and his horse went down before a perfect smother of shell. A large splinter entered just under the unfortunate young fellow's right arm, and part of it protruded from beneath the left arm. The horse was raked from end to end, and absolutely smashed to pulp. No more demoralizing instance of the effect of their heavy shrapnel could be given. Of late we had certainly paid for our immunity during the earlier half of the siege, and not a day passed without some deaths.

For its best shelter during this trying time, Ladysmith was indebted to Australia. Standing on a point above the town one noticed squares of trees that far overtop the camel thorn, syringa, umtola, and carob bean which grow locally. They were Australian gums, most of them filled with the swinging-cot nests of the weaver bird, and sheltering also hundreds of the volunteer tents. They had helped to improve the health of the town also, though it is something of a fever bed, and in common with hundreds of others I had suffered with a kind of fever, which made anything like active exertion almost impossible. One longed to be up in the clear air of the higher veldt again, even though it meant exposure, cold nights, and long day marches.

This civilized, long-settled Africa is still a country of plagues, and were it not that the farmer gets his land, as a rule, for ten shillings an acre, has no clearing to do, and pretty well escapes taxation, farming in Natal would be impossible. In addition to the horse sickness, most of his cattle are infected with pleuro-pneumonia, and occasionally swept clean away by rinderpest; his sheep are afflicted with blue tongue, and his fowls have some other horrible disease, so that the flocks of Angora goats which range the rocky hills seem to be the only really healthy stock. Thus it is that in the heart of a farming and pastoral district studded with agricultural societies and show-grounds, one finds Australian butter, meat, honey, cheese, and bread on the tables, side by side with Californian fruits, English hams, and other imported food products. Mealies are the staple crop, and their yields would be laughed at by our maize growers on the Snowy River.

Saturday, December 2, came. For a week the relief column had been in touch of us almost, but it came no nearer. Amid all our tribulations the Scottish portion of the besieged garrison did not forget St. Andrew's night. At the Royal Hotel, temporarily re-occupied for the occasion, there was "a braw Scotch necht" of a unique, even an abnormal character. It is probably the only great Scottish gathering recorded at which not a drop of whisky was obtainable. The toasts were drunk in brandy, in champagne while it lasted, in Cape Drachinstein, and in Ladysmith ginger-beer, but in Scotia's drink – not once. It was otherwise in the Gordons' lines, where for "Auld Lang Syne" the officers of the regiment, with Colonel Dick-Cunyngham in the chair, entertained their old Colonel, Sir George White. The pipers marched round the table, played Highland airs, and there was much enthusiasm. The prevailing tone was that of the Scotch orator, who on a festive occasion began with, "The man who would attempt to talk sense at a time like this would be a fool." A good many were surprised, though, at one assertion made by the Commander-in-Chief during the evening. "In spite of appearances," said Sir George White, "I do not believe that the enemy have deliberately fired a single gun at our hospital in the Town-hall." "I don't agree with you, sir," said Captain Lambton, of the *Powerful*, with the freedom of opinion which prevails at social gatherings on St. Andrew's nights, and a storm of approval showed that very few acquiesced in the favourable view of the commanding officer. The evidence that the Boers deliberately fired upon the one building which with its tower stands up so defiantly in the centre of the town was so strong that they must either admit the odium or confess themselves shockingly poor gunners.

Men who have attended both sides say that, whatever may be their respective merits in action, the British soldier showed more fortitude than the Boer when wounded. Many men of both sides had after a late action to lie all night untended on the veldt, and by morning the Dutch had invariably quite broken down, while Tommy, even when hard hit, bears up wonderfully. Young Crickmore, of the Natal Mounted Rifles, was a marvel of physical endurance. A boy of nineteen, he had hurried up from the Cape on the outbreak of hostilities to join his corps, and one morning he was riding up the street for a packet of cigarettes. The shell that killed him absolutely tore away one of his lungs, and his internal injuries were otherwise so frightful that, according to medical science, he should have been killed instantly; but he lived for hours, saw many of his comrades, laughingly expressed the conviction that in spite of it all he would get through, and then, in the height of good spirits, his head dropped over and he died. After Tinta Inyoni a wounded man walked a mile to avoid falling into the hands of the Dutch, yet was dead before daybreak.

The expedition with which the doctors work after a fight is marvellous. The chief runs his hands over each wounded man, pulls away the temporary dressings, and, if no extraction or amputation be necessary, calls up one of the young dressers, tells him in a few words what to do, and passes on to the next case. The dresser sets to work quietly, just as quietly the little Indian dhoolie-bearers are at his side, with every instrument and bandage ready to his hand, as though the science of advanced surgery were one of their every-day accomplishments. I saw one of the infantry, who had a large bullet in his arm, beckoned to the operating-table. He had been chatting about the fight, and turned a little white when he saw the instruments. A mere whiff of chloroform was given him, and in a few minutes the operating surgeon was handing the big bullet over to the sufferer, with, "Keep that, my lad, to show to your family." The soldier stared at him, shook his head to dispel the fumes of ether, then, putting his good hand in his pocket, pulled out three sovereigns and some silver. "Thank God they didn't get that," he said, as he straightened himself up and went his way. Close by there was a little German prisoner crying. He had been wounded three times in the right arm, evidently with Maxim fire, but was quite convinced that the snub-nosed Cockney who kept guard over him was responsible for his misfortunes. "He shot me," he whimpered, pointing to the stolid guard. "I didn't want to fight; I have no grudge against the English; but I was a burgher, and I had to go." It is always the same cry, – duty, not inclination.

I met a Melbourne man, a Captain Clarke, who had a nerve-trying experience some few nights ago. He was on outpost duty on a very dark night, and got separated from his men. Finding himself at one of the railway bridges, he met several Kaffirs, who assured him that mounted Boers were close up to him. Captain Clark, who had lived much of his life in the saddle, was more disposed to trust to his horse than to the scared Kaffirs, and when he saw his charger suddenly raise his head and prick his ears forward he knew there was something in it. Soon he heard the clatter of hoofs in the scrub near him, but dared not fire lest they should be his own men; so there was nothing for it but to wait quietly and take his chance, holding his horse by the nose in the meantime to prevent him neighing. Repeatedly during the siege the horses were the first at night to warn our outposts that the Boers were on the move. In this respect their keen sense of smell and hearing, if not their intelligence, has proved valuable.

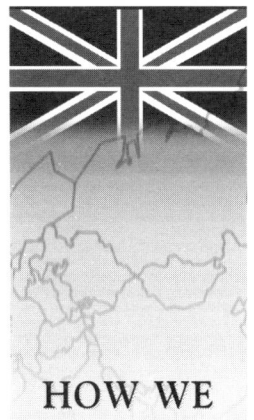

HOW WE KEPT THE FLAG FLYING

CHAPTER 12

A NIGHT OF SORTIE

*News of Buller – Mysterious preparations – Biltong –
The Ladysmith Lyre – A dash for Long Tom – Blowing up a gun
– Exultant volunteers.*

A WEEK had gone by since the relief column – or the reinforcements, as the military authorities preferred to call them – entered Frere. For days we spoke to them by heliograph, and from the round shoulder of a hill away to the south the sun instrument winked at us through the haze. On Sunday it was never idle, and the communication was so complete that the General decided that next day each war correspondent should be allowed to send thirty words by heliograph to his paper – all the official messages, including particulars of the casualties, having by that time got through – but, to the mortification of all, when our morning shell woke us a little after five on Monday there was a dead grey sky and light rains. The chance had gone for a time. Then came the news from an unquestionable source that General Buller was in Maritzburg, and that, so far from being a lone little band cast away in the wilderness, we had become the centre of interest. Coincident with this came also the gratifying news that Lord Methuen had three times beaten the Boers over Kimberley way. It had been a gloomy garrison that rushed for shelter when the first shell came that Monday morning, but by breakfast-time every one was in splendid spirits, and the most truculent of the civilians wanted to go up on the ridges and shoot something. The full text of this message, which sent the spirits of the depressed garrison bubbling up like the mercury in a Christmas barometer, was as follows:- "Sir Redvers Buller was at Maritzburg on the 29th ult. Sir George White has much pleasure in publishing the following extract from a despatch of that date received this morning by runner – 'Methuen is at Modder river *en route* for Kimberley, having defeated the enemy in three battles, in the last of which they were 8000 strong, and entrenched, under command of Cronje. Adverting to affairs in Europe, no chance of intervention.'"

During that week the movements of our own troops had been most puzzling. All day they were lying perdu, ready only to resist a Boer advance on the town if it were attempted, and replying only at rare intervals to their ever-roaring artillery. But as soon as the darkness covered our movements the whole force was astir, and the different corps mustered silently at given stations, all in flying order. This really means fighting order, with saddles stripped of blankets and all the impedimenta that men carry on the march. There is nothing in war so impressive as these night movements. The order had been given that all lights should be out on the ringing of the town bell at half-past eight – this with the double object of not confusing the flash-light signalling, and giving the enemy no guide as to the movements of the troops.

The inference from these nightly parades of the troops was that Sir George White anticipated two possibilities, and was equally ready for both, viz. a desperate midnight rush by the enemy to get possession of Ladysmith before relief came, or an equally sudden effort by General Clery to effect a junction. The streets were literally lined with men, the cavalry and mounted infantry sitting on the ground at their horses' heads. It was a remarkable bit of quiet organization – nothing seen but the flicker of a match as a soldier lit his pipe; nothing heard but the occasional clank of a bit, the stamp of a hoof, the flutter of bat wings, or the calling of a veldt plover high in the air. Thus they waited until midnight, and then began to move back to their lines again. The horses were too well-behaved even to neigh, and we who watched everything spoke to each other in whispers, without quite knowing why we did it. It was the natural consequence of the silent, stealthy preparation, the self-contained, subdued power which might at any moment flame out into death, destruction, and the soul-suppressing din of a night conflict. At no time, I think, are the soldier's nerves so tried as when thus waiting in the darkness for the unknown.

That day, for the first time, I tasted the biltong of which you have heard so much as furnishing the Boer fighter with his chief food supplies when on a campaign. It looks leathery and uninviting, but, if well made, is palatable, and even dainty, while its nourishing qualities are declared to be exceptionally high. It is not, as some may imagine, just a strip of sun-dried beef, but requires some skill in the cutting up. Commencing at the hock, they strip the meat away in natural rolls from the haunch, rarely using the knife; dry it in the sun during the day, and roll it at night in a green hide. It hardens so that, uncooked, it is best cut in thin layers with a carpenter's spokeshave; but these layers make a perfect sandwich, and biltong made from the bluebuck especially is a great delicacy. The settlers of Natal when out on a game hunt invariably equip themselves with biltong, and I have met few who are not fond of it. With biltong, coffee, and flour, the Boer is not badly supplied, and Tommy Atkins, with his biscuit, tinned beef, and no beer, has by no means the best of the comparison.

The local paper, *The Ladysmith Lyre*, had reached its third issue. It was brought out by war correspondents temporarily out of employment. The editor explained that all truthful news would be found under the heading,"Fact" – beneath which was a blank space. Here are some extracts, with explanatory notes where necessary:-

LEADING ARTICLE.

THE SITUATION.
The situation is unchanged.

NEWS.
We are informed that the colony of Natal is safe. Then "God Save the Queen."

Whisky is selling at 35s. a bottle. The Army Service Corps are waiting until the price is £2 before disposing of the 11,000 bottles in stock.

The remarkable nature of the rumours circulating in Ladysmith for five weeks was fairly reflected in the following extracts from

THE DIARY OF A CITIZEN.
Nov. 9. – Tremendous battle to-day. Enormous victory. Enemy's losses prodigious. Fifth Lancers galloped two Maxims up to Limit Hill, and then trotted back. Boers followed, when up jumped Liverpool regiment and shot 600. Boer cavalry charged up Observation Hill, tripped over wire; then up jumped 60th Rifles and shot 600. Dublin Fusiliers drew enemy across Leicester Post, when up jumped Leicester regiment and shot 600. Gordon Highlanders surrounded 600 Boers, when up rode Sir George and all surrendered.

Nov. 14. – General French has twice been seen in Ladysmith, disguised as a Kaffir. His force is entrenched behind Balwan. Hurrah!

Nov. 20. – H.M.S. *Powerful* ran aground in attempting to come up Klip river. Feared total loss.

Nov. 21. – Hear on good authority that gunner of Long Tom is Dreyfus.

Nov. 22. – Dreyfus rumour confirmed.

Nov. 26. – Boers broke Sabbath, firing on our bathing parties. Believed so infuriated by sight of people washing that they quite forgot it was Sunday.

NEW SONGS.
(Sung by the Leading Vocalists.)

"Oft in the Stilly Night,"
Boer Artillery Chorus.

"Oh that We Two were Maying,"
Sung by Sir G. F. White and Sir C. F. Clery.

"Over the Hills and Far Away,"
Relief Column Chorus.

"They're after me, they're after me,
To capture me is every one's desire;
They're after me, they're after me,
I'm the individual they require."
By Colonel Rhodes.

Note – I have mentioned the remarkable persistency with which the Boer shells followed Colonel Rhodes, however frequently he changed his residence.

SKILL COMPETITION.

A bottle of anchovies – useless to owner on account of prevailing whisky famine – will be awarded to sender of first opened solution of this competition:– "Name date of relief of Ladysmith." Generals and inhabitants of Ladysmith who say "Ja" instead of "Yes" will be disqualified as possessing exceptional sources of information. Send answers, with small bottle of beer enclosed, to Puzzle editor.

THEATRICAL.

The amateur theatrical club have for the last five weeks been rehearsing "Patience." Their next productions will include "The Case of Rebellious Susan" and "The Liars."

WHERE TO SPEND A HAPPY DAY.

To the Ladies of Pretoria. – Messrs. Kook and Son beg to announce a personally conducted tour, Saturday to Monday, to witness the siege of Ladysmith. Full view of the enemy guaranteed. Tea and shrimps (direct from Durban) on the train. Four-in-hand ox waggon direct from Modder Spruit to Bulwan. Fare 15s. return. One guinea if Long Tom is in action.

This was the explanatory note to one of Maude's cartoons, showing the women and children of Pretoria pouring out of the train, while Joubert invited them to try three shots at the Ladysmith Town-hall from Long Tom for a penny.

ACKNOWLEDGMENT.

General Joubert has acknowledged with thanks the receipt of a railway engine.

The point of this lay in the fact that some little time ago the expedient of sending an engine full speed up the line with the intention of wrecking a Boer transport or ammunition train, and perhaps blocking their communications, was hit upon. An engine was specially stripped for the purpose at the Ladysmith railway station; the driver took it out a bit, then opened the valves to full speed ahead, and jumped off. It was a plan full of dramatic and sensational possibilities, but it failed badly. The Boers had not torn up the line, but had thoughtfully widened the gauge, so, long before their terminal station, Modder Spruit, was reached the engine ran off the line and fizzled itself cold on the veldt.

The days dragged their weary length along with no change

for the better in the position. With Macbeth, the tired citizen of Ladysmith cried, "To-morrow, and to-morrow, and to-morrow creeps on this petty pace," but finally came a feat which cheered our drooping spirits, and won in a single act a reputation for the volunteers of Natal. On Thursday, December 7, just at dusk, Long Tom – who, as I have already said, had been shifted from Pepworth's Hill, on the north, to the shoulder of Lombard's Kop, on the north-east – fired his good-night last shell into the town, and it burst in a building next to our quarters, which the military authorities had only that day commandeered for a post-office. The fragments proved of greater value as mementoes than we then imagined, for it was the last shell from the throat of a gun which for weeks had held the people of Ladysmith in terror. It was nearly ten o'clock on Thursday night when the volunteers – some of whom were already in bed – were ordered to turn out in forage caps and light boots, armed with rifles and revolvers only, and without their horses. Every one knew that something interesting was afoot, for General Hunter, the chief of Staff, was there wearing his sword, and evidently out for business; while fifteen of the Guides, led by Major Henderson, were also ready.

Very quietly a force of four hundred volunteers was got together, the men being told that excessive quietness was the first thing required of them. They had repeatedly asked to be allowed to take one of the Boer guns, so Sir George White was giving them their chance with one of the finest fighting men of the empire as a leader. A small party of engineers were also in attendance, confirming the impression that the destruction of a gun was the object of the night expedition. They waited until the moon went down, then had a fine starlight night.

Halting occasionally for a few minutes to let the Guides feel the way, they found themselves at a quarter to two o'clock in the morning within fifty yards of the foot of Lombard's Kop, yet so silent was the march that the Boer pickets, then within revolver shot of them, had not been alarmed, and those in the

In trenches

front of the column could hardly hear the tramp of the eight hundred feet behind them, though the front rank was not more than fifty yards away. In a brief halt General Hunter explained what was intended; one hundred of the Imperial Light Horse and one hundred of the Carbineers would creep up the mountain and take the Boer guns, while as many more of the Border Mounted went round on either side of the hill to protect the assaulting party from a flank attack. The Engineers, with guncotton and appliances for breaking up artillery, were close upon the heels of the stormers. They crept on, amazed that there should be no outposts, when, apparently fifty yards behind our men, who were creeping up the steep hill on hands and knees, came a hoarse challenge, "Wis kom dar?" In the dark we had passed the Boer sentry without noticing him, and it is just possible that he had been dreaming in the warm sultry night. "Wis kom dar? Wis kom dar?" He was getting impatient, and roared out his challenge again and again, and our fellows sat still on the slope above him for a minute, laughing to themselves, and made no answer. "Wis kom dar?" This time there was an unquestionable note of alarm in the Boer challenge, and an English voice said, "Hit that fellow in the stomach with the butt of a rifle, and shut his mouth."

The Boer knew now who was coming there. "Zoo waar as Dod hier is hulle," he yelled in Transvaal Dutch, which in English means, "God's truth, they are really here." His next remark indicated a very natural desire to get out of the district, for after firing his rifle he called to his after-rider, "Bring my peart," or "Bring my horse." That was the last we heard of the vigilant sentry, who had let the enemy past him first and challenged afterwards. A second rifle was heard further up the ridge, and a shrill, squeaky Dutch voice shouted, "Martinas, Carl, der rooinek, der rooinek." A couple of volleys were fired, most of the bullets going over the heads of our men, one of whom shouted, "What ho, she bumps!" The red necks were clambering up the hill like cats, quite prepared for a desperate fight at the summit.

"Stick to me, Guides," General Hunter shouted, and "Take a breath," he called at intervals, but the Guides noticed that Kitchener's fighting general was going on all the time without taking a breath, and they went after him, with a cheer that rang all round the hillside. Colonel Edwards, of the volunteers, shouted, "Now then, boys, fix bayonets, and give them the steel." There was not a bayonet in the whole party, for the volunteers, who are all mounted infantry, did not carry them, but there were Dutchmen up there who understood English, and they waited for nothing more, but went clattering, tumbling, and stumbling down the other side of the mountain. It was all over in less then five minutes from the first challenge, and as Major Henderson jumped up beside Long Tom, who was pointing apparently at the stars, and loaded and laid to a range of 8000 yards, not a Boer was in sight. Away behind the mountains we could see two camp fires shining brightly, but though Umbulwana, with its big guns, rose a black mass not more than half-a-mile away, not a shot was fired from these, and every one regretted that both guns were not being taken. The riflemen ran on to the opposite crest of the mountain, and fired volleys down the slope to keep off any of the enemy who might be coming up as supports.

It was a lesson in military expedition then to see the Engineers going to work at gun destruction. Some of them whipped out the breech-block; others ran a charge of gun-cotton half-way down, plugged the muzzle and the breech, after first chipping away part of the screw, so that it could not be used again. Then they ran a necklace of gun-cotton around the outside of the barrel, and all was ready for Long Tom's funeral.

The gun had been beautifully set on a traverse of solid masonry. It was mounted on huge iron wheels, and a little railway-line had been laid down to run it up to the firing position. Over it was a thick bomb-proof arch, and huge stacks of shells lay round about ready for use. The gun had been stripped by our men of everything that could be carried away as trophies, even the heavy breech-block being brought down. Close by were a howitzer and a field gun, which were soon smashed to pieces, while a Maxim, which had not been fired, so precipitate had been the flight of the defenders, was brought away by the Engineers. Occasionally a Mauser bullet came in amongst the men, but they were few and far between, and within from twenty to thirty minutes of reaching the top, the Engineers, who reminded one all the time of a horde of cats clambering on a rooftop, announced that they were ready. The firing apparatus was attached, and the key pressed. There was a dull roar from the charge, not nearly so loud though as one would have expected, though the whole mountain flamed up with a flash of light. For a minute there was a fear that the gun-cotton had not done its work, but on the Engineers going back, they found that the barrel had been rent asunder, and part of the muzzle torn away. Long Tom would shoot no more. Combustion of the bowels had placed the poor fellow beyond all aid.

The word to retire was given, and nearly every man brought away some souvenir of the fight. One had the tangent-scale of the gun, another the sights, a third the rammer; some had biltong, some tinned beef; even a tin of baking-powder was amongst the trophies. One of the Boers had left without his trousers, in the pockets of which was £4 10s. in Dutch money. Another had thrown away his waterproof coat, which fitted the finder exactly. Back to cover at the foot of the mountain, and the night still dark, we had time to count the cost of this brilliant little rush, which every one had expected would prove difficult. We had looked for such unpleasant entanglements as barbed wire, and the Guides carried wire-cutters, but there were no impediments of any kind.

Major Henderson, the smiling Intelligence officer, for whom all correspondents had so warm a regard, had been twice hit. A shot had almost torn away his thumb, and a couple of slugs had cut their way through the flesh of his thigh, just above the knee. He had been hit at the first volley – the slugs evidently fired from a fowling-piece – yet he never halted, but was the first man on the gun, while afterwards he marched back to camp without the help of the friendly arms so freely offered him. Godson, of the Guides, had also been hit in the thigh with slugs and loupers – the latter a large buckshot, something like swan-drops – so that the Boers must have equipped themselves freely with shot-guns, as likely to be the most useful in stopping a night rush.

It was found afterwards that the Boers had used as loupers the hard steel bicycle-balls looted from the Johannesburg cycle-shops. Godson still has some of them in his leg, and is probably the only man in the British Empire going about on ball-bearings.

Private Nichol, of the Light Horse, a sturdy giant, 6 ft. 6 in. in height, was badly hit, one shot passing through his arm and two through the right side of his chest, just under the shoulder. Private Williamson, another comparative giant, was shot in the thigh, and Private Patterson in the right arm. A bullet ricochetting from a rock had hit him just above the wrist, and torn the flesh away almost up to the elbow. Lillywhite, of the Guides, was grazed across the knuckles, and Corporal Hume, of the Carbineers, had a furrow cut in his cheek with a Mauser bullet. This was the casualty list, and Nichol was the only one so badly hurt that he had to be left where he fell, in care of his surgeon, until the ambulance came.

There was tremendous cheering when the volunteers came back to camp, and that morning at breakfast, in the officers' mess-tent of the I.L.H., Long Tom's breech-block was the centre-piece, and held a bunch of flowers. General Hunter, before leaving, complimented the volunteers warmly, both on their silent march and plucky rush, and said he had no wish to lead better men – a compliment which, coming from the source it did, was the more greatly valued. Later in the day Sir George White repeated the congratulations.

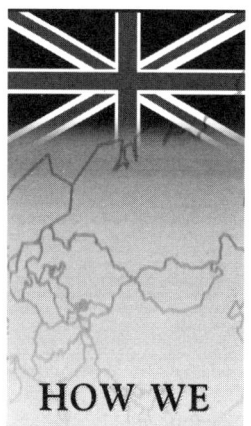

HOW WE KEPT THE FLAG FLYING

CHAPTER 13

A SURPRISE ON SURPRISE HILL

A night raid – Dilatory Hussars – A plucky Australian – A Boer letter – Physiology of funk – The rush on Surprise Hill – Deadly bayonet work – A resentful enemy.

ON Friday, December 8, the people of Ladysmith overslept themselves. There was no Long Tom to wake them with its morning shell, and when Long Tom had set himself to wake the residents there was nothing half-hearted in his way of doing it; no one turned over drowsily and asked for another half-hour. It seldom happened though that we had any little success in the siege without its counterbalancing failure. This took the shape of reconnaissance by the Hussars. The idea in sending them out was to create a diversion toward the northwest, while to north-east at Lombard's Kop the volunteers carried out their task of destroying the big gun. The cavalry burned some Kaffir kraals in that direction, and, as instructed, made a considerable flare, but repeated the mistake which has so often been made in this campaign, of so long delaying their return that they had to come back in daylight under a heavy fire, for if there is one thing in which the Boer excels in war it is the feat of promptly following up and peppering a retiring enemy. Where upon a determined advance not a man is to be seen, they appear as if by magic the minute the foe turns his back, and rarely is their fire so hot as then. They pour it in as fast as they can load and fire, and their haste to make the most of an opportunity, which involves no risk to themselves, is the one fault in their method. It proved the salvation of our men upon more than one occasion.

From the Convent ridge at half-past four in the morning we could see a body of horsemen coming leisurely in from Pepworth's towards the town. As the Boers opened on them with every arm available, the 100-pounder on the top of Bulwan, the lesser siege guns, field guns, Pom-poms and rifles, the blare of sound was imposing. All along the western Boer ridge it equalled the crash of a general engagement. Then, too, the enemy got some idea of what our naval guns could do if fairly put to it. The pivot gun had hitherto confined itself to silencing their fire when it became at all heavy, or to dropping a couple of shots at dusk on a spring, where the Boers came late to water their horses. It commanded every hill within a radius of eight miles of Ladysmith, and now poured its shots upon the Bulwan gun so fast that the gunners dared not work it, and were silent. Two others searched the length of Pepworth's Hill, where, judging from the sound, their machine guns were stationed. A battery of our field guns searched the low ridge on which the Boer rifles crackled.

Under cover of this fire the Hussars made their dash for home in three separate squadrons. No sooner were they in the open, having to cover an even stretch of grass, than the rifles burst tempestuously, and the sun being up we could see the Mausers flicking the dust all around them, while an occasional shell fell dangerously close. It was a long-range fire, but it was none the less remarkable that the squadron got across without leaving a man on the green grass, which the field-glasses on our ridge were searching anxiously. The cavalry had the shelter of a donga for some distance; then more open ground, where the Boer fire was even heavier. Here there were several men down, and every one drew a long breath when the last of them was in. That last man, in this case, rode alone quite half-a-mile behind the others, and galloped his hardest, drawing at one stage of his run the fire of almost every Boer rifle within range. Yet he lived and finished his ride, though the dust from the bullets hung like a low rising fog upon the veldt. The instant he had dropped behind the hills the fire ceased. On our ambulance going out they found two of the Hussars dead and quite a dozen wounded. The Boers on that side evidently knew of the loss of their guns that morning, and were burning for vengeance. Red crosses and white flags commanded no respect then. They fired on the ambulance as soon as it appeared, and shot one of the leading mules.

Dr. Hornabrook, riding out to attend to the wounded, stirred up the fire again, and the bullets were dropping all round him. He waved his white handkerchief, the signal the doctors generally adopt, for the white armband with the Geneva cross is invisible at the distance. The waving of the handkerchief only appeared to exasperate them, and as the fire grew hotter the doctor got back to cover. Out of this affair the Hussars came with a loss of three killed and about a dozen wounded, but it was an entirely unnecessary and aimless sacrifice, as there was nothing to prevent mounted men getting back to camp before daylight. The carelessness of our men in this respect is a complete mystery to the Boer. While Dr. Davis was waiting beside some wounded men that day a few Boers came down to him and chatted about the fight. "Why do your men always let us catch them in daylight?" one man said. "It is very foolish; cannot the English horses march home in the dark?"

When the volunteers carried the gun position at Lombard's Kop on Friday morning, and the Boers went down the back of the mountain, some of them shouting in falsetto notes that were almost a scream, there was some curious loot taken on the mountain-top. One of the Free State burghers had evidently just written a letter to his sister and left it behind. It was addressed, strangely enough, to Balaclava Farm, and a translation of that part of the letter dealing with the war shows that however the people of Pretoria may be gulled by the imaginative accounts of the siege published by *Diggers' News*, some of those in the commandoes have no delusions about it. The writer, Wessel Groenwold, gave his address as Head Laager, Ladysmith, care of Major Erasmus. He says –

"It is one month and seven days since we besieged Ladysmith, and don't know what will happen further. The English we see every day walking about the town, and we bombard the town every day with our cannon. They have erected plenty of breastworks outside the town. It is very dangerous to take the town. Near the town they have two naval guns from which we receive very heavy fire, which we cannot stand. I think there will be much blood spilt before they surrender, as Mr. Englishman fights hard and well, and our burghers are a bit frightened."

That hint as to the feeling of the enemy tallied with what we have heard from other sources.

The list of narrow escapes continued always to be more amazing than the actual casualties. Yesterday Mr. King, the district superintendent of public works, had two shells bursting simultaneously, one close in front of his horse's head, the other at its tail. Those who saw it waited very anxiously for the smoke to clear away, but neither horse nor rider had a scratch – though the concussion was so severe that Mr. King was ill for an hour afterwards. On the same day a small shell ricochetted from a higher ridge and rolled down the road like a hoop, close upon his horse's heels. A few days ago a party of ladies were walking down the Crown Hotel garden to a large apple tree, on which the red-cheeked Margarets were just ripening. They stayed for a minute to talk to the gardener, and that minute just saved them, for they were within twenty yards of the tree when a 15 lb. shell struck it just below the branches. It was a very old tree, umbrageous and gnarled, but the butt was snapped clean, the top of the tree thrown some distance away, and even then the shell did not burst until it had buried itself in the earth. The ladies had no difficulty in picking apples. A man in one of the Carbineer tents was taken out for dead, a shell having pitched close to his head as he slept. He suffered only from concussion. A still more wonderful escape occurred in the same camp. This time the shell pitched at the man's feet as he faced the gun. The explosion tore away his clothes, burned his chest with the flame of the powder, and plugged his nostrils with earth. In an hour he was walking about all right. From November 1 the casualties amongst the military forces in Ladysmith, taken from the official list, were 23 killed and about 180 wounded, while with civilians and Kaffirs the death-list for a six-weeks' siege reached less than 40.

On Sunday, December 10, the Boers fired a number of heavy shells into the town, this being the first Sunday during the siege on which they had seriously bombarded. It must, therefore, have been a matter of urgency. In the dusk of the morning there was a heavy fire of rifles and Maxims on the top of Bulwan, the result of a little ruse on our part. It was known that the Boers had concentrated a lot of riflemen on the mountain in anticipation of another attempt on our part to take a gun. It was thought that if our pickets went close up in the darkness, fired a few volleys at the crest of the hill, and then promptly retired, the enemy, confused by the darkness, which they hate, would probably fire into each other. Their firing was certainly furious, but whether the anticipated effect followed we could not say. Next day the fantastic crowd of Dutch prisoners and suspected spies imprisoned in the Boer church sang "God Save the Queen," but from the remarks of the corporal's guard they would have been rather more respected had they sung the Boer anthem. Tommy admires stubbornness in an enemy, and has a distaste for "rats," which will, I think, become so plentiful as to be almost a plague two months hence.

Students of human nature had an excellent opportunity in Ladysmith of studying the physiology of funk, the lesson being presented in many and peculiar phases. There were members of the volunteer corps – and the volunteers won a name for daring in all that they have been permitted to undertake – who had never accompanied their corps into action. They simply lost their nerve, and were quite incapable of fighting. They were pitied rather than despised. Their colonel took them aside, and appealed to them to pull themselves together and act like men, but not the example of their comrades round about them, nor their own shame, nor their desire to overcome their fears was of the least use. They were for the time being incapable of fighting, and pitiful as such an exhibition may be, none felt it so much as the men themselves. There were others who funked shell, and nothing else. They had the nerve to do anything required of them with the rifle, but a shell found the weak spot in their moral armament. Neither ridicule nor argument could prevent them ducking when a shell passed over, however high in air, though with all the corps it was a question of honour when on parade to pay no attention to a shell, however close it fell. Early in the siege an old major, whose fighting record is beyond question, was lecturing his men on the folly of ducking to shell. "When you hear it, men, it's actually past, so that ducking your heads is quite useless." Just then came a hissing shell from "Silent Sue" close over the major's head. He ducked. The men laughed, and the major observed, "Ah, well, I suppose it's just human nature." An enemy rather more feared than shell was amongst us in typhoid fever. The outbreak was due no doubt to the impossibility of enforcing anything like sanitary observances upon the hordes of Kaffirs and coolies camped about the hills. Cases were pouring in daily, and no one was more anxious for the appearance of the relief column than the doctors, who were seriously alarmed for the health of the town.

Having so brilliantly, and with trivial loss, taken the gun on the formidable position at Lombard's Kop, our men burned for further enterprises of the same dashing character. As the Boers were certain to be on the alert after their first humiliation, it was decided to let Saturday and Sunday pass without any further effort, but on Sunday night men were moving about with an air of studied secrecy so plainly written on their faces that even the novice in military movements knew some further enterprise was afoot. Surprise Hill, due west of Ladysmith, was appropriately the point aimed at. It had been so named because there the second gun placed in position by the Boers early in the siege opened fire upon us one morning before even our outposts had an idea that it was being placed in position. At ten o'clock on Sunday night the first move was made, and as the storming party was picked from the Rifle Brigade, which held a high point on that side of the town known as King's Post, the preliminaries were carried through with even greater secrecy than usual, and the Boer spies in the town had no chance of sending or signalling a warning to their friends.

This time the attacking force consisted solely of regulars, five companies of the Rifle Brigade – the biggest lot of men in the Natal column – being led out by Thornhill and Ashby, of the Guides, who, both being residents, know every foot of the country. The same plan that proved so successful at Lombard's Kop was again adopted, 200 men making the direct attack while 150 were thrown out on either wing to check any attempt at outflanking, and in this the retaliatory effort of the enemy was exactly anticipated. Moving out slowly and reconnoitring every few yards, it was two o'clock in the morning before the battalion arrived at the foot of the hill, and halted not more than a hundred yards from the summit. Running obliquely up the hill was a wash-out by storm waters, and this sheltered them for another fifty yards at least, when Colonel Metcalfe, who was in command, gave the word to move on still stealthily, each man passing the order in a whisper to his left-hand support.

Still not a challenge, and everything round about as still as death. They were within ten yards of the crest, when those directly in front of the redoubt were seen to throw themselves flat on the ground. Through the faint light they had caught sight of the 6 in. gun, drawn out of its pit right forward to the brow of the hill, the muzzle depressed and pointing straight down at them. For a second or two the men in front crouched in momentary expectation of being blown to eternity almost from the gun's mouth. But there was no sound of men about it, and the position flashed instantly across the minds of the British infantry. The Boers had brought their gun forward from the redoubt in expectation of just such a surprise movement as was then being made, yet kept so poor a watch that we were upon them before they knew it. Our men could no longer control themselves. As a unit the assaulting column sprang forward. A man started up out of the gloom with a low exclamation of surprise, and the next instant there was that dull lunge of the bayonet as the first man on the crest drove it through the breast of the Boer sentinel. "Oh, God!" the poor wretch screamed in Dutch as he fell writhing on the ground, clutching with both hands at the weapon that had transfixed him. Before the man who killed him could withdraw his weapon a second Boer, standing further back, sprang up and shot him, and Briton and Boer, the first two victims of this dramatic night fight, lay side by side dead. A sweeping cut from an officer's sword almost decapitated the second burgher, and in an instant the men of the Rifle Brigade leaped into the redoubt.

Some twenty men of the Staats Artillery, the squad who worked the gun, were sleeping there and they had no time to use either rifle or revolver – they woke only to die. There was a confused shouting and screaming, a few appeals for that mercy which could not be given, for unpoetical Tommy Atkins is a very demon of death when with bayonet fixed he gets amongst the enemy at night. He may himself be overwhelmed by numbers in the next instant, for there is necessarily great uncertainty as to what may follow, so there is no time for making prisoners. The dismounted Boers behind the gun fired two hurried volleys, which did little damage, and then fled, the clatter of their veldt-schoen being heard down the stony slope. Most of our men ran forward one hundred and fifty yards and fired after the retreating Boers, and when the section of Engineers and Royal Artillery, who followed up the storming party to destroy the gun, jumped into the redoubt they actually stumbled over the dead and dying artillerymen, nearly all of whom were lying on the gun-floor. Everything was ready for action; there even the gunners had slept in their clothes; but the national torpidity of their sentinels had betrayed them. Their magazine was open, and four of the large brass cases which hold the charge for the howitzers lay in a leather case close to the breech of the gun. Charges of gun-cotton were quickly placed both in the gun and the magazine, but at the first attempt only the magazine blew up, the fuse laid to the gun having proved defective. On the explosion there was a roar of cheering from our infantry, echoed by a triumphant shout from the enemy, who thought the magazine had accidentally blown up, with our men all about it.

No less than twenty-five minutes of valuable time were lost in preparing another fuse to the gun, and this gave the enemy a chance to recover their senses for their favourite style of fighting – rifle fire on retiring troops. In a few minutes a large body were working round the mountain on both sides, assuming that, on the first explosion, our men would retreat. When the gun blew up they had almost outflanked us, and, sudden and successful as had been our assault, it looked as though our retreat might be cut off at any moment, and a heavy toll taken for the splintered gun and the dead men we had left upon the summit of Surprise Hill.

"Straight through them with the bayonet," was Colonel Metcalf's order, and the men rushed back, with a cross-fire already opening on them, though, in the darkness, the Boers fired high, and most of their bullets went harmlessly overhead. The fire became heavy, and men were falling out, though as the bulk of fire was still overhead, it is just possible that the enemy fired into each other as well as into our men. One of the first who fell there was a sergeant of Rifles, upon whose breast were four medal ribbons; and what a satire on the triumphs and trophies of war these scraps of silk appeared when, a couple of hours later, the man who had won and worn them with such pride was brought in dead. Another man was killed by his own weapon. Some of the Boers, in their eagerness, came down the hill, and, as our line brought their bayonets to the charge, this poor fellow stumbled over a rock and fell upon his own steel. A comrade stopped to help him and withdrew the bayonet, but he breathed brokenly once or twice, and with these few respirations had gone. Even then it seemed that we might get back with a loss of not more than five men killed, but, in the confusion which always attends a night attack, our men and the enemy got mixed up on one flank, and some murderous work at short range followed.

Before the attack, as I have already said, one hundred and fifty men had been sent out on either flank to meet the enemy should they rally upon our retreat, and attempt to outflank. Both parties worked rather wide, so that the two lots of Boers who first cut round the shoulder of the hill passed between our wings and the mountain without being seen. It was a third body of the enemy hurrying up to reinforce that came directly upon our right wing. Although the light was growing fast, they were within thirty yards when they opened with a volley, and so confident were our infantry that the clatter ahead was that of their own men returning from the gun, that they shouted to them, "Don't fire; it's A Company." They were soon undeceived. A second volley was fired, and the Boers, shouting to each other to kill the "verdomed rooinek," came surging on. That was their mistake; better had they stood off and kept silent, but, confident in their superior numbers, they thought they had the British at their mercy.

In those first two volleys several of our men fell, including Lieutenant Everton mortally, and Captain Pavey seriously wounded; but, before a third could be fired, the British infantry were amongst them with the bayonet, fighting in the old style, as under Wellington, Raglan, and Lord Clyde. The whole situation changed again like magic. Guided by the spurts of flame from the Boer rifles, Captain Gough – whose conduct was highly praised – shouted "Follow me, lads," and went straight at them, shooting the first man he encountered with his revolver. The Boers were once more surprised, dazed, demoralized, and again the revolver, which might have served them at close quarters, was never drawn. On one side it was lunge and thrust, on the other scream and scuttle, but they were so dazed by the suddenness of the move that they showed anything but their usual promptitude in getting away. Some of the Dutch shrieked like women, and nearly fifty of them were left lying amongst the rocks after that short, grim fight. One officer of Rifles counted twenty-three dead Boers in a donga, and all had fallen to the bayonet. Having scattered them our men drew off without further loss, and, for a time, knowing only our own casualties, it was generally assumed that we had paid rather dearly for our success. Eleven of the Rifle Brigade had been killed and 43 wounded, while 6 of our men were taken prisoners – 60 men of the 200 who an hour earlier went up Surprise Hill out of action. The missing men were captured while helping wounded comrades off the field – a thing which, according to military usage, they had no right to undertake, and the Boers were fully justified in holding them prisoners.

The Boers were determined that we should learn as little as possible as to their actual loss, and sternly ordered our ambulance wagons to halt until they had first removed their own dead and wounded. They even marked their determination in the matter by firing a few shots. But when the bayonet is the weapon used there are means of guessing at the enemy's loss. On the inspection of our bayonets after the fight 96 were found smeared with blood, and some of them may have been used more than once. Those red blades were a horrible proof of what the Boers had suffered. Later on they admitted a loss of 28 killed and 23 wounded, but in those little professional confidences which the surgeons exchange in the field, their doctors told ours that the loss was really heavier, and the call upon their services more severe than on any other occasion since the opening of the campaign. Little wonder, then, that when Major Duff, from our camp, had occasion to meet General Schalk Berger, a couple of hours later, to ask why he had detained the first surgeons we sent on to the field, he found the Boer commander dazed with the magnitude of the loss, and much more curt in his negotiations than usual. The whole thing had been done so silently that the enemy were unable to realize that so many of their men had fallen, accustomed as they are to judging the fatalities solely by weight of rifle fire. If anything could be humorous on so grim and bloody an occasion it was the remark of Colonel Erasmus, commander of the Staats Artillery, to one of our surgeons, "Who is going to pay for these guns?" It was very brave, Erasmus thought, for our men to have taken their guns, but what a pity to have destroyed them, and he said it with the almost paternal concern of the bombardier for his beloved guns. They took especially to heart the destruction of the long gun on Lombard's Kop, their very best. It was such a beautiful gun, Erasmus declared, and they had, in a spirit of satire, named it "The Franchise," so that any Uitlander who wanted the franchise could get it for nothing. "And we got it for nothing," observed the doctor, "which makes the allegory complete."

The astonishing point of all others is that after their first experience the Boer should have been caught napping. As a fighter he has his limitations, and one of them is disinclination to, or complete unfitness for sentry-go. On the other side, our supports had almost failed. The British regular, unlike the Natal volunteer, has no bump of locality, and but for the Boers blundering upon our infantry as they did, we might have had on a lesser scale a repetition of the disaster at Nicholson's Nek.

All the Mauser rifles brought away from Surprise Hill that morning had their rangers marked in metres, and it is thought that the Boers read them as yards – hence their erratic shooting on occasions. All their lives they have been accustomed to rifles sighted for yards, and the Boer is not a man to readily accept innovations.

The Gordons were extremely anxious to have their turn at a night attack, and aspired to nothing less than the taking of the big gun on Umbulwana mountain, but Sir George White was disinclined to waste more life in the temporary occupation of positions which could only be held by the enemy a little longer.

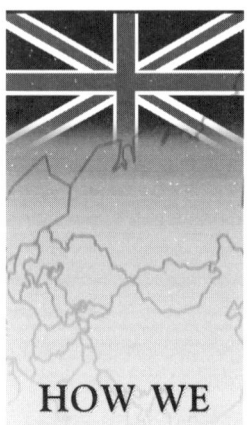

HOW WE KEPT THE FLAG FLYING

CHAPTER 14

BLACK MONDAY IN LADYSMITH

Hope deferred -- The distant guns – Enteric fever – A gloomy garrison – Bad news from the Tugela – The bombardment increases – A shell amongst the Carbineers.

STILL that hope deferred which maketh the heart sick, and, still worse, is provocative of indigestion. It was three mornings since we first heard the cannon of the relief column – "the deep thunder peal on peal afar" – and this morning (December 15) we heard the same distant rumble, no nearer, no further off. At daylight it was constant as the beat of a drum; at noon we heard it in fainter bursts. There was heavy fighting down there on the Tugela river, and we were out of it. Interlarded with the distant cannon came Rumour with tales more or less roseate, taunting us with tidings of victory in which we have no share. That first far-away roar, the Kaffir runners said, was the heavy English guns shelling the Boers out of their picked positions on the western bank of the river. They stood miles off, said the black scouts, and threw their great shells without the Boers being able to reach them in reply. The need for relief became more urgent daily. We had only five days' supply of fresh beef, even on half-rations, 8000 lb. being the ration daily, instead of 20,000 lb. in the earlier part of the siege. The butchers were no longer allowed to supply their customers with meat. Every one must draw his ration. The herds of Angora goats that whitened the hills before the Boers came had almost disappeared, but fortunately the bread, cheese, bacon, and pickles were still plentiful. Quaker oats was our sheet-anchor.

The bombardment continued intermittently, though at times severe. In the cool hours of the morning they did their best or worst, and, taking it at its worst, one might still hope to live to a ripe old age in Ladysmith, though accidents were possible even in a Dutch bombardment. The Boer artilleryman – that is, the son of the soil, as apart from the Staats artilleryman, usually an alien – has methods which our Queenscliff gunners would consider singular. I watched them from King's Post on Wednesday through a first-rate glass. The gunners came up on horseback, went through their work, and retired, perhaps a quarter of a mile to the rear, leaving one man to fire the gun. He had a fast horse and a long lanyard – about two hundred yards I should say for he went quite that distance back before the gun was fired, then galloped off hurriedly to join the rest. They stayed under shelter for a time, and if our guns did not reply came slowly back again to the redoubt. Caution ever marked the guarded way of the Dutch artillery, and it was very hard on those of their gunners who had to stay on the hill-tops, having no horses. Our naval men had been kind to them latterly. When Bulwan opened on the town the Powerfuls no longer fired at the Dutch guns, but pitched their shells right over the mountains, to where the burgher in his laager was masticating his morning biltong. They always know when they have reached the spot, for the Dutch guns at once ceased firing, in the hope that ours may follow their example. We had generally a couple more shells to spare for that particular elevation.

The slackness in the Boer fire was, no doubt, due to the fact that most of their guns had been hurried southward, to face a more aggressive enemy. The conduct of the residents had become correspondingly callous. No one paid any attention to the shells until one pitched remarkably close to them, when they started hurriedly for shelter. The consequence was often a careful shutting of the stable door after the horse has been stolen.

To be careful of oneself for days during a bombardment is easy enough; it is even easier when the siege stretches into weeks, for one has shocking samples of the sort of thing he does not wish to become; but when the weeks stretch into months one goes quite away to the other extreme, and, as I have said, nothing short of the bursting of an adjacent shell, and the ominous fusillade of its shrapnel upon the iron roofs, turns one's mind to the first law of nature. It is the general experience. Those who were a little bit afraid at first became quite indifferent; others, who were very much afraid began to regard themselves as, upon the whole, rather brave. Life would have been tolerable did its bare necessaries not so egotistically pose as its luxuries.

The *Natal Mercury* told us that we of the three beleaguered cities – Ladysmith, Kimberley, and Mafeking – were heroes. We were. Any man who could face the flies of Ladysmith for a month, and its mosquitoes at night, was a hero. Our courage was being tried, however, by something more distressing than Boer shells, for the camp reeked of dysentery and enteric. No fewer than fifty of the Light Horse were invalided, and, in face of this new danger, faces wore a greater gravity than the Dutch siege train had ever been able to stamp upon them. There was a train-load out to Intombi every morning, and the condition of those who had sought refuge there was truly miserable – sickness, gloom, stagnation, and sometimes next door to starvation. Enteric is just typhoid under another name – though Drs. Buntine and Hornabrook say that they have adopted local usage, for the mention of typhoid generally kills the patient through fear, though most of them are confident of being able to grapple with enteric. Other diseases, attracted by congenial surroundings, had come and established themselves, and the one thing from which we were singularly free was delirium tremens. The stagnation was killing. One sometimes got a ride out in the cool of the evening, though at midday even a single horseman appearing on the table-land for a breath of fresh air drew the fire of one or other of the Boer guns. It was a distinction in a way to secure the undivided attention of a 6 in. Krupp gun and ten artillerymen, but even with an egotist it adds little to the pleasure of a ride. The balloon had not been up for days, we had only one fill of gas left, and reserved it for an emergency. A shell fired by the relief column fell within four and a half miles of one of our hill camps. So near and yet so far.

Saturday, December 16, was the anniversary of the declaration of Transvaal independence – the last probably they shall celebrate as a self-governing people. They celebrated it by opening on us with twenty-one guns, thus repaying in kind our Prince of Wales's birthday salute. Their salvoes were more deadly than usual, two men being killed, and another severely wounded. A gunner of the R.A. was hit fairly in the middle of the back with a large shell, and fearfully mutilated. Major Valentine, a young officer who had won his brevet rank rapidly owing to the many fatalities amongst the officers in his brigade, was about to saddle his horse, when a shell came through the stable and cut off the animal's head as cleanly as though it had been done with a butcher's cleaver. Every day less attention is paid to fatalities from shell – every one being so sick of the situation that there was room for no other sentiment than selfishness. Two months ago a few rifle-shots would have sent every correspondent to his saddle in anticipation of a fight; now we paid scarcely any attention to it. Men engaged in a game of whist were rarely so distracted either by bomb or Mauser that they failed to return their partner's lead or overlooked his demand for trumps. Some one would languidly remark, "Rifle fire at Cæsar's Camp," and the game continued.

Declaration Day of the Dutch closed in eclipse literally, for that night there was a total eclipse of the moon, which we regarded as emblematical of the eclipse of Boer independence. Just then they had less reason for thinking so. They knew what we learned for the first time on Sunday, December 17, that Sir Redvers Buller had had a reverse on the Tugela – "failed to make good his footing," as the official account curtly and enigmatically put it. Correspondents, who had been wagering as to whether Buller's advance guard would be sighted at noon or not until sundown, were invited to the intelligence office to hear this chilling news first, and it struck them like a bombshell. Later the town was placarded with the dispiriting announcement, to anticipate the more sensational accounts of the fight which were sure to reach us from the Boers *via*, Intombi Camp. Public feeling, like a barometer in hurricane weather, had been always moving for the last week. With the far sound of the cannon came hope deepening to expectation as the sounds of the battle died away. Then came doubt, and with this last announcement of failure utter despondency, which found no reflection, however, in the heliograph press messages sent away that day. By request, correspondents ceased to dwell upon the fever and sickness with which the town reeked, though that morning we knew that in the 19th Hussars alone there were ninety-six men down with enteric, and the fever season was not due until the middle of January, and on through February, when it is usually at its worst. What wonder, then, that on this Sunday a great despondency fell upon the town, affecting different men in different ways. Then we realized that strategy rather than audacity had brought the Boer out of his own level country, where the superior British artillery and our long-range volley firing would have smothered him. His position on the Tugela was almost unassailable. His front was covered by the river, beyond which for miles lay an open valley, across which the British must come without a particle of cover. On the enemy's side of the river the hills rose abruptly from the water, the reverse slope so sharp that shrapnel, to be effective, had to burst with the nicest accuracy, otherwise it was lost in the valley beyond. One such hill would have gained tactical prominence were it the only one in a province, but when you reflect that such ridges, each of them a natural fortress, were packed over the whole eighteen miles between Colenso and Ladysmith, just as though some Titanic ploughman in ages long gone by had turned up the sods, you may realize the tremendous difficulties an invading force had to encounter, even where the number and excellence of British troops would, under ordinary circumstances, have given them the right of way.

Monday, December 18, – only a week till Christmas Day, and no expectation of getting out. Fired with their success on the Tugela, the Boers had been at us since dawn with a cannonade more murderous than anything previously experienced, though they had not, I should say, more than half-a-dozen guns in position firing from west, east, and south. But they had tested every range exactly. They knew their own gun errors, and their first shot from Bulwan on Monday morning was one of the most disastrous we had in camp. The Carbineers had just returned from outpost duty, and off-saddled. A party of them were on stables when the first shell from Bulwan came at them with its threatening scream. It struck a horse fairly on the quarter, otherwise it might have been less disastrous. The shock was sufficient to burst the shell – one of those thin skins of steel, loaded with large-sized bullets – and it flew, spreading forward. The rising smoke revealed a dozen men and horses on the ground, some writhing in agony, some still in death, and from the poisonous shell fumes rose the awful groans of men shockingly mutilated. Troopers Buxton and Miller, of Maritzburg, lay dead. Close to them was Craig Smith, the dashing full-back footballer, of Dundee, his body partly across that of his youthful townsman, Elliott – a cadet who at the age of sixteen had died a soldier's death. Poor little chap! his comrades had tried often to shield him, keeping him in camp upon one pretext or another when they went to fight, though all their generous deceit had proved vain. Nicholson, another private, lay close by, his right leg hanging by a tendon, a piece of the thigh-bone blown yards away. Five other men were badly wounded. A three-legged horse was plunging amongst the tents. Eleven others, dead and mutilated, made the place a horrid shambles. This was the shocking sight that met us in the Carbineer lines, a camp that had been fully exposed, and every rood of which had been seamed with shell, yet with slight loss to the corps until this devastating bomb came amongst them. The escapes were, as usual, wonderful. Craig, a trooper who affected the baggy riding-cords of the British officer, had three bullet-holes in them, yet was not scratched; another had a box on which he sat blown from beneath him. The base of the shell – the only heavy bit of metal in it – ricochetted across the river three hundred yards away, and killed a sapper who, having just come off duty, was lying down to rest. Only four rounds were fired by their big gun that morning, and one of them, pitching near the river, killed four of a fatigue-party of Kaffirs and their white overseer, while, at the other end of the town, a Kaffir woman was blown to pieces. The Blauwbank gun to southward also pitched a shell amongst the Manchesters, killing one man and badly wounding another – a bad butcher's bill for half-an-hour's shelling. The South African is like the Australian in many things. I heard one of them say, "There's poor Auld Robin Gray killed." Looking in that direction I saw a grey horse, a crack hurdle-racer, well known on South African courses. Even in that *mêlée* of dead and dying men there was a regret to spare for a race-horse.

It needed only such a disaster as this of the Carbineers to deepen for all in Ladysmith the natural gloom of the situation. For the rest of the day men moved about silently and alone, saying little, thinking much. It was the day of light living and deep thinking, for everything in the shape of luxuries had long since disappeared, even in the best-kept houses, and the town was on army half-rations, and having, for the time being, something the worst of the comparison with Tommy Atkins. In the fits of moody abstraction that came upon us, memory, like a magician, opened up her treasure-box to show us all the joys of life we had so lightly valued – the treasures made sacred by time and distance and contrast with the harshness of our environment. It would be harder still a week hence – on Christmas morning. Even those things that were but the commonplace of life came to us, took possession of us, stayed with us. At the close of one of the burning days, a Melbourne doctor dropped in for a chat, and after we had been silent for a while asked, "How would you like to be taking a header off the springboard at St. Kilda now?" "Or riding out to Keilor on the bicycle," I suggested, "for a quiet tea at Hassed's in the evening?" "Or sitting in the Melbourne pavilion, watching Bruce and Trumble bat?" And so we went on, putting ourselves upon the rack for pleasant torture.

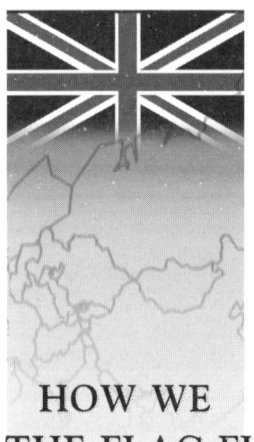

HOW WE KEPT THE FLAG FLYING

CHAPTER 15

WAR WITHOUT GLAMOUR

The Ladysmith oven – Dodging the shells – Burials after dark – Flies and mosquitoes – Our estimate of the Boer – Sickness and wounds – A threat of assault.

TAKING it in all and all, Monday, December 18, was a day that the besieged of Ladysmith will not soon forget. It was 104° in the shade, a temperature which in South Africa makes our 110° seem a pleasant summer day by comparison. The iron roofs become an oven, and on the slightest exertion in the clammy dead air the perspiration streams from one. It was quite trying enough without the 300 rounds of shell that the Boers flung into us. They fired perhaps twenty shells at a time, then rested from their labours, and began again, a plan always likely to be destructive, for people, finding a lull in the firing, venture out in the open, and are caught. The fire appeared to be directed largely on Sir George White's quarters and the ordnance stores at the foot of the western ridge, once well protected from their gun on Pepworth's, but now fully exposed to the fire from Bulwan Range. A shell passed through the roof of Colonel Ward's quarters, bursting in a bedroom in which Colonel Ian Hamilton and Major Ludlow were lying down. A large splinter of shell struck the bed on which the major was sleeping without injuring him. A much narrower escape was that of a civilian named Marchant. He was sleeping in his room when a shell came through the window, passed between his feet, carried out the end of the bed, and burst beneath the floor. There was not a foot of that room which was not shot-torn; the floor was mostly sticking to the ceiling, yet its occupant came out unhurt – came out at the window, bringing the sash with him, as the door was blocked with *débris*. A colour-sergeant of the Leicesters had just finished with a squad of men, and sat down in the shade of a rock, when a shell struck the rock on the opposite side, the shock throwing him head-over-heels. The sergeant got up, dusting his tunic, and making observations picked up in the ranks long ago, but which had fallen into disuse since he got his stripes.

The melancholy sequel to this day of shell was the burial of the dead. There was little delay, for the graves were always ready, seven and eight at a time waiting for the sleepers, and the white crosses grew thicker every day in "the haven under the hill," where so many of the Ladysmith garrison are waiting for the *réveillé*. The honours of war are sparse. No gun-carriage, no coffin, no band playing the "Dead March," and no last volley over the soldier's grave. We waited until the darkness to bury our dead, and then the men, who at sunrise were flushed with all the aspirations of war and of life, were taken away on a field-stretcher, wrapped in the brown blanket which is at once a coffin and a shroud, the one scrap of military circumstance being the little knot of marching men with reversed arms. So the burying parties came to the cemetery with the stealth of body-snatchers. There was a service, doubly impressive as read by the faint gleam of the dark lantern, and with the dimly-seen men in khaki gathered about the grave, and as they made way for another funeral. It was the burial of Sir John Moore on the ramparts of Corunna over and over again. One burial party was coming down from the hill just before dusk when a shell came straight at them. For a second it seemed that they would be slaughtered, but they dropped the body, fell flat upon their faces, and the shell, just clearing them, swept its desolating course beyond. They rose, picked up their dead comrade, and, swearing with that fervency which only the soldier knows when deeply moved, went on their sad errand. You saw all this, and came home worn down in body and spirits by the strain and the heat, too tired to talk, too hot to sleep, too apathetic to eat, and with nothing to drink. And back to you like a mockery, like the whisper of doom, came that Shakespearian expression of despair, "To-morrow – and to-morrow – and to-morrow." Lastly, the mosquitoes took you to their keeping until daylight, when the flies carried on the work, and a sick and sleepless man cursed from the very depth of his soul all who would appeal from God's high gift of reason and justice to Satan's remedy of the sword. And came to one then, as a lightning flash, the thought that even in our greatest, most inspiring victories, when the bubble of enthusiasm, for the brief moment ere it burst, was glorious in the sunshine, the other side were suffering and dying. When we have inoculated some great fighting general with the virus to kill personal ambition, we shall have created the humanitarian of the age – a most eloquent preacher against the multitudinous horrors of war.

Hot as was their fire on Monday, we never replied to it. Two of our guns had been moved in anticipation of the relief column coming in from the south-west about Sunday, but in this we had been premature, so had to move back again. The result was that all our guns were down, and we had to suffer their three hundred rounds without effective protest. For the first time, too, one of our howitzers was hit. A Boer shell struck it obliquely on the muzzle, fortunately without quite destroying it, and during the night the armourers were hard at work getting it into fighting trim again. The Boer gunnery was very effective that day.

Thirty rounds were fired at one of the howitzers, and there was not a bad shot amongst them. Finding the most dreaded of the naval guns silent, they sought to smother it up with weight of iron, and quite one hundred rounds must have been fired at it – one of the Boer 6-inchers being busy all day, and the scream of its shell splinters flying off the rocky hill had become a characteristic note in the siege of Ladysmith. The day's experience sufficed to show how badly we should have fared without the help of the naval artillery from the *Powerful*. To use a current siege phrase, we should have been "blocked out."

For the balance of the week preceding Christmas the firing, both near and far away, was generally heavy; but still the distant conflict came no closer, though kind rumour was again busy granting us victories. The best that our Intelligence Department could give us was that the news was a little more cheering – a very little, I should say, or it would surely have been made public, for the benefit of a town that was dying of despair and stagnation, and for which good news would have been the best tonic. Then it was rumoured that Buller had carried the Tugela heights by a night attack, and bayoneted the Boers in their own trenches, so that, this position won, succour was measurably closer. And, oh! the pressing need for it. On every side death, sickness, and despondency. It was not enough that Nature seemed to have designed this Natal to be one great battle-ground for the game of manslaughter, but she must needs throw pestilence into the scale against us. And, as though both were insufficient, we must give ourselves opportunities for dramatic dying, as we had done more than once in the sorties about Ladysmith, as we did in the fatal fight of Lombard's Kop early in the siege, as our artillery are said to have done in this blind advance at the Tugela, as we went on doing, in spite of warning or experience, until we learned the bitter lesson that in nothing that he did of his own choice was the Dutchman to be undervalued. It was exasperating to find our men persistently making targets of themselves. They were slowly grasping the fact that modern warfare with a civilized nation is something utterly different from the tribal fights of India and the fanatical charges of North African warriors, to which we have been so long accustomed.

In Natal war was divested of absolutely everything that once lent it meretricious glamour – no bright uniforms, no inspiring bands playing men into battle, no flags, no glitter or smoke or circumstance of any kind, but just plain primeval killing, without redemption, and with every advantage taken that international law allows. The loss in artistic effect was prodigious. The war artist had to presuppose, the war correspondent to imagine, much. But tradition was still strong in Tommy Atkins, and in most of the younger men who commanded him. He wanted to go out and wipe this half-civilian horde from the face of the earth in the fine old way; and thus far the wiping had been effectually done only at night, and even then it is impossible on a large scale. For it is a desperate resolve at best to turn a lot of men loose in the darkness, with the difficulty of keeping touch of each other, or being kept in hand at all, and to find perhaps when the affair is over that the bloodiest fighting has been between men of the same side. Were it not so, our best plan for the balance of the Natal campaign would have been to sleep all day and fight all night. The only bit of colour in the uniforms of the Natal Field Force thus far had been the dark kilts of the Gordon Highlanders. Even that was now abandoned as undesirably conspicuous, and, pending the receipt of khaki kilts, with perhaps just a glimmer of the Gordon tartan, the men wore khaki aprons.

That you may have some notion of the awfulness of life in Ladysmith at that season of peace on earth and goodwill towards men, let me give you one day of the incidents that converted this town by the Klip river from a jewel set in the midst of the veldt into a den of horrors. On Friday morning the train to Intombi Spruit (invalid camp) took away fifty men stricken with dysentery or enteric, and brought back nine dead. That was about the average in illness, if not in deaths. That morning, before breakfast, the remnants of the Gloucester regiment had joined the Devons on the exposed north-eastern ridge of the defence. The Boer gunners saw a group of them full exposed, and planted their big canister shell with murderous accuracy. It went through them as a reaping-machine through ripe wheat, and in the swathe of mortality upon the ground were six men quite dead, five others so fearfully hurt that their wounds could not be looked upon as otherwise than mortal, and five more less severely wounded. It was a horrible holocaust for the one bomb. At another point a number of officers of the 5th Lancers were talking together, when a shell fell almost on them. They were all hit, Colonel Fawcett having one of his fingers shot off, and two shrapnel bullets through his legs. Major King was also severely hit, and the others more lightly. Latterly, it was noticed that their shrapnel had been bursting better than formerly, though still too high to be very effective. This is one respect in which we quite outshine the Boer, the perfect timing of our shrapnel, which invariably bursts twenty feet or so above the point aimed at. A curious example of the effects of shell fire was seen in the artillery camp a few day ago. A number of mules were feeding near a gun, when a Dutch shell cut the heads off five of them, without greatly damaging the rest of the carcase. That was sheer waste. When cattle were thus ruthlessly cut down we had a reasonable chance of fresh meat next day to relieve the monotony of canned meats, but mule – it came not yet, though running a neck-and-neck race with the relief column. Even then our transport cattle – the gaunt, black, high-shouldered, light-flanked South African bullocks – were being slaughtered. The supervision of food supplied became every day more rigid. People who had treasured secret milk supplies, and passed on bottles of it to their neighbours, were ordered to bring their cattle to the show-grounds for milking, so that all might share equally in the luxury, or that, at any rate, those sick of enteric should have first call upon the supply available.

For the few days preceding Christmas our guns had been so silent that the Boers, presuming our ammunition exhausted, showed themselves for the first time in the open. First their gunners came boldly outside the redoubt to watch the result of their shots; next, a little knot of riflemen clustered just below the gun, and, with continued immunity, others joined them, until there were quite fifty of them assembled half-way down the slope of Bulwan. When a well-placed shell carried away part of the tower of the Town-hall, which had so long been a prominent target for their guns, the Dutch on the mountain side swung their hats, and that was the psychological moment for the men at our 4.7 in. guns. The Boers saw the smoke, and scrambled wildly for cover, but our guns have a much greater muzzle velocity than theirs, and the shell burst right amongst them, causing havoc, as one might easily see. They brought six wounded men into hospital at Intombi Camp, and stated that five others had been killed. They were very fierce with their return fire for some time afterwards, and a bit nettled, no doubt, that, with ammunition still to spare, we should have ignored their fire for days. It was no fault of the military authorities, though, that we were compelled to economize ammunition. Two 6 in. guns, with a thousand rounds of shell for each, and a thousand extra for each of the 4.7 guns, were on the trucks at Durban, but the railway authorities failed to get them away, though they were ready two days before the line closed. With that extra armament Ladysmith might still have been besieged, but its bombardment would have been rendered much more difficult. On the evening of December 22, the Boers made their first attempt to approach our guns – a half-hearted advance under cover of darkness against one of the 4.7 redoubts, which a few volleys checked. As they swung away they menaced other points in the ring of defence, but never for a moment probably contemplated carrying the assault home. It is not their game, though the fact that they had already held so much of this colony of Natal for two months against an English force, which at one time would have been thought sufficient to carry the campaign to its climax, disposes for all time, I hope, of the foolish impression that the Dutch are not fighting men. Though the Boers were slow to come on, our sentries rarely relaxed their vigilance. Tommy's shot, too, came so promptly on the heels of his challenge that the usual formula when one was challenged at night was to shout "Friend!" with unmistakable earnestness, and get down flat on your face, to be ready for every emergency.

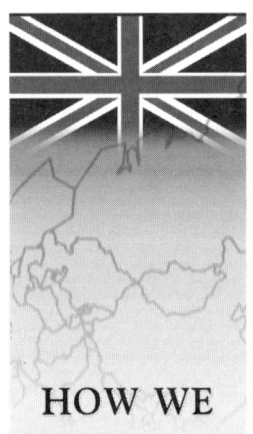

HOW WE KEPT THE FLAG FLYING

CHAPTER 16

CHRISTMAS IN LADYSMITH

*"A Merry Christmas" – The waits – A Christmas text – A Boer joke
– Dead on the veldt – Hospital scenes – New Year greetings
– Remarkable wounds – Commandeering supplies.*

CHRISTMAS DAY! And what a satire the season's compliments sounded. Peace on earth, goodwill towards men! Even as the thought occurred to one, overhead with a scream went the 6 in. shells from Bulwan, for they were earlier at work than usual. "A Merry Christmas, old man; where did that last one drop?" So we mixed up the season's greetings with inquiries as to shell. Had it been only the shells we should have spent the day merrily enough, but the death's-head at every feast was the knowledge of the awful amount of sickness that was cutting some of the corps down to mere skeletons. The squadrons of the Light Horse were usually composed of 75 men each. The largest they could then parade was only 40 strong, and at Saturday's parade one of the squadrons mustered 12 men – the rest were in hospital. Yet on Christmas Eve we had the waits, who borrowed a harmonium from the Dutch church, and made all Englishmen miserable with the recollections of Christmas Eve at home, so utterly different from this one. The Natal Mounted Rifles made us laugh when we felt least inclined for laughing, with their amusing burlesque of a cavalry band, everything improvised. The drums swung across the withers of the gaudiest horse in camp were a pair of empty carbolic oil drums. The cymbals were the ends of a kerosene tin, the triangles the work of the local blacksmith, and the only instruments that by any stretch of imagination could be called musical were the tin whistles. The uniform of the band was weird, mostly gauze and tinsel, and from an Oriental or a Kaffir point of view the drum-major was a magnificent spectacle, his bâton surmounted by a boy's tin top. The amazing thing was the really good music that with constant rehearsal the N.M.R. had got from his queer jumble of makeshift instruments. At a little distance one mistook it for a real drum-and-fife band. The Boers no doubt still found promise of victory or consolation in defeat from the Scriptural texts, in the choice of which they are adept; but looking at the psalm for this Christmas Eve, Sunday, December 24, and remembering the composite character of the Dutch army, there appeared to be something singularly appropriate to our situation in Ladysmith –

"All nations compassed me round about, but in the Name of the Lord will I destroy them.

"They kept me in on every side, they kept me in, I say, on every side; but in the Name of the Lord will I destroy them."

The difficulties in celebrating Christmas are best indicated by a few quotations from the prices at the Christmas market: Ducks, a guinea a pair; fowls, a guinea; eggs, 12s. 6d. a dozen; 28 potatoes for 30s.; a water-melon, 6s. 6d.; Australian butter, 6s. 6d. per lb.; apples, 9s. 3d. a packet; cigarettes, 4s. a packet: sardines, 2s. 9d. per box; tomatoes, 5s. 6d. per plate; brandy, £7 per bottle; whisky, £5 per bottle; Cape port, £1 per bottle. The youngsters were not forgotten, Major "Karri" Davies, of Johannesburg, and Colonel Dartnell issuing invitations to a

Christmas tree, or, rather, four of them, labelled respectively Great Britain, South Africa, Australia, and Canada, and each represented by a typical tree – Australia by a gum, Canada by a fir, and South Africa by a Kaffir thorn. A big trooper of the Light Horse was splendidly got up as Santa Claus, and the wonder was where all the children came from. For months we had lost sight of them; now every burrow of the river-bank poured them forth, starched and radiant as though such a thing as a siege had never been.

The mention of Colonel Dartnell reminds me that we had in the chief of the Natal Police a fine officer, whose services were not used to the extent that they might have been. He was with Lord Wolseley in the 27th during the Crimean War, and has a fine fighting record. On that famous retreat from Dundee his military knowledge, coupled with his knowledge of Natal, prove invaluable, and when most of the officers of the column – with the exception, perhaps, of Major Murray – had, in the expressive language of the men of Natal, "gone in," Colonel Dartnell, with the assistance of the Guides, brought the column through by a circuitous rout, and, helped by opportune fogs and rain, completely baffled the Free State Boers, who, the day before Elands Laagte, told the prisoners they had taken that there would be a big fight next day, and that the Dundee column must be captured or utterly destroyed.

As I have said, the Boers bombarded us before breakfast and again in the cool of the evening, but, though one of the Natal Police had a sensational escape, there was no one killed on Christmas Day. This man was shaving, when a ninety-pounder passed between the mirror and his face. The shock of the passing shot left him grovelling on his face on the ground – as I have seen a beaten pugilist after the knock-out – and for an hour the poor chap could only sit with his head in his hands, and, in reply to questions, murmur, "Not hurt; not hurt." On the morning of Boxing Day we again heard the distant cannon on the Tugela, and the only fear amongst the troops of

Ladysmith now was that the great battle for which we had so long waited might be fought down there, and we should have no share, save listening to its distant echo. The hope was that the Boers might be rolled back upon us beaten, and that our cavalry, for what they were worth, might get amongst them. It was for that they had been pinching and saving in the horse lines, killing every useless animal with a merciless severity, so that the sparse forage could be used to the best advantage.

Although humour is not the strong point of the Boer, he had his grim joke at our expense during Christmas week. A common shell was dug out, upon which a Dutch artilleryman, with some knowledge of English, and the social observances of the time, had cut the message, "Compliments of the season." A wooden plug had been substituted for the fuse, and the shell was stuffed with plum-pudding. It was a characteristic Dutch pleasantry, for the practical joke is the Boer's ideal in fun. On Christmas Eve a dare-devil vedette crept down in the dark quite close to the Manchesters' ridge, emptied his clip of bullets into them, and called out, "Merry Christmas, rooineks." Our men tried to cut him off, but he was too clever. Our acknowledgement of the plum-pudding courtesy was barbarous in the extreme. The vedettes had brought in word that every evening, at dark, a number of Boers were accustomed to come round to the end of the Bulwan, and camp for the night in the dense grove of Kaffir thorn at its foot, directly under their own guns. The object was the double one of getting better shelter from the frequent thunderstorms, and massing men in a convenient place to resist a possible night attack on their guns. They left early each morning, before firing commenced, but Captain Lambton, of the *Powerful*, asked permission to give them a few shells on the morning of the 28th, and as soon as there was enough light to lay a gun on the thorn plot the Navals opened with a swift and sudden storm of metal. There had been heavy rain during the night, the air was clear, and the moon still luminous, when the crash of our guns brought the people of

Ladysmith tumbling out of bed in the fond hope that the relief column, so often in their minds, was at length within their field of vision, for the echo of the few guns rolling, ringing, crashing down the valley made the din of a general engagement. Those at Intombi Spruit, who were close enough to see the result of the fire, say that it must have been disastrous. They saw one man – the first riser in the Boer camp – walk out into the open, and stretch his arms. He heard our shot, and turned to look at the redoubt above him, then realized that it was coming his way, and tried to dart for shelter. He was too late, and when they saw him last, as the shell burst, he was whirling through the air. Four shots were fired in about twenty seconds, a proof of what the *Powerful* guns could do with ammunition plentiful, and then it was all over, and a crowd of Boers were hurriedly saddling up and flying round the shoulder of the mountain. After all it only squared a bloody debt standing over from the day before. The Liverpools had had so little respite in their exposed position that a few days earlier the Devons took their trenches on Helpmakaar ridge nearest to the Bulwan guns. The officers of the regiment were sitting in their traverse on Wednesday morning, when a Dutch shell just cleared the edge, killed Captain Dalziel, who was seated at a camp table writing a letter home, and wounded nine other officers, two of them severely. Poor Dalziel's body was a shocking spectacle, for the shell took his head clean off, and his brains were literally blown in the faces of his comrades. All through Wednesday night there was the crackle of rifle fire, very heavy at one time upon the Devons' post, though what they could see to fire at just then was a mystery, for the rain was falling in tropical flakes, and six feet away it was impossible to distinguish any one in the dense blackness. These wet nights in the trenches were very trying to both sides, trying also to the poor Kaffirs and coolies, who went out in hundreds to cut grass under cover of the darkness, and so eke out our short supply of forage. Though every scrap of grass was eaten away round about the town, there was a splendid crop, that had been growing untouched for months, in the belt of debatable ground between the Boer outposts and our own. A few nights before, Lord Cardigan, going out with the grass-cutters, lost his way in the darkness, and at dawn found himself much nearer to the Boer lines than our own. He would probably have been shot in trying to get back, and wisely determined to lie by in a donga all day, and reach his own lines on the following night. His friends, who assumed that he had been captured by the enemy, were immensely pleased to see him back again.

To those who had their baptism of fire in Ladysmith for sixty days, no horrors that war can offer will now appal, inventive and original as war is in designing the gruesome. Death from shell is not death alone, but butchery; while most of the dead I saw at Tinta Inyoni and the fight at Lombard's Kop were just sleeping with their faces almost always to the veldt. And if the faces be hidden one is soon accustomed to the brown figures lying so limply and so flat amongst the grass, that but for the gleam of a rifle-barrel or a bayonet or the glitter of the chain epaulettes on the shoulders of a Lancer, one might suppose it a bundle of clothes thrown down carelessly. But there is often one ghastly distinction between those who die in bed and die in battle, especially where the circumstances do not permit of an early burial. There is no tender hand to close the eyelids or bind with the face-cloths, so that the dead have that blessed aspect of serene sleep. With these poor neglected dead of the battlefield the chin has fallen as the facial muscles relaxed in death, and the mouth and eyes are generally wide open. The vignettes of the dead which photograph themselves most firmly upon the mind are those in which the pose suggests some action of the living. These will stay with us as long, I think, as life and memory last – such a pitiful pathos is blended somehow with their dead helplessness. Twice we found dead Boers sitting in their little hill redoubts, and coming to them from behind, the only conclusion was that they were still alive and waiting for the enemy. I saw the second one on a kopje of Tinta Inyoni. He was sitting with his back supported by a rock, and in the aperture of the little breastwork in front of him rested the muzzle of his rifle; on a flat rock handy to his right hand were the rows of Mauser bullets in clips of five as they are pushed into the magazine. From the rear was no suggestion of death, save the black stain of blood upon his left hand; but from the front the same staring eyes and open mouth that haunt one, and kill every feeling of exultation in the downfall of an enemy. The views of battle are necessarily distant, but these are impressions that fix themselves by repetition. You rarely see men fall, that is, infantry. They go down quickly with the suddenness of the shock, and the first sight you have of them is the man left lying upon the grass as the fighting line moves on. Then there is nothing more characteristic in action than the swing of the kilt, with its pendulum-like accuracy, as the Highlanders go forward to the assault, never hurrying, never slowing down, but always with that regular, irresistible, unswerving stride. It is an illusion of the bright sunlight, something corresponding to our mid-Australian mirage, which always makes the horses of the retreating Boers appear to be rolling away from us rather than galloping. Where there has been a heavy loss in horses, the poor wounded brutes are ever raising their heads from the ground in pain, and letting them fall back again – an appeal which brings only a merciful revolver bullet to end their sufferings.

Anything that occurs in actual fight pales, though, beside the sufferings of the hundreds of fever patients in the hospital at Intombi Spruit. Only those who know with what care the patient convalescing from typhoid is fed and nurtured can realize the suffering where every medical comfort is exhausted; no stimulants, jellies, beef-teas – nothing fitted for the starving sufferer but the smallest ration of tinned milk. Doctors grew despondent at times, and almost broke down with the strain of unceasing labour. Scores of men, I am told, died of sheer starvation. It was a hundred times worse than anything we had suffered from shell; and is it any wonder that knowing it, feeling it, sympathizing as men must with the sufferings of friends and relatives, they cried out in bitterness of heart, "Why, in God's name, this eternal waiting? Are we to stay here till we rot?" The plight of the well and able-bodied was bad enough, but insignificant by comparison with the occupants of these overcrowded hospitals, where one doctor had as many as forty patients and forty convalescents to look after. As far as possible the men in camp assisted in fatigue work, seventy of them being employed as orderlies, and assistance was needed, for there was not more than one nurse to every sixty patients. Worse still, the medical chests were getting low, and many of the more valuable drugs already exhausted; while, owing to the great scarcity of milk, the doctors heroically struggled to coax typhoid patients back to health on a diet of rice or barley-water. Rations had become scarce, and many were unable to obtain more than a little rice and mealie meal for porridge. The ingenious shifts to secure tobacco were amusing only as against the more vital needs. The man with a pipe was fortunate in being able to secure Boer tobacco – the home-grown, home-cured leaf, which the Boers prepare by first soaking it in the juice of peaches, and then working it into rolls. It has a great fascination for smokers, and when once accustomed to it they never again use American tobacco. The hunt for cigars was eternal, and a few death's-head weeds were picked up occasionally in the coolie shops, even the butts of which were broken up and rolled as cigarettes.

By New Year's Eve it was estimated that since they shut us in they had fired 8000 rounds of shell. That estimate is, I think, a bit over the mark; still, making the most liberal deduction, it was a lot of iron to have thrown upon one small town. I should say that 3000 rounds were fired from the 6 in. guns, or 90-pounders, 2000 rounds from the 4 in. howitzers, or 40-pounders, and 2000 from the 3 in. and smaller ordnance, from which, however, I except the one-pounder Nordenfelt as not being a siege gun, and used as a rule only upon our outposts or the

Devons' ridge. Personally, I had wonderful luck. We were in the direct line of the Bulwan guns, and I suppose 1000 rounds of shell have passed directly overhead since the siege began. Some had gone twenty yards over us, some twenty yards to either side – we could muster, perhaps, 50 100-pounders within a radius of forty yards – yet, save for the rattle of shrapnel on the roofs, our bedrooms had not been hit, and the only shell that was short, and might have done mischief, buried itself without bursting. Beyond us to the town ridge every building had been hit, some of them half-a-dozen times, and the whole of the open place strewn with shells. Considering our position in the line of fire, our luck was just phenomenal. On New Year's morning especially the big shells were hissing almost within reach, it seemed, yet we were so familiar with their music that we could resist the impulse to duck after the shot had passed, and that takes long experience or stern self-discipline. We bowed, perhaps, to one or two that morning, just after we had seen an officer's orderly cut in two within twenty yards – for such sights, though familiar, are shocking, and always temporarily unsettling to the nerves. Soon after midnight the firing began – cannon, machine, and rifles – and continued in an intermittent spluttering fashion all night. We had no ears, though, for anything close at hand; it was the far-away boom, heavier than ever on this early morning of 1900, that interested us. But we had ceased to expect much; we only waited, and in the mean time things were said that I dare not repeat here. It would be high treason. The civilian element in this camp was hard to please. True, as they pointed out, people were dying weekly by scores for want of the common necessaries of life – at any rate, of hospital life – but, on the other hand, we had a military sports meeting.

I must not omit a message sent in by the Boers as a New Year's greeting. It read, "You d---d cowards, why don't you come out of your holes and fight us?" The obvious reply was the old school-boy invitation, "You come half-way." They found Colonel Frank Rhodes again on New Year's Day, a shot going through his house and killing a servant, who was just preparing breakfast. An officer of the Lancers was sleeping in the house, and the explosion fairly buried him in shattered timber. A door thrown fairly on top of him protected him from the fusillade of brick and splinter. When they pulled the timber off him he was rubbing the dust out of his eyes, quite unhurt. That house was one of the first hit from Pepworth's early in the siege, and on the same day a room occupied by Mr. Pearce, of the *Daily News*, was also gutted. Here was the coincidence. On New Year's Day Mr. Pearce's room was again wrecked by a 6 in. shell.

Living in the next room to me was Private Edmunds, a young Englishman, of the Border Mounted Rifles, whose escape from death was one of the miracles of the siege, fruitful as the time and occasion were in hairbreadth ventures. In the very centre of his broad chest is a red indentation, the spot where a Mauser bullet passed through his lungs. A little lower a red mark, the point of entrance for another Mauser bullet, that raked his body, and came out in the thigh without smashing a bone. He lay for days almost pulseless, with ashen-blue swollen lips, and the doctors had already allotted his bed to another wounded man. A severe attack of pleurisy followed the wound in the lungs, and he was almost convalescent, when, in the midst of one of the tremendous thunderstorms so frequent during the Natal summer, the electric current struck the hospital tent, and Edmunds, who was lying with his hand resting on the tent-pole, was again nearly killed by the shock. He got his wounds in the fight at Bester's Farm, which we officially call by that convenient name for failures, a reconnaissance, but which, inasmuch as both cavalry, artillery, and infantry were in action, and a general officer commanded, was really an engagement. One of the heroes of the campaign I may have mentioned earlier, the bugler boy of the 5th Lancers, who, after sounding the charge at Elands Laagte, drew his revolver, rode into the thick of it on his colonel's flank, and shot three Boers in less than as many minutes. There is no doubt about it, for the colonel saw the feat, while scores of officers each gave the boy a sovereign for his pluck. Prancing down the streets of Ladysmith, he was the envy of every boy in town, and he knew it.

Time hung heavily on the garrison with the brief excitement of the Christmas and New Year past, and the only variation to the day's duty of lying behind the stone sangars, and ducking to the Dutch shells, was the gruesome task of grave-digging. That exercise was always with us, for of the garrison of 10,000 fighting men that the Boers shut in here at the end of October, not more than 7000 were efficient. For days we had heard nothing of Buller's guns – not even that faint, faraway roll which at least gave promise of a good time coming – though coming slowly. If in the town there were narrow-minded, nervous people, whose belief in England's might was shaken, who shall blame them? If those who, with the blend of the fatalist and the martyred, placed themselves wholly in the keeping of God, and their countrymen, could not at times fathom a plan of action which condemned them to stagnation and death, be not too hard on their transgression, you far-off critics, who slept in peace, and had three wholesome meals a day. Round about them every day they saw despondency, mutilation, sickness, pestilence almost, and death, and these were not things to stiffen the sinews of the weak-kneed or buttress the faith of the heart-sick and smitten. But the MS. Journal, the *Bombshell*, on one of its rare appearances, satirically parodied –

> "The columns are coming from near and far,
> The columns are coming from Helpmakaar,
> The columns are coming from Frere and Van Renan,
> But no one on earth knows where they are."

"What had you for dinner to-day, doctor?" I asked one of the ambulance staff. "Maize meal and gravy," he answered. They had been served with meat, but it was the tough, sinewy flesh of an old transport ox that had trekked over half Africa, opening up roads for civilization and field guns, and was too awful to tackle in cold blood. The best thing was to chop it and mangle it, and coax as much gravy out of it as possible to help down the unsophisticated mealies, and in doubtful kindness to throw the carcase to the dogs. When an officer – and especially a commissariat officer – ended a series of kindly inquiries as to your dietary scale, with the innocent observation, "How are you off for tinned stuff?" the common practice was to lie bluntly, but with some regard, of course, to artistic verisimilitude. "We had a fair stock, but, unfortunately, we've just finished it." To acknowledge the possession of anything in the way of preserves was to have it commandeered, and if you were in luck to get a little of it back as luxuries.

No news that filtered through to us during the siege caused more regretful sensation in Ladysmith than the bare announcement by heliograph that Mr. Harry Escombe was dead. The leader of the Opposition in the Natal Assembly, he was by far the strongest man in colony, and every one looked forward expectantly to his figuring prominently in the discussion of those great national questions which would face the whole of the South African states upon the conclusion of the war. He strove hard to avert war at the outset, having many Dutchmen in his constituency, but when the die was cast his sympathies were clear. He stood in the open at Dundee and watched the fight – the only really conspicuous man on the field, clothed in black frock-coat and belltopper – a rare sight there, where the Englishman had at least done something in emancipating himself from the manacles of dress. One met the Briton in all types – the soldier, the tourist, the adventurer, the speculator, and the pioneer – and more than ever his capacity for colonization was a mystery to me. He is an Englishman, first, last, and always; he talks of home, thinks of home, dreams of home, and all the while is steadily building up the new branch of empire in which he has so little personal interest beyond the winning of fortune. Yet he relaxes guardedly, blends slowly with his new environment, has in his new chum stage especially a distinct insularity which repels the stranger, and yet with all the national aloofness he is a colonizing success. Why? First, I think, because England seems to pick always the newest, the most remote, the deadliest of her possessions as the outlet for young, strong men, who find no scope in their own land. Educated mostly in the public schools of England, they have a high sense of national honour and duty, a strong, unobtrusive racial pride, which makes them endure much while saying little; and, above all, the love of adventure and travel which is foster-mother to colonization. One thing that surprised me was the number of young Englishmen in the volunteer corps of Natal. For the most part they had no previous military training, yet they were amongst the most daring, and endured silently the hardships over which men less delicately bred grumbled greatly. One could easily overlook the little English angularities in respect for the grit beneath.

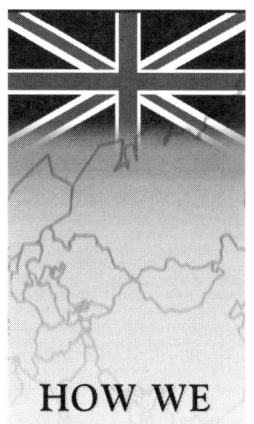

HOW WE KEPT THE FLAG FLYING

CHAPTER 17

A DESPERATE ASSAULT

The Boers come on – The rush on Cæsar's Hill – Bravery of the Imperial Light Horse – The Manchesters' resistance – A stubborn enemy – The inopportune thunderstorm – Charge of the Devons – A costly fight.

EVER since New Year's Day we had heard persistent rumours that the enemy contemplated some decisive step in the investment of Ladysmith. Generals Joubert and Schalk-Berger had gone back to Pretoria to a council of war, and as the sequel, Ladysmith, we were told, was to be taken at any cost. The price had been paid, and the town was held by a British garrison, but there were hours on January 6 when the question of ownership hung suspended in the balance. Monday, January 8, was the date generally named by the Kaffir spies as that upon which the attack might be expected. The truth was that some of the investing forces, and especially the Free State commandoes, were as tired as ourselves of this long siege. "Let us fight or go home," was their appeal. Accordingly a force of picked men was massed to the south-east of the town – 5000 in all, a young Free State Boer who was brought in wounded afterwards declared. The point chosen for assault was known as Cæsar's Hill, being the south-eastern end of the horseshoe forming the "outline" of our defences. The range was irregular here, something in the form of a triangle. It was the highest of all the hills surrounding Ladysmith, and the possession of it would have given the enemy such absolute command over the town, not only by artillery, but long-range rifle fire, that Ladysmith would have been tenable only at a heavy cost. In fact, it would have cramped every operation of our troops, and even the ridges still left to us would have been under fire from both sides. In this respect it was absolutely a life and death struggle, and, having determined on a course of action, the Dutch carried it out with a magnificent daring and disregard of consequences worthy the finest trained troops in the world. Once again they did all that men could do, all that it was anticipated they would not do. Every student of Boer tradition, tactics, and character had declared that they would not attack in the open, that above all they were averse to night movements; yet they did both, and did them splendidly, their stealth and bush-craft enabling them to get right up to our pickets unnoticed, while their quickness of resource in an emergency helped them to delude our men with the idea that friends were approaching, and to get the full advantage of a night surprise. They did all but succeed in their attempt, and thus lavished life to no purpose.

The attacking force was made up largely of Free State Boers, and the Transvaal commandoes, chiefly from Heidelberg and Wakkerstroom. Fortunately for ourselves, we had been steadily bracing up the defences of this particular hill for some days, and, at the very hour the assault was delivered, were placing in position one of the 4.7 naval guns from the opposite side of the town. The Manchester regiment held possession on the left, their redoubt being one of the prominent landmarks there, though to screen it from artillery fire it was placed some distance back from the brow of the hill up which the enemy delivered their assault. Close to the Manchester post Major Aberdy,

A Desperate Assault

of the 42nd Battery, had six field guns in pits, the Naval Brigade had a 12-pounder, and the Natal Navals a 7-pounder. On the extreme right of the position three squadrons of the Imperial Light Horse were in occupation of a point known as Wagon Hill, so called from the curious shape of a tree growing on its crest. In between these two points were scattered at intervals four companies of the King's Royal Rifles. The Light Horse were covering a working party of Highlanders, who were placing the gun in position. All had pickets forward, some little distance on the enemy's side of the hill, the Manchesters lying in stone sangars upon its crest. The face of the hill in front of them was steep almost as a wall, and covered with tremendous boulders, piled in such confusion that amongst them men were absolutely safe except from shrapnel bursting directly overhead. Beyond that, and stretching right across the valley to the Boer ridge, the country was covered with Kaffir thorn. Although the Boer attack, which covered a front of over two miles, was very well

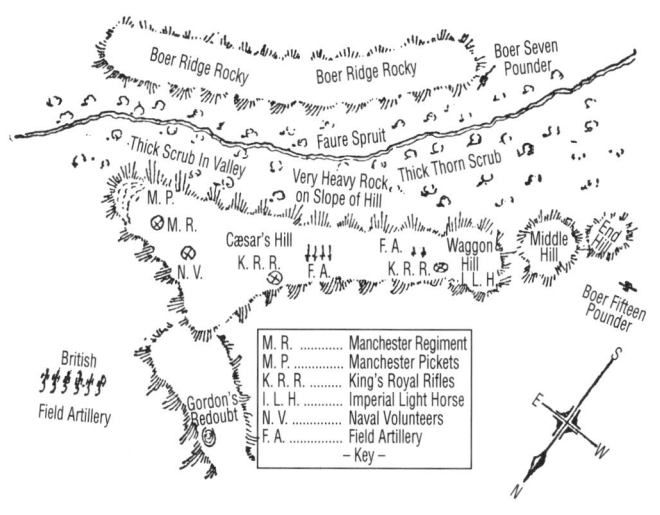

Rough map sketched during fight, showing position of our troops when the enemy attacked.

timed, they got home first at Wagon Hill, upon the extreme right of our position.

The night was very dark, and the Imperial Light Horse sentries, hearing a slight rustling in the brush in front of them, challenged. The reply, "A friend," came in excellent English, but instantly the enemy opened fire, and the sentry was killed. The noise of the men at work on the 4.7 gun probably drew the enemy sooner to that point, for as the pickets came back they followed on, and firing upon the Cossack post at a distance of not more than ten yards, killed five of the men at work there. A working party of Gordons, who were also warned, were captured in a trench, but most of them escaped later in the day and got back to their lines. As the Boers came on, Lieutenant Walker, who had a Hotchkiss, opened fire. They dropped for shelter at every shot, and the delay gave the Light Horse time to line the inner crest of the hill, the Hotchkiss, after about a dozen rounds, being withdrawn to the redoubt. About twenty Highlanders and King's Royals came to their support, and there on the extreme right of Wagon Hill a grim and deadly fight went on for four hours, the defenders being cross-fired at a distance of not more than thirty yards. Quite 500 Boers came to the assault on that side, yet the little band of Britons, lessening every moment, held the post, which was the key of the position, with splendid tenacity. The Light Horse did many fine things in the campaign, but did never more for their country than during those few hours of darkness on the morning of January 6. Briton and Boer lay close fifty yards apart, each keenly on the look-out for his enemy, and after daybreak, when the light increased, the casualties were heaviest. One Dutchman, believe to be Ardendall of Harrismith, carried a particularly deadly rifle. In turn he shot Lord Ava mortally through the temple, Lieutenant Palemon through the spine, killing him instantly, and put a bullet through Captain Fowler's hat. In his eagerness he exposed himself slightly, and one of the Light Horsemen shot him dead through the side. Lord Ava, a fine athletic young fellow, and a son of the

Marquis of Dufferin, was acting as galloper to Brigadier-General Ian Hamilton. He carried a sporting magazine rifle, and had just put his head over the rock to fire at a Boer when he was hit. He uttered the one word "Done" and rolled away from the rock. On Sunday his chance seemed hopeless; on Monday, the 8th, he had a slight pulse, and his splendid constitution would, it was thought, pull him through, but it was only a faint chance. In this four hours' murderous work no fewer than fourteen officers went down, dead or wounded, and at times there was confusion as to the command. In this emergency Lieutenant Digby Jones, of the Engineers, who had been supervising the erection of the gun, went into the fighting line, and as the Boers came into the sangar he shot four of them dead just outside the wall. I saw these men lying where they fell later in the morning, and amongst them were Field-Cornet Viljoen of Harrismith, and Acting-Commandant Van Wyk, two grizzled old Boers, who had come forward with all the impetuosity of youth. Poor Digby Jones did not survive them long, though had he lived he might have won a Victoria Cross. As he went forward with the fighting line later in the day he was shot dead. Shortly after seven o'clock supports of the Gordons and the Devons came up, and the Dutch were driven off that end of the hill, leaving many of their dead behind them to mark their first failure. The fight there was assumed to be over, but in this we underrated both the Boer determination and their resource. They had come to take the position at all cost, and there were yet more of them for the sacrifice. On the extreme left of the position the enemy came forward just as silently, but just as surely. So quietly was the attack made that they were within a few yards of the Manchester pickets when the "Who goes there?" checked them. "Don't shoot," said a voice in excellent English. "We're the town guard." The answer was so ready that the pickets stood irresolute for an instant. "I don't believe you're the town guard," one of the men said. "How the devil did you get out there?" The answer was a yell and a volley, and our poor deluded pickets went down as the Boers came on. They got between the little stone walls where our outposts were lying, some of the Manchesters being shot from behind almost point-blank ere they had awakened to the fact that the enemy were upon them. Those who survived the first rush were driven back on their main position, and it was said unfairly that they had too soon given way. The fact was that they were outnumbered ten to one, and when I rode along that ridge at daybreak on Sunday, the melancholy proof that the Manchesters had not given up the ground readily was afforded in the number of their dead who lay there. No men could have done more than they did against this sudden overwhelming rush.

The Boers, however, had won possession of the extreme left of the hill – a high rocky, thorny peak. Their trouble was to hold it. Colonel Royston sent forward detachments of the Border Mounted and Natal Mounted Rifles to the foot of the extreme left of Cæsar's Hill, where, covered by the thorn, they kept up a guerrilla fire on the Boers above them, while a battery of artillery on the outskirts of the town and firing over their heads, both percussion and shrapnel, searched the hill from crest to foot. Stubbornly as they had held their place against the rifles, the shell fire was too much for them. The biggest rocks were useless against the downward burst and the hail of splinters, which searched every corner, and after the fight no corner of that bloody field was so horrible a spectacle. There were men lying there who apparently had not a whole bone in their bodies. They were literally torn to shreds. On Sunday I saw men who had not yet accustomed themselves to the carnage of battle turn sick when they came suddenly upon the awful slaughter-pen. The big gun on Bulwan, and two lesser ones, concentrated their fire on this battery, in the effort to silence it, but in vain. When the big gun had almost got their range, our gunners changed position so quickly before the smoke had cleared from the Dutch muzzle, that the enemy's artillery went on firing for some time before they discovered that the guns had moved to a new point. Our Royal Artillery were right in the open, as they generally are, but very few of them were hit.

Human nature could not long stand the tremendous fire from the field battery, but until eleven o'clock the gallant Dutchmen held possession of that hill corner. Then they moved round it to their own side of the range, where their retreat was cut off by the Manchesters and King's Royals, who had worked forward to the Boer side of the hill. Sheltered from our artillery fire amongst the rocks, the rifles could make no impression upon them, and there they lay all day, like rabbits in their burrows, nor could our men go down the hill to take them without subjecting themselves to a heavy fire from the Boers, who were lying behind rocks all the way across the valley, while their reserves held possession of the main ridge. By mid-day the whole of the hill was once more in our possession, and with the defenders reinforced by heavy drafts from the Gordons, the Rifle Brigade, the Devons, the Mounted Infantry, and Dismounted Cavalry, it looked as though the fight would drag itself on till dark, and then fizzle out.

As soon as the rifle fire slackened the artillery duel began – which is the reverse of the procedure in action – and a more remarkable artillery duel was never fought. It was a geometrical puzzle, such a curiosity in warfare that I went to some pains to get as good a diagram of the fire as possible. The dotted lines represent the Boer gun fire; the black lines our own.

Of all calibres, short of machine guns, there were no fewer than sixty in action, ranging form 90-pounders to 7-pounders. The big fellow on the Bulwan was particularly busy, and fired no fewer than 130 rounds during the day, yet there was not one of our field guns in action which did not kill at least twice as many men. Their 40-pounder shot much more accurately, yet the whole of their guns combined did not kill as many men as the two field-pieces, the 15-pounder and 7-pounder, which were able to bring a cross fire of shrapnel upon our rifle lines on Cæsar's Hill. At about four in the afternoon especially these two burst quite a score of their shells over Wagon Hill, where our men, with their attention concentrated on the Boer lines at right angles, were exposed to the flanking fire, and many of the Gordons got their death messenger then. I saw them next day frightfully torn with the splinters, which showed often on their bare knees, yet not so terrible a spectacle as the Boers I have already mentioned – killed by our shrapnel.

Last of all came the closing epoch of the fight, a gallant effort by an already beaten foe to turn a chance circumstance to their advantage, and take the hill where so many of their dead and wounded were already lying. At about three o'clock black

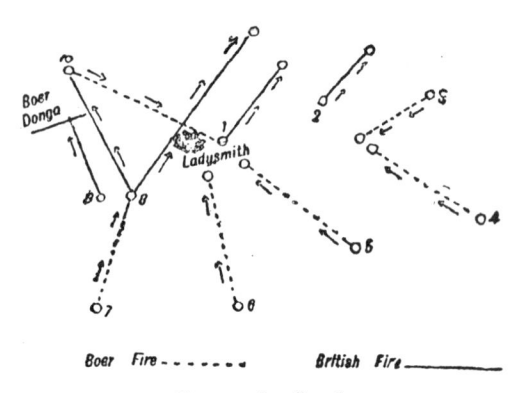

Diagram of artillery fire.

clouds rolled up from the south, and one of the heaviest thunderstorms I have ever witnessed burst over Ladysmith – burst thickest of all upon that hill round which the fight had raged all day. Hail fell in blinding flakes as large as a shilling, and no one can estimate the suffering of the wounded who lay upon the field, many of them too badly hurt to shield their faces from the lashing fusillade. It was as though an offended heaven were visiting upon men her punishment for the carnage there. Everything was blotted out. At fifty yards figures of men were seen as faint shadows through a fog. The sixty guns were silenced in a moment in the face of heaven's more vivid and deafening artillery. Was there ever such thunder, and lightning that ran in long trickling streams down the black sky? The surroundings all combined to make it awe-inspiring. It was not in human nature to face such a storm, but the Boers had it at their backs. It may have been that the God to whom they had so often prayed for aid had come to their help at last – little doubt but that many of them believed it a supernatural intervention that was to give them the victory for which during the fifteen hours they had struggled. Anyhow, in the very climax of the tempest they gathered up their smitten ranks, and came on again to the hill, already drenched with so much of their best fighting blood. We were crouching behind the rocks wherever a ledge gave shelter, when a loud hurrah and a burst of firing told that they were upon us. In an instant the hurricane was forgotten. With the hail beating in their faces, our men sprang to their positions, and these indomitable foes were all in an instant engaged in another death-clinch, firing their rifles into each other at short pistol range, wild with excitement and the anticipation of victory. Once again the best men of the Boer army led the way, but all their desperate valour was in vain. For the third time that day the Boer had possession of the hill, but it was only permissive occupancy. Twice the number could not have taken it then. For half-an-hour it was little better than a *mêlée* in which, but for the distracting surroundings, the carnage would have been twice as great. Slowly the Boer was forced back. The Devons, fixing bayonets, drove forward, the last of them were pushed over the brow, and as our riflemen lined the crest the Boers trickled back across the valley, still taking full advantage of the matchless cover. Faure Spruit, which at mid-day had been a mere trickle, was now a raging torrent, and as the enemy halted irresolute on its banks, their dark figures loomed up against the white water like giants. So they looked, at least, as seen through the field-glasses, the enlargement of the figures being some optical illusion of the moist atmosphere. There many of them died. In the water we could see them throw up their arms and fall under our volleys, fired at nearly a thousand yards, and the current swept them away. Then the darkness came, and after seventeen hours' continuous fighting, this heroic effort to take the defences of Ladysmith failed. That it was so nearly successful was due in great measure to the completeness of the surprise. Ten weeks of immunity from anything more serious than sniping had given our men a false sense of security, and had it not been for their magnificent stubbornness they must have been swept away in the first Boer rush. To the Imperial Light Horse especially immeasurable honour was due – and they paid for it dearly, for that night there were only three unwounded officers in the regiment.

The crowning episode of the day, the move that more than anything else contributed to the final discomfiture of the Boers, was the charge of the Devons. They had come up late in the afternoon, drawing a heavy fire from the guns on Bulwan as they climbed the hill. They were full of ardour, burning to avenge their fallen comrades, and were luckily in a good position near Wagon Hill when the Boers came for their last rush. When Colonel Park gave the word "Forward!" his men charged in a line straight up the steep. They had to some extent, however, miscalculated the centre of assault, and when they reached the crest of the ridge found the Boers pouring forward through the river on their extreme right. Their left swung round instantly, and it was in the very act of effecting this movement that a withering fire at short range caught them, and the gallant Devons went down literally in dozens. They neither halted nor faltered, but swept resolutely across the hill, for the close work in which the Briton has always revelled. It was too much for the Boers, and as they came forward at the double the Dutchmen stopped, wavered, and fled, a half-dozen of them only waiting for the *coup de grâce* with the steel. Little wonder that Sir Redvers Buller, an old Devonian, sent his congratulations to the regiment, or that the Queen cabled her admiration

The charge of the Devons.

of their gallant deed. The Devons had had a singular experience that day. Early in the morning a hundred of them had repulsed an attack by double their number of Boers from the eastward, while on the north they also held the ridge at which the enemy directed their third attack, but which the fire of the 13th Battery checked before the Boers had got within effective range of the rifles. The climax was the charge through the thunderstorm on Wagon Hill.

I have more than once had reason to admire the British soldier in battle, but never was there such good ground for admiration as in watching him prepare. All the blare and tumult, the death and disaster of actual conflict have no such tense, dramatic, nerve-trying moments as when a regiment is making ready for some great enterprise. The fight is a medley of mixed impressions, jostling each other for a moment's existence ere passing away, but the getting ready is unforgetable. Everything is clear-cut and within the sum of human emotions – eternal. So it was with that last grand charge of the Devons, which swept the Boers from their fringe of the little plateau and finished the long seventeen hours' ordeal. The enemy were on one side of the Table, we on the other. A tropical hailstorm howled across it, and beat heavily in our faces, as Colonel Park led his men up the sheltered face of the hill, and halted a moment within five yards of the crest, to make ready. The men knew exactly what they had to do, and the solemnity of a great and tragic undertaking was upon and about them. All the world for them – the too brief past with its consequences, the fast-flying present, and the mysterious beyond – might concentrate in a short desperate dash across a storm-swept African hilltop. It was the sublimity of life – the anticipation of death. The Devons were making ready for it, and how unready a man might feel at such a moment! The line of brown riflemen stretched away to the left of us and it seemed that every trivial action of every man there had become an epic. One noticed most of all the constant moistening of the dry lips, and the frequent raising of the waterbottles for a last hurried mouthful. One man tightened a belt, another brought his cartridges handier to his right hand, though he was not to use them. It was something to ease the strain of waiting. Every little thing fixed itself on the mind as a photograph. There was no need of mental effort to remember. One could not see and forget, and would not, for his patriotism and his pride of kinship, forget if he could. Then the low clinking, quivering sound of the steel which died away from us in a trickle down the ranks as the bayonets were fixed – and a dry, harsh, artificial laugh, in strong contrast to the quiet of the scene – everything heard easily somehow above the rush and clatter of the storm, and lost only for an instant in the sudden bursts of thunder. A bit of quiet tragedy wedged in the turmoil of the great play, and all unspeakably solemn and awe-inspiring. One must see to understand it. One may have seen yet can never describe it. The situation was not for ordinary language; it was Homeric, over-mastering.

"Now then, Devons, get ready." There was a dry catch in the colonel's voice as he gave the word – and the short sentence was punctuated by the zip-zip of the Mauser bullets, that for a few precious seconds would still be flying overhead. There was a quick panting of the breath, a stiffening of the lines of the faces, that with so many of them was but the prelude to the rigidity of death. It was waiting for them only a few yards up, and their manhood was being sorely tried. But the Devons squared their shoulders, gripped their rifles – bringing them up with the quick whip of the drill, that was too well ground into them to be forgotten even then. A prompt dressing by the left, and, as though eager to get it over, the Devons sprang forward to the word into the double storm of hail and nickel-plated bullets. The killing suspense was over – they were in action at last, one's whole heart went with them, and just for one moment, as they stood fully exposed upon the plateau, it seemed to the watchers that there might be disaster. As I have already told, they had slightly miscalculated the enemy's strongest point, and had to wheel by the left. As they did so the line faltered for a moment. A shiver, a pendulum-like swaying seemed to run down it; that was the history-making moment, when the regiment might either do something that ever afterwards they would try to forget, or that all their countrymen would be proud to remember – the moments in men's lives which, measured by emotion only, stretch out into centuries. It was the moment of a life, too, for the commander of men. His chance had come.

"Steady, Devons, steady," came the clear ringing call, and then, with one great surging rush, that gathered momentum even as it lost in fallen units, the regiment went on.

Boldly though they had taken and held that hill, prudence came to the Boer riflemen as these eager bayonets bore down upon them. For a moment they shot the Devons through and through, and then they ran. At that moment not a man amongst our commonplace, drinking, swearing Tommies but was exalted, deified – but so many of them were something less of interest on earth than even a common soldier. Where the regiment had gone seventy of its dead and wounded littered the hill-top, but still it was the moment of victory, not of lamentations. It may sound strange to say that the prelude to a battle, like the preface to a book, can be greater than the actual battle or the book. But so it seemed to me. Others might view it differently, but challenge our impressions as we may in the light of riper history, we shall never alter them. They are indelible. Overhaul the plates again and again as we please, it will always be the same picture.

It was purely a soldiers' fight. There was no time for a concerted plan of action; every one had to rush forward and fight in his own way, driving back the foe by sheer doggedness. Then the fatalities amongst the officers were as usual exceptional. At one time the Gordons and King's Royals were absolutely leaderless, and faltered for want of direction, for "Tommy" without a leader is as a rudderless ship. It was impossible for the Boers in this bad light to have picked out the officers, they simply were the more frequently exposed, and so they suffered. When an officer rises to advance with his resolute "Come on, men," he is the first one seen, and becomes a target for a score of rifles. It is not sufficient either that he should lie close and pick his man, he must get some idea of the position, and of the everchanging phases of the fight, and in doing so he courts disaster. Latterly, the officers had laid aside their swords, and each carried a rifle. Thus two of the leaders came to their death in the last stage of this fight. Major Miller-Wallnutt of the Gordons, and Commandant De Villiers of Harrismith, one of the bravest of the Boer leaders, fired at each other in the same instant. The officer of the Gordons was struck fairly in the temple, the bullet passing out at the back of his head. De Villiers was shot through the chest, and neither lived ten seconds. Major Miller-Wallnutt was a magnificent specimen of the British soldier, standing nearly six feet four inches in height, and with the physique of a giant. He would have succeeded to the command of the regiment had he lived through that fight. For a time the only surgeons on the field were Dr. Hornabrook of the volunteers, and Dr. Wood of the Manchesters, and both were wounded while attending fallen men. Dr. Hornabrook had a miraculous escape. As showing the cosmopolitan and confused character of the fight, he had, within a few yards, attended a Natal Mounted Riflemen, a King's Royal, and a Manchester, and went a little way down the Boer side of the hill to where one of the Gordons was lying. "Don't come here, sir," the poor fellow said, "they'll knock you over." The young South Australian, ordering his dresser to stay under cover, went down the slope, and as he knelt beside the wounded man, one bullet cut away the star from his shoulder, another passed through the flap of his coat. He bent over slightly and so saved his life, for a bullet cut through his side, just above the hip, making a nasty wound, but fortunately missing the vital parts. Though his clothing, when I saw it later, was matted with blood, he stayed on attending to the wounded until Major Heslop, his chief, ordered him into camp. Dr. Wood, of the Manchesters, was shot through the arm. "Have a drink of water, old man," said a commiserating soldier to an old Boer, who lay wounded. "I don't want your filthy water," the old man snarled, unrelenting to the last. Amongst the Manchester wounded was Major Thessiger, son of Lord Chelmsford, who led the British troops in the Zulu war.

I saw another Australian stripling on the field who had taken a man's part in the fray, for there were many boys on both sides in this bloody feud. This was little Jack Plunkett, a Queensland boy, from Roma, and one of the best horsemen in South Africa. He and another lad – both of the Imperial Light Horse – lay behind the same rock, watching three Boers, who were just as carefully watching them, and shooting even at a finger if it came in sight. Each of the youngsters got his man, the third being killed by a flanking shot. Young Plunkett had come out in a blue jersey, as he was in too great a hurry to find his jacket. One of the first of the Boer wounded brought into our camp was a mere lad, though big and sturdy – young Schultz of Harrismith, who talked freely of the fight. He had seen his father killed just before he himself fell wounded – shot in three places. This boy, with many others who were in this fighting line, had been brought away from Grey's College in Bloemfontein to take the field against the rooineks, for whom however, he declared he had no personal hatred. The whole of the men in this assault, he said, were Dutch, most of them the old Dopper Boers, whose hatred of Englishmen, bred of ignorance and tradition, will die out only with themselves. They had held a meeting, had asked to be allowed to take the town, had sung their national songs, and while shaking hands with each other had vowed that if beaten back they would come on again and again until they died, or Ladysmith was taken. This youngster still wore on his hat his Grey College badge – it was his only uniform. His statement was confirmed while they were collecting the dead on Wednesday. Captain Blore, adjutant of the King's Royals, while amongst the thorn, met two Dutchmen, who were also searching for their dead, and they exchanged notes on the fight. "You did well to get on the ridge the second time," said the adjutant. "You did better to hold it," answered the Dutchman. "But you would not have held it if all our men had come on at the right time." One of these Dutchmen signalled to the captain to come to one side, and he did so. "I'm not a Dutchman," said the enemy. "I'm English, and there are hundreds like myself in the Boer lines – English, Scotch, Irish, and German. We had to take the field, or we should have been shot. But they don't trust us. They would have none of us in this assault, but we were to have come up and garrisoned the hill when they had taken it. We shall be glad indeed when the British are in Pretoria." He went on to explain to the captain the Boer method of fighting. "They've done with the sangar," he said; "it's played out. The Boer just throws about three rocks together, screens it with a tuft or grass or a thorn-bough, and pokes the muzzle of his rifle through. That's better than a sangar. It does not draw the fire."

One of the Imperial Light Horse, after firing on the Boers, dropped behind a rock, and the enemy, thinking him dead, rushed right over him. Then he fired at them from their rear. There were rumours that some of the Dutch wounded, finding themselves down and badly hit, committed suicide rather than fall into our hands, and two significant circumstances lent colour to an even more ugly suggestion. One of the wounded Imperial Light Horsemen was found dead with a strap drawn tightly round his throat, as though he had been strangled. A dead sergeant of the Highlanders, one of the working party, had neither bayonet nor bullet wound on him, for some of the Boers carried bayonets in this charge, presumably taken from the captured Gloucesters. This man was bruised to a pulp, and had evidently been kicked or beaten to death in a fit of pure savagery. Of such acts of brutal cowardice the great majority of the more enlightened Boers are incapable, but there are a few of the old stubborn stock, the unspeakably bearish Dopper, who will do anything to an Englishman – do it for his own soul's salvation and to the glory of God. It may have been some of these who in their flight took shelter behind a wounded Englishman, so that they could not be fired upon without killing him. It may have been yet another of them who shot one of our wounded, and while drinking from his water-bottle was himself killed. For once the usual condition of things was reversed. Ours was the composite force in the early hours of Saturday morning. It consisted of police, soldiers, and civilians. Bell, a wagon-driver, and one of the best shots in Africa, left his team, and was fighting for fourteen hours at a stretch. All kinds of weapons were used by the Boers, and the mangled condition of some of our men who fell to the rifle was only explainable on the theory that the explosive bullets kept for game had been freely fired. One of our men was wounded in the arm by an elephant ball, and the youngster whom I have already mentioned as being brought in wounded, had the tops of all his Mauser bullets filed, so that they might spread and wound more seriously. When a boy without much racial animosity could do this, what is to be expected from the old rigid rooinek haters?

All over the crest of the hill one saw the clips of Mauser bullets behind rocks, where the owners had left them when they retired in a hurry. When the King's Royals went into action their regimental dog accompanied them as usual. He has never been out of the fighting line, and has never had a scratch. In riding up the hill on Sunday morning I met a little red, three-legged dog coming pottering down. "That's the Hussars' dog," said a corporal; "he's always in it when the guns begin to shoot. He lost his leg in India – it was smashed up so that the doctor had to amputate it." I had another look at the little red mongrel, who was threading his way through the medley of mule-wagons and water-carts. He was at least two miles from camp.

Boer trickery sometimes recoils upon themselves. All Saturday night one poor fellow was calling for help not fifty yards in advance of our outward pickets. They were anxious to help him, too, but feared further trickery, so no one would go forward. But all the wounded suffered greatly in this fight. They lay all day between the contending lines, spent a horrible night, and it was late on Sunday before many of them reached the hospital, some of the ambulances taking eight hours to come from the battle-field, owing to the block on this two miles of rough road. Lieutenant King, wounded early in the fight, was down for some time, and tried to get back for surgical treatment. As he staggered weakly along, the poor fellow was shot through the spine and killed. On Sunday morning I saw five Boers lying dead just outside one of our redoubts. They had fought their way right up to the sangar wall, and had fallen there dead in a cluster. The fact of men lying dead together, though, is not always a proof that they fell together. I saw many a bloody trail on the hill-top, which told where a man mortally hit had dragged himself up to another fallen man, as though the companionship of a comrade in misfortune were a comfort to him when he felt the end drawing near. It is an awful death, that of the lonely man on the battle-field – the glazing eyes looking for a friend, the twitching fingers feeling for that touch of a hand which comes not until the cold finger of death chills him for ever.

In the fighting on the left corner of Cæsar's Hill there was one tall Dutchman, who exposed himself like a dare-devil, and did it once too often. He sprang upon a rock, waved his rifle over his head, and shouted, "Here we are! Come on, you dogs!" Then he pitched slowly forward, face first, as though taking a header from a spring-board, and never stirred again. When they took his body down on Saturday, it had stiffened as he fell, and there were four bullets through him. They had all been watching for him. The crest of that hill was the last place upon God's fair earth for a vaunter. Had a man the capacity to shrink to the dimensions of a mouse, he would have been none too small for the situation. Bitter to the end was another Boer, who, when offered a drink, turned his face away in loathing, and murmured, "I'll meet you again, you wretches."

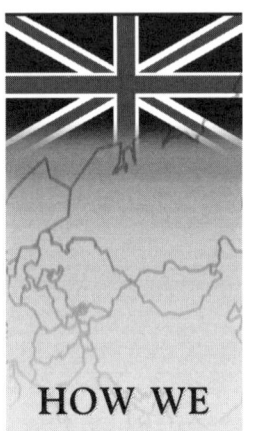

HOW WE KEPT THE FLAG FLYING

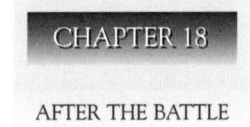

CHAPTER 18

AFTER THE BATTLE

*The Gordons' loss – Incidents of the fight – A field of the dead –
Greathead of the Guides – The Boer loss – Father and son – A stubborn foe
– Why the attack failed.*

THE casualties of the day were not limited to those round about Cæsar's Ridge. Early in the morning, Colonel Dick-Cunyngham had just ordered out his men to reinforce the defenders, and was walking over the bridge a mile and a half away from the fight, when a Mauser bullet, almost spent, passed through his body. The wound was mortal, and to the great sorrow of his regiment, he died a couple of days later. He had been very seriously wounded at Elands Laagte, and only returned to duty during the siege. No regimental commander in the British army was better loved than Colonel Dick-Cunyngham. He was a V.C. man – modest, brave as a lion, and as much liked by his brother officers as by his own men. It was cruelly hard luck for a grand fighter to fall to this one chance shot.

Bullets were flying freely into the town that day, and one of

Sir George White's orderlies was hit standing at headquarters. Two Border Mounted men, of very different type, were killed side by side. One was a lad of nineteen, just stepping into life; the other a grizzled old soldier, Trooper Fox, once a captain in the Royal Artillery, and who had long since given up soldiering. The temptation of active service was too strong, and he joined the Border Mounted Rifles as a trooper. There are scores of such cases in Africa, some of them, I am afraid, rather "hard cases." After the first rush our men were thoroughly cool, and never thought of failure. Here is a typical scrap of conversation between a crack shot of the Gordons, who had crept up to the same rock as a Light Horseman. "What ye shootin' at, matey?" asked the Highlander. "At six men in that patch of scrub." "Well, now, see me fetch out; what's aboot her range?" A Boer lifted his head to fire, and the Highlander grazed him. Then the enemy broke cover over a little bit of open ground, and two were killed before they reached the rocks. All the senior officers of the Light Horse were down at the position they had so gallantly defended, Colonel Edwards being hit in the shoulder and buttock, and Major Doveton very seriously in the shoulder, while Major Karri Davies was shot through the thigh, but went on fighting. At one time, when the Natal Mounted Rifles and a small body of Gordons were firing upon some Boers on the end of Cæsar's Hill, one of the enemy called out "Surrender!" "Go to blazes!" was the curt reply of the Britons, as they went on fighting. Indeed, the word surrender had no place in the vocabulary of either side that day. It was "No surrender!" always. One of the dead Boers was found completely dressed in the uniform of the Manchester regiment. He had probably stripped one of the dead pickets on the slope of the hill, and was killed as soon as he reached the summit, with some plan in his head which he never lived to carry out. Captain Carnegie, of the Gordons, was three times hit, two being severe wounds in the arms, yet, though bleeding freely, he stayed with his men, and led them on, fighting nobly, until the enemy were finally driven off the hill. He knew that most of the officers were down, that his men might be leaderless at any moment, so he stayed. Even at midday the fire was so keen that the medical officers, moving from one wounded man to another, had to worm themselves snake-like along the veldt.

On Sunday morning that battle-field was a woeful spectacle. Our mortality list at daybreak on Sunday was one hundred and twenty of all ranks killed, and two hundred and fifty wounded, but that terrible waiting for succour had been to the wounded so great a strain that every hour added to the numbers of the dead. One sad illustration will suffice. At midday on Sunday the Imperial Light Horse had lost just twenty men. By sunset on Monday their dead numbered thirty. Fourteen officers were instantly killed, and twenty wounded. Many of the deaths were due to exposure, and a score at least might have been saved had the surgeons been able to get on the field freely immediately after the action. In this sense there were all the drawbacks of savage warfare. Some of the wounded were lying where they fell for twenty-seven hours. Remember the circumstances, and imagine the horrors of that dreary, deadly waiting. It was pitiful, revolting! In moving amongst the dead one could distinguish between those shot in the early morning and the men killed after the thunderstorm. There was little blood about the former – the rains had washed it out, leaving only a dull brown stain on the uniform. Those killed by the bullet were mostly placid, and there was an infinity of difference between the faces of the men who died with their heads up the slope and those who had fallen head downward. In the latter case the blood had rushed to the head, and the faces were absolutely plum-coloured. At first sight there seemed to be many black men in those ghastly lines of British dead. This was the explanation of it. Other wise, the faces were perfectly white and waxen.

Most impressive of all sights was the burial of our dead. The spot chosen for the graves was a little plateau halfway down the defenders' slope of Cæsar's Hill. The short grass was vividly green after the rains, and dotted with low thorn trees. The spot gave a far view to northward over leagues of rolling veldt right away to the foot of the Drachenbergs. It was an ideally peaceful scene – such a spot as one would have chosen for a mountain home – and as the stoical Kaffir boys dug the long, shallow graves in which the dead of each regiment were to lie, there were skylarks trilling blithely just overhead, though higher still the wheeling vultures. The dead, as in life, were shoulder to shoulder, the men of each corps side by side; here the bare knees of the Highlanders, next the brown putties of the Light Horsemen; all of them young men, nearly all shaved, except the moustache – while the Boers were invariably bearded. Most of them had the knees drawn up, and there was something dramatically suggestive in the attitude of the dead arms. Men had died face downward with their arms stretched out. By the graveside they were upon their backs, so that the chin-straps of the helmets might be cut away, the face fully exposed, and the dead identified. Thus the arms came upward, raised in the air, and in very many cases the poise was pathetically life-like. The outspread palms and outstretched arms seemed to ward off something – yet it was only the loose-flung attitude of death. They were buried so, their hands under the brown blanket, the last thing seen above the mould. It was the most impressive note in the whole grim death scene. Then came the friends and comrades of the dead, cutting off a button or a badge as a memento; last of all the burial service, with the Commander-in-Chief standing bare-headed seeing the last of his brave soldiers. Less than a hundred yards away the camp butchers of the King's Royals were cutting up a beast for dinner – perhaps an artillery horse killed during the fight, for it had come to that. Before this came a private of the Manchesters. "I hear my brother is missing from the King's Royals," he said: "I hope he's not in this lot." He walked along the row of brown-clad riflemen, who wore the black cross-belts, then sank upon one knee, with his hands over his face. He had found his brother, the most boyish-looking of all that grim group. I put my hand upon his shoulder, and offered him the consolation of sympathy, which at its best is weak and insufficient. "He was the youngest of us," the poor chap said. "I always hoped he would go back to the old people; I myself never shall." I had my own shock a little later. Passing along the foot of the hill, I came upon a single man lying rolled in a brown blanket. The little slip of paper pinned to the head attracted me, and I read in pencil the word "Greathead." My friend of the Guides – sturdy, handsome Greathead! I lifted the blanket; the face was smeared in blood and looked thinner than in life, but the heavy moustache, that at least was recognizable. I came away more sad and sick at heart than ever, and one of the first men I met on returning to town was Greathead himself. This poor fellow at the foot of the hill was his brother, of the Light Horse.

Next over the hill to the enemy's side of the slope, where the Boer dead were lying. Their Red Cross men were dotted amongst the thorn in the valley. Close to me was a wagon, upon which the dead were piled one upon another, anyhow. Twenty-six bodies were still lying on the grass, five wagon-loads had already gone. Across the valley I could see through the glass some sixty others in a row upon the veldt. About ninety of the Dutch dead were taken off the hill they had come to capture. Thirteen of them could not be moved, they were in that pen of death where our shrapnel fell thickest, and, much as we in Ladysmith had seen of the destruction of shell fire during this past ten weeks, we had witnessed nothing quite so appalling as that. These men could not be removed for burial – they were too shockingly mangled; so their graves were dug beside them. Many of the Dutch dead at other points were only partially clothed. Some had disrobed themselves in their last agony – all had been searched by the Natal Mounted Police for identification papers, the invariable practice where the Boer dead lie within our lines. The instructions were to keep a record of all the dead, but especially of those men who were resident in

Natal and naturalized British subjects. "This is the worst day we have ever had," said one of the Dutch searchers to a surgeon whom he met. The same story was told to the adjutant of the King's Royals, whom I have already mentioned. From the Intombi Spruit camp, which lies parallel with the Boer ridge, and gives a full view of their position, our people saw long lines of wagons taking away the enemy's dead and wounded, and at dusk on Sunday night their search parties were still moving about the valley. Their loss on the main ridge must have been great; we know what our field-gun shrapnel can do – so does the Boer. When he opened on the town with his heavy guns on Monday morning he laid them first on the artillery camp, and kept them there all day – anxious to pay back in blood the debt he owed the Royal Artillery. I have mentioned the big Boer who stood on a rock, dared us to come on, and was shot there. A sporting Mauser rifle lay partly under him, with the letters H.V. deeply cut in the stock. There was also an envelope, the address partly obliterated in blood, but at the foot the words "Heidelberg Laager, Ladysmith, Z.A.R." Thus they had proclaimed the town a part of the South African Republic, and thus tragically they had failed in their brave effort to take possession. Eight hundred killed and wounded was the first estimate, but later the official estimate swelled to one thousand. While we were on the hill the enemy fired once on a burial party – a dozen rounds or so from their Pom-pom – but those were the only shots, and by common consent the search parties on both sides were undisturbed for the rest of the day.

At two other points that day the Boers made an assault upon our defences, but as the attack was in neither case carried through with anything like the determination shown at Cæsar's Hill, these were presumably intended as feints to divert attention from the main assault. At Observation Hill, on the extreme west, where a post of a hundred of the Devons were in possession, some two hundred Boers came forward in the early morning, and got as far as the Free State railway line which runs at the foot of the hill. In doing so they lost eight killed and fourteen wounded, and were finally forced out of the position by the Hotchkiss machine gun. Two of the Devons were killed, and one wounded. What at one time appeared to be a much more imposing move was made on the north-east from Lombard's Kop. The enemy came half-way forward to the Liverpools' ridge, and occupied a deep donga. Our 13th Field Battery had been posted to command this position, and as soon as the shrapnel began to drop there the enemy came no further, and in an hour or so were glad to creep out at the top end of the donga, and get back to their lines again. Following upon the attack on Cæsar's Hill we had several anxious nights of heavy rain, during which it was feared that the enemy might again come forward to the assault, but they shirked it, though on Monday, January 8, we could see them massing heavily towards the east.

After the bloody struggle at Cæsar's Hill came a few days' calm – a period never free, however, from illness, apprehension, privation, and anxiety. There were nearly two thousand sick and wounded at Intombi Camp, and all civilians in the town, whose work at the moment was not one of public importance, were required to go out as hospital orderlies and nurses to the sick. There were no eaters of idle bread in Ladysmith. Some of the corps had suffered so heavily that they were almost skeleton regiments. The Liverpools had a hundred and seventy men down. The Imperial Light Horse, who took the field with a strong force of young, stalwart, seasoned South Africans, could only put about a hundred men in the field. The enemy, who were well informed as to all that occurred here, counted on this, I understand, in their assault on Saturday morning. They know now that British valour is not entirely dependent upon British beer, but thrives fairly well even upon maize meal. The Boers spoke of their loss as a national calamity. The Free Staters were much incensed at the failure of the Transvaal Boers to carry out a preconceived plan of attack. They were to have assaulted our defences determinedly and in force on the northern side at the same hour that the assault was made on Cæsar's Hill. The Transvaal men dallied with the task, were driven back from the one point where they showed in the open, and otherwise only occupied late in the day a donga which proved to be a shell-trap, and which the longer they held it the more men they lost. I have not seen better shooting than our artillery did at that point – and in this arm, it seems to me, alone rests our superiority to the Dutch. The Royal Artillery dare everything for a good position in the open, and gaining that nothing can stand against them. It was that knowledge, I feel sure, born of bitter experience, which induced the enemy to attack at night.

One heard every day of new and remarkable experiences in the fight at Cæsar's Hill. Colour-sergeant Bryce, of the Gordons, died at Intombi Camp three days after the fight, and had no fewer than fourteen bullet-marks on him. One of the Imperial Light Horse had four bullets through his hat, and a fifth grazed his temple and partly stunned him, but he was about in a few days. There was one Boer marksman firing through a narrow slot between two rocks who, it is said, hit no fewer than six of our men, and upon whom four of our crack rifle-shots had finally concentrated their fire ere they killed him.

On January 10 we were indulged with a budget of news by heliograph – the first we had heard of the outside world for some time. We were told of the settlement of the Samoan question, of the settlement of the Alaskan boundary, of Chamberlain's "clean slate" speech, of everything and all the world excepting that little strip of country on the Tugela where our thoughts and anticipations so often centred. Late in the day came General Buller's congratulations to the garrison on the success of Saturday, flashed by heliograph across the intervening hills, with an assurance of his early advance to the relief of Ladysmith. There was an indefiniteness as to the time, however, which left much to the imagination. The one reassuring thing was an announcement by the Commander-in-Chief that the

Cæsar's Hill.

rations to the troops would be increased, and it was welcome. They had been "whipping the cat" for weeks, and were sorely in need of a better fighting ration than maize meal – the only difference in the supplies to horse and man being that the meal in the one case was boiled. In the meantime some few of the garrison had rivalled the besieged of Paris in recourse to horseflesh. On Monday a fat, five-year-old horse in the volunteer lines had his head blown off by a Dutch shell, and the carcase was cut into joints and sent to several of the messes. Those who were hungry enough to try it declared that the flesh was much more palatable and tender than the fresh beef with which they had lately struggled, and that it tasted like venison.

Five days after the battle of Cæsar's Hill the Dutch were still searching for their dead. Some of them were found as far down as the Tugela – carried away by the flood waters of the swollen spruit. Some were being picked up every day amongst the clefts of the huge rocks approaching Cæsar's Hill, which hid them so well both in life and death. On Thursday their officers complained that their search parties were being fired on from Cæsar's Camp, but once their object was known they were no longer molested. Our Lancers found a great many of them in an overlooked donga some days after the fight. They found also one man who lay on his face partly behind a rock. His attitude was that of a sharpshooter lying forward to fire, and in that position nearly fifty bullets had been fired through his body after death, our men, on catching a glimpse of him, imagining him to be alive. Five hundred rounds of ball cartridge were lying ready to his right hand.

One of the sad phases of this war on the Boer side was the number from one family killed – father and sons had taken the field in company, had gone into battle together, and were found dead together. I saw one such case on Cæsar's Hill the morning after the fight. Two Boers were there killed by shrapnel. Both had been hit in the body, and there was no mistaking the likeness between the two faces – the similarity of the reddish-brown hair – they were father and son. Not far from them lay a stalwart, handsome Boer with fair, curling hair. His blue eyes, wide open and staring at the blue sky, seemed strangely alive. Young Schultz, who died in hospital three days after the fight, saw his father killed before he fell. When John Smith, the British soldier, falls in action there are a thousand John Smiths ready to fill the gap in the ranks. When Jan Schmidt, the Boer farmer, falls there is no other to take his place, but all through the Dutch possessions there are relatives to mourn his loss, and so does the blow reach further with the Boer than with the Briton.

From Intombi Camp the approach of the Boers towards Cæsar's Hill was noted in the early daylight while the attention of its defenders was concentrated on the firing at the other end of the position, where the attack had developed earlier. With mixed emotions, our sick and wounded saw the enemy halt at a crest in a donga 200 yards from the British lines, and gather their forces for a final move, and they would have given much to have sent a warning cry over the veldt to their comrades. Next they saw the figures silhouetted clearly against the skyline, and the tension eased only with the splutter of the defending rifles and the occasional toppling over of a Boer rifleman. On this point of the hill a new gun, the Colt automatic, a machine gun, smaller and more portable than the Maxim, and without the encumbrance of a water-jacket, did great execution, sweeping the whole crest of the ridge once the Boers had gained a footing there. It is an American invention, proved to be very deadly in the late war with Spain, and was brought out to Natal purely as a speculation. One of the men connected with it is said to be a well-known socialist leader, whose projects for levelling the masses have evidently taken a new turn. The company sent out an expert, who was eagerly waiting a chance to try the weapon under new conditions, and this is surely the most up-to-date development of the commercial traveller. On Sunday morning that soldierly bagman was calmly refilling his feeding belt.

One remarkable feature of modern warfare with the small-bore rifle is the erratic course taken by the bullet. It has frequently turned out that where a man appeared to have been hit by several bullets the wounds were all from a single shot. I know of one case where the bullet struck a man in the back of the head, passed through his ear, entered the shoulder, passed out again, entered the thigh finally, and lodged near the knee. It seems an impossible course for a single shot to follow, even though partly accounted for by the fact that the man was lying down when hit. There were scores of such instances. Our death list for Cæsar's Hill had, a week after the conflict, been brought very nearly to 150, and with their shrapnel wounds the mortality amongst the Dutch wounded must have been proportionately greater. When, on the day after the fight, six of the Dutch wagons on their way to the base halted near Intombi, Major Bruce and some of his medical officers humanely went forward and volunteered their services. They were not needed, however – each wagon was a mortuary stacked with dead.

Four days after the fight poor Lord Ava died of his wounds, and on the following day amongst the victims of enteric was Mr. Robert Mitchell, a Scottish and South African journalist, who had been acting with Mr. Maxwell as representative of the London *Standard*. It became a question then whether enteric, if given a little while longer, would not kill more men than the Dutch shell, though were it not for the defective fuses, which caused Joubert such consternation just before the war began, the mortality, both amongst soldiers and civilians, would have been enormous.

One pair of eyes can never see the whole of a fight, nor one memory keep every impression. Fresh vignettes of battle, lost for the moment in some new and overpowering impression, came back to one every day.

The Dutch fought bravely on Cæsar's Hill, as bravely as men could fight, but they were the flower of Joubert's army, and had volunteered for what they knew to be a desperate task. There was no need of corroboration upon that point from the wounded prisoners. To those who know the Dutch, the dead upon the hill told the whole story. An infallible sign of the superior classes amongst the Boers is the wearing of elastic-side boots, and those men who died nearest the British lines all wore them. I saw three in one group. De Villiers, their valiant leader, was one – a finely-built man, with crisp black curling hair, and a brown, weather-tanned face that suggested my own ideal of Longfellow's Village Blacksmith. Near him lay a man with a decidedly English face, and the trimmed, pointed beard of our naval officers. There was a third whose face I could not see. He had fallen face downward, as most men fall when shot dead with a bullet on level ground, and – another invariable mark of those killed in battle – had his arms and legs drawn up in a dying contraction. All three wore elastic-side boots; but such boots were far less common amongst those who had fallen some distance away from the British position – that is to say, the men who had come forward a certain distance, then taken cover, and fought there in Boer fashion until the Lee-Metford bullet found its billet. Some of these looked pitiably destitute in death. The soles were worn off their boots; some of them were actually wearing women's underlinen. It looked anything but a prosperous and conquering army, and in face of it every emotion of racial animosity died away, and there was only a great pity that such things should be – an appeal not to valour, but to humanity.

The cause of failure with the Boers was that too few of them – in proportion to the number who started – had the courage to persevere to the bitter end. Had they done so, one trembles now to think of the possibilities, though I firmly believe that Ian Hamilton would have squandered British blood and given his own life recklessly rather than have yielded the position. No; there is no disguising the fact that even though at the last stages of the day the Boer supports came well within hitting distance of our lines, in the earlier part of it their assaulting columns were badly supported, even shamefully abandoned by their more timorous countrymen. There is, to my mind, too, one default in the official account of that gallant fight which history will require to make good. The Queen cabled her admiration of the Devons. In that message a word for the Imperial Light Horse might well have been included, without in the slightest degree lessening the compliment paid to the Regulars. It was a *corps d'élite*, none being taken but smart young fellows, who were both good shots and accomplished horsemen. Many of them were young Englishmen, barely yet acclimatized, and few, on joining, anticipated the thrilling experiences through which they were to pass. They typified the fighting spirit of the nation as apart from the trained and disciplined soldier, and on Wagon Hill their conduct was worthy the best traditions of a warrior race. It will never, in Africa at any rate, be forgotten. In the fiercest corner of that fiercest fight, when vastly outnumbered, they stood their ground, and died like men and heroes. What more could men or heroes do? There was one of them, Gorton of Maritzburg, who fell wounded between the contending lines. As he lay bleeding another bullet hit him. He raised his handkerchief as a signal for help. It only drew a hotter fire upon him, and four times more the bullets found him. Still he was alive. He lived through the burning heat of the day, the storm that followed, and still through the dismal night, but man could not bear such a strain, and four days later he died. Some of the Imperial Light Horse did try to help their wounded comrades, and their loyalty cost them their lives. Young Tucker, son of a Johannesburg stockbroker, crept forward to where one of his friends lay, and, in the act of binding up his wounds, was shot through the heart. Their capacity for sticking in hot corners was indirectly recognized. They were at once equipped with bayonets and revolvers – the only mounted corps in Natal who carried them. Better still, the brigadier commanding in the fight wrote the following letter–

"To the Officer in charge of the Imperial Light Horse, – I write these lines just to let you and your brave fellows know that in my despatch it will be made quite clear that the I.L.H. were second to none. No one realizes more clearly than I do that they were the backbone of the defence during that long day's fighting. Please make it known to the men that to have been associated with them I have always felt to be the highest privilege and honour." Brigadier-General Brocklehurst, commanding the cavalry brigade to which they were attached, also wrote– "I'm very proud that the I.L.H. belong to my brigade." A high testimonial from trueborn fighting men.

The more I saw of our two young Australian doctors, the greater my pride in my countrymen. In the hottest of the fight at Wagon Hill, Dr. Buntine, exposed to a cross fire, sat down calmly, and performed the delicate operation of tracheotomy upon a wounded officer who had been shot through the throat. His conduct was everywhere the theme of admiration. Hornabrook, much against his will, was sent on duty to Intombi, and his friends were glad that, for a time at any rate, he was unable to expose himself to the risks of bullet and shell.

On the night of the 13th we correspondents buried our poor colleague Mitchell, of the *Standard*, skulking to the grave by moonlight, as though on some shameful errand. It was the usual way. Alongside us some soldiers were burying a comrade, and very few minutes elapsed before the blare of the bugles told that the interment was over. There was little waste of time on ceremony, for burials had become a matter of routine. But wherever the dead were taken through the streets every soldier turned and lifted his hand in salute; every civilian uncovered his head. In the short range of bedrooms, one of which I occupied, there were three men down with enteric, and disease simply stalked brazenly through the streets of the town. To arrest its progress was hopeless. We could only wait and hope for General Buller's coming, and the chance to get away from the pesthouse into a purer atmosphere. If waiting be ever weary work, how trebly weary under these dismal circumstances. "A breath of unadulterate air, a glimpse of a green pasture." How we longed for both, after the stench of that plague-smitten town and the eternal brown of the prison hills. At an earlier period of the siege we wondered always what the enemy expected to achieve by sitting down upon their seven hills and potting us at long range with their cannon. It was such a hopeless thing, with the relief column coming on from the coast. We laughed then at the bombardment, but the humour soon faded from the situation. We forgot that sword and pestilence could be just as much twin destroyers in this enlightened age as in the days when the germ theory of disease was unknown, and realized that the Dutch had an ally in disease far more effective than their inferior shell. Sometimes on one day there were as many as sixteen dead waiting for interment at Intombi. Why should the Boers waste powder when sickness could do that much for them? On January 15 – one month since we had listened to the sound of Buller's guns upon the far Tugela – things were very nearly at their worst with us. Fever, grim and gaunt, stalked the streets, for Ladysmith had a town-hall – or as much of a town-hall as the Boer cannon had left – a coat-of-arms, a common zeal, a mayor, all the requirements of modern municipal civilization – excepting drainage. They had gutters which, after heavy storms, become fever-beds, stewing and sweltering under the fierce Natal suns, but drainage in its true, wholesome sense was unknown. They had methods of sanitation entirely worthy of the people by whom it was mainly carried out – coolies and Kaffirs. No cause for wonder, then, that ninety per cent. of the people in Ladysmith were, during this awful three months, down with some form of sickness, or that the doctors, struggling heroically with their work, one day in the field, the next in the hospitals, had thin, worn, haggard faces, with lines of anxiety ever deepening upon them. It made many of them older men. Yet, for humanity's sake, they held up bravely. There were seven of them down with fever in the officers' hospital at Intombi. The Imperial Light Horse, who came in 475 strong, paraded less than 150. The Border Mounted, who came with a strength of over 200, mustered 96.

The Devons, who marched in 984 strong, had 480 on parade, and the missing ones had gone down in greater numbers to fever than to the bullet. The proportion ran much the same through every corps. And never were poor, famishing, despairing wretches so tormented by illusive rumour as the garrison of Ladysmith. There were relief columns on all sides of us, but they came not –

"not yet, but he whose ear
Thrills to that finer atmosphere"

might imagine upon every side the faint, very faint boom of guns – but they remained always faint, and were generally but the phantasy of a sick man's brain. The bombardment fell away slightly, but we ceased to notice it – fever had supplanted shell as the universal peril.

The heart-breaking thing to the physicians was that though they might pull a man safely through the crises of his illness, they had no chance of building up his strength again. There were no suitable foods for the purpose; no chance for that careful nursing which, to fever patients, is half the battle. Those to whom money was no object could buy eggs at 20s. a dozen, but these were luxuries far beyond the means of the man in the ranks, hundreds of whom were invalided home unfit for further soldiering and with constitutions hopelessly broken down. Thus, in the slow stages of convalescence, died G.W. Steevens, one of the best-known of war correspondents, holding, as an attractive writer on war, the position that was once so universally accorded to Archibald Forbes. Steevens was one of the first men smitten with enteric, but thin, wiry, cool, self-contained as he was by nature, he passed very successfully through the trying stage of the illness, and seemed to be quite out of danger, when some slight indiscretion brought a relapse, which, in a few hours, killed him. Next to Bennet Burleigh – who, from the strictly newspaper point of view, the capacity to get early and accurate information, had no peer amongst modern war correspondents – Steevens was by far the most able writer in the field. He was through the short Græco-Turkish campaign, where, like Kinnaird Rose of Brisbane, he made a reputation with his book, *With the Conquering Turk*. He went to Chitral later, and, last of all, described the downfall of Mahdism as no one else has described it. Then, at the zenith of success, mourned by many comrades, as by those who wept for him in their English home, died in this wretched, man-eating Ladysmith, an able correspondent. We buried him at midnight, with the Boer search-light from Umbulwana playing inquisitively upon his coffin. On the spot where Colonel Dick-Cunyngham, of the Gordons, fell wounded on the early morning of the battle of Cæsar's Hill, the regiment built a cairn bearing this inscription:–

"On this spot

LIEUT.-COLONEL DICK-CUNYNGHAM, V.C.,

Commanding 2nd Gordon Highlanders,
Was mortally wounded
On Jan. 6, 1900."

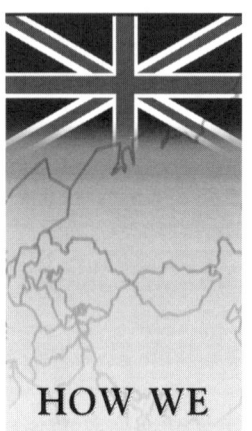

HOW WE KEPT THE FLAG FLYING

CHAPTER 19

THE GUNS ON THE TUGELA

*Distant shell fire – Lyddite on the hills – The garrison underground –
The town signals – Half rations.*

ONE point of controversy that had lasted pretty well throughout the siege was settled by the resolute effort of the enemy to break through our defences at Cæsar's Hill. Civilians in Ladysmith had always contended that Sir George White was guilty of a tactical blunder in not including both Umbulwana and Lombard's Kop in our ring of defences. No doubt it would have deprived the Boers of two most commanding points for the bombardment of the town, but the real point was, not whether the hills were worth holding – that was beyond argument – but whether doubling the length of our line of defence (for that is what it meant) would not have left the chain dangerously weak at any point where the enemy chose vigorously to test its strength. Cæsar's Hill settled that point beyond all question, and admittedly justified the Commander-in-Chief's disposition of his forces and choice of stations. Had we attempted to hold the two big hills, a Boer assault half as impetuous as that of January 6 would have isolated a large portion of our forces, and left the town pretty well at the mercy of the Boers. It was due to the tried soldier, with the gift of looking far ahead, of gauging the task, not by his present strength, but by what his strength might be in months to come, that we were still in possession of even such a sorry harbour of refuge. Most of us in Ladysmith had, I think, been a little precipitate in our judgement of the military authorities. We had suffered too much personally to be calm, unbiassed judges of the situation. In face of daily peril and discomfort, the severely judicial attitude was not easily assumed, and we were apt to be carried away by individual grievances. It had been a trying situation, and the Staff, whether fighting men or executive, had risen to it. Upon Sir George White the strain must have been tremendous, for probably only he and General Hunter, his Chief of Staff, knew that when Buller was repulsed at the Tugela it meant two months waiting. And in General Hunter he had just the man to help him to carry the burden. Through it all the great fighter of the Soudan was cool, cheerful, courageous, hiding all trace of anxiety, carrying always that cheerful face which gave strength to his subordinates.

By the middle of January we knew that the repeated rumours as to the disposal of General Buller's troops on the Tugela had some foundation in fact. Sir Charles Warren, it was said, had moved up the river, and would attempt the crossing at Potgieter's Drift, eighteen miles from Colenso, and the nearest ford that gave suitable passage to an army. The heights were further back from the river than at Colenso, giving us a better chance – once we had shelled them out – to make our footing good. The key of the Dutch position was a high, doubled-pronged mountain, known to the Kaffirs as N'taba N'Yama, or the Black Mountain, the Dutch name being Spion Kop. For some few days after their heliograph, working from the new position, had told us that our countrymen were at Springfield, we waited in hourly expectation of hearing their guns, and we were beginning to despair again, when at dawn on the morning of January 17 the long dull roar came to us, and we knew that the expected battle had begun – the battle that was to bring us early deliverance, or – well, we hardly liked to think of the alternative. Death from stagnation or imprisonment at Pretoria were both unpleasant. All day the faint roar of the cannon continued, just as we heard it on the Tugela a month before, when we expected so much and realized so little. The sky was overcast, and there was no chance of signalling, but the fact that the guns were going until ten o'clock that night told that no definite stage in the fight had been reached. They were more tardy in beginning next day, and we were in suspense for a while lest again the relieving column might have failed to "make good its footing". Later we heard the Titanic duel raging once again, and no music ever sounded sweeter to ears long dulled to close, but ever sensitive to distant, cannon fire. Pulled down though we were by dysentery and bad diet, fit rather for the hospital than the field, there was that thrilling promise in these far-off guns which made it impossible even for a sick man to stay a-bed. I rode out to Observation Hill, to get a far-away view of the country in the direction of Potgieter's Drift, where there are fewer hills than towards Colenso. Beaten from their main position there, the enemy had but one or two points where they could make a stand. The guiding point was a British war-balloon, its oiled silken skin shining in the sunrise like a new sixpence suspended from the sky. As we watched, a gun flashed from the side of a black hill across the river, and though over twenty miles of rolling veldt lay between, we could see the British shells bursting about the tops of the enemy's hills, huge pillars of red and black smoke – a mixture of South African dust and British lyddite. Occasionally a dense cloud of white smoke, like one of the woolpacks that float across Australian skies in the early autumn, burst from the top of the nearer hills – the black powder of one of the big Boer guns. On our side of this ridge we could distinctly pick out with the glass two large Boer camps, sheltered from Warren's guns, and hidden even from the war-balloon by the lofty tops of N'taba N'Yama. We were able even at that distance to co-operate with our friends. Observation Hill was a heliograph station, and we could see behind the presumed position of the British lines their heliograph, resembling in the distance a bright brass gong, with yellow prismatic rays thrown across it. We told them of the Boer camps, and a huge laager of some forty wagons – their transport trains in waiting – and saw the sequel later in the afternoon. It was between three and four o'clock that the steady fire ceased for a little; then burst out again in salvoes as yet unequalled. Suddenly we saw the shells bursting, a half-dozen at a time, around about the left camp of the enemy, whence the white tents, or wagon buck-sails – which serve the purpose of tents with the Dutch – soon disappeared. Shells fell amongst the wagons also, and the naval gunners through their powerful glass could see the enemy's ambulance vans at work. It needed nothing of the kind to assure us that the Boers were in a hot corner. Lyddite shells falling as these fell must wreak awful havoc. Before sundown the whole of the left position of the Boer forces at Potgieter's Drift seemed to be deserted, and our shells were falling on their right only. That was the best night we had spent in Ladysmith for many a week. Unless we had lost faith in the evidence of our own senses, we could not but believe that the relief column had "made good its footing" at Springfield.

Even the enemy's gunners around Ladysmith appeared to realize that it was the beginning of the end, and that their three months' fun was almost over, for they pounded us with redoubled energy. Best of all, our guns answered them shot for shot, showing that the need for husbanding ammunition was almost past. It was while we rode back from Observation Hill in the evening that a shell from Bulwan fell, with a demoralizing crash, almost on us. The scream, the concussion, the roar of the explosion nearly hurled us from the saddle. My chum Greenwood, helped by an alarmed double somersault from his terrified Basuto pony, was thrown, and then I realized that the admiration of a true horseman for his horse is something that passeth human understanding. Badly bruised and partly stunned, the correspondent sat up in the dust, and, looking at the offending pony – which stood with spread nostrils, pricked ears, wide eyes, and quivering flanks – gasped in unmistakable admiration, "Isn't he a little picture?" "If he were mine," retorted the *Central News* correspondent, "I'd knock the picture out of its frame with half a brick."

Shriller than ever in Ladysmith rose the different alarm notes, which told that Bulwan is in eruption. There was no longer any false pride as to taking shelter from Long Tom. The men were commanded to go to earth; each camp had its own shelters, and its own signalman always on the look-out for the first puff of smoke, between which and the shell there were over twenty seconds to get to cover. From the volunteer camp came the warning in a three-note blare of the bugle. From Helpmakaar ridge, held alternately by the Liverpools and the Devons, there was a shrill whistle, while a Hindoo sentinel perched on one of the railway-station buildings, gave the signal to his countrymen with a high, piping cry of "L-o-o-o-n-g T-o-o-o-m" – that to Oriental ears sounded like the Mussulman call to prayer. One heard that shrill call quite as far off as the bugle or the whistle.

The 20th and 21st – two roaring hot African days, on which the 105° in the shade was more trying in Ladysmith basin than 110° in Australia – passed without developments of any decisive character, though the cannon fire was still heavy to the south-west, while the fight appeared to shift still further towards the great chain of mountains cutting off Natal from the Free State and the Transvaal. On Sunday we judged, from the white smoke bursting in puffs along the escarpment of the foot-hills, that our forces had pushed the enemy back from their position at Potgieter's Drift, and, leaving their siege guns, were following him up with field artillery. Towards evening on the

20th a squadron of British cavalry – presumably an outpost – was seen upon a distant hillside, and it looked alluringly easy then to link hands with our friends across the veldt, but we knew perfectly well that the prelude to that was battle, and it might be heavy slaughter, and the British forces in Ladysmith stood ever prepared to take a share in the conflict. The cavalry and mounted infantry had three days' rations and fodder packed ready to move out at an instant's notice, and they waited the development of what we believed to be a far-reaching plan for cutting off and cornering the Boer army. Information was exceedingly meagre; we had to guess at everything, for it was not a time when generals exercised candour or communicativeness. Badly as we needed succour, we were content with such a possibility ahead to wait a little longer, and as a germicide to drip carbolic in our drinking-water. There was no choice in the matter of diet – bread (rather sodden), biscuit (tremendously hard), canned beef (objectionable only when the cooks made a well-intentioned effort to disguise the fact that it was tinned stuff), and tea without milk or sugar. Half rations of each. Occasionally transport oxen were killed to save them from starvation, and then fresh meat was served out. Human teeth were powerless to make an impression upon thews that had done transport work through the whole length of Africa, and with soldiers and civilians the universal plan was to boil this meat for hours, and use the soup only. We mixed with it for vegetables a variety of wild spinach, the only objection to which was its tenacity in holding to its native sands. A few fortunate ones had the softer tendrils of pumpkin vines for vegetables, but the veldt is singularly destitute of any native plant that can be so used. Neither nettle nor marsh-mallow seems to have penetrated to this part of Natal. The result of it all was hollow cheeks, sunken eyes, and flapping waistcoats. Men had ceased to fit their clothes, and the garrison was the flabbiest, shabbiest, and sorriest lot of human beings ever gathered together.

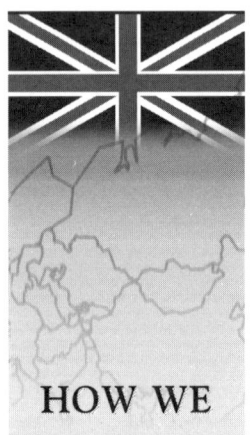

HOW WE KEPT THE FLAG FLYING

CHAPTER 20

IMPRESSIONS OF BATTLE

*The folly of inaction – The first battle – A nasty few minutes –
The impressive sequel – Conduct of the enemy – The lonely dead –
Confusion of fight – How historians disagree – Night and the bayonet.*

THE one thing brought home to all of us in Ladysmith while we waited for the end was the suicide of inaction. We rose early and rode early ere yet the Boer gunners were about to make horse exercise on the outer veldt at all perilous. To talk, to write, to play a game of whist, anything were better than to sit still and think and ponder over dour possibilities. Just as it became necessary to prevent, by a fine, men talking of appetizing dishes between meals, so it was necessary to get others out of themselves, out even into the danger zone, so that they might at least have the melancholy proof that there were hundreds in worse plight than themselves. Sometimes for days there was the monotony more trying than actual peril. Let me take advantage of one such period to try and convey to you some of the emotions of battle with which we are now at least fairly well acquainted. They may sound strange perhaps; it may be strained and overdrawn, but remember that we speak of war – and that war touches, it seems to me, almost every string in the gamut of human emotions. There may be something that is very nearly hysteria – there can never be indifference. It is but the record of individual impressions, and different men are differently affected.

I had long been impressed with the idea that the first battle was the great ordeal – that no stone could be too large for cover, no shelter too insignificant. It is not so. Until one has realized something of the effect of fire, he is not in any sense overawed by it, and even then he is apt to magnify the lesser danger and ignore the greater. The Boer artillery fire was, with us, never at any time terrific. It brought to mind, indeed, a homely saying I once heard in the mouth of a Scottish member of the Victorian Parliament –

"Great cry and little wool,
As the devil said when he clipped the bull."

But to the novice the artillery fire is everything. The roar of shell to those who hear it for the first time is impressive, and there is an overmastering impulse to duck and hide from shells that could not hit one though he stood as high as the loftiest gum tree in Australia, a corresponding tendency to ignore the unobtrusive, imp-like buzz of the Mauser bullet. It takes time to discover and guard against the real danger, and if you have bad luck you may die before you make the discovery. In my first fight I was lying close to one of our batteries, not knowing then the undesirability of such neighbours, and the Boer shells were bursting at intervals round about. A horse plunged in the traces just behind, yet no shell had burst there. A gunner running past with a shell in his hand dropped down suddenly on the veldt, spat blood, quivered, and was still. The shell, painted in red, white, and blue bands, rolled down the slope a bit, and was caught by a stone. The gunner was dead, yet no white puff – like the bursting of a bag of flour at a lively election meeting – told of shrapnel exploding near enough to be effective. Then I began to grasp the vital fact that noise is not necessarily danger, and that of two evils it is best always to choose the louder and the least, to be keenly alert for rifle fire, and take the risks of shell. Caution grows with experience, and one has never such an eye for cover as in his very latest fight, though he may have become apathetic in some respects. Apart from obligation, one's own desire to see as much as possible of the greatest game in the world makes him think less of personal risk, while mechanically almost making the most of all advantages in cover.

If the hour of victory is the hour of exultation, it is the moment of revenge too, and of all that is worst in warfare. The hour of pity and forgiveness is not yet. The dominant note is pure savagery, the overmastering emotion – Destruction. The foe are flying, and the one desire is Kill, Kill, Kill – for this is a flight turned to rout and demoralization. It has ended perhaps with such a charge as those at Dundee, Elands Laagte, and Cæsar's Hill. All day men have seen their comrades dying round about them, and, as yet, have not realized the full measure of loss. They are panting for close quarters, for the wild, indescribable bayonet *mêlée* – most of all for revenge. They cannot be turned loose at such a moment and play the saint. Those who have long crouched behind rock and kopje rise as one, and, with every nerve thrilling savagely to the spirit of the wild charge, "like reapers descend to the harvest of death." "Now then, give them hell!" is the wild cry, and God help those whom the British soldier reaches with the bayonet while his dead are yet in sight, and the blood lust shines ensanguined in his eyes. For them is no salvation, save from the Conqueror who is all mercy. There was abundant mercy in the earlier stages of the fight, ere the victor had been mauled and mangled by his enemy. Killing, like increase of appetite, grows upon what it feeds. The difference between the civilized man and the savage is but a veneer – the centuries of civilization, sentiment, and culture seem only a dream in the presence of the primeval emotions. It is the old rugged, untutored man killing in a delirium of anger and exultation. I felt no qualm of pity when I saw the flying Boers tottering against the yellow background of the flooded spruit as our guns and rifles cut them down. We had been long with our dead, had seen them killed, had felt the tension of waiting, the sullen resentment of possible defeat, and then came this maddening, inhuman impulse. Those who have not experienced it will think it unworthy, and it is unworthy, just because human nature, freed from restraint, is at best a poor, savage, uncultured thing, that the years have not greatly bettered. It had one redeeming quality, and only one. It was but for a moment that the curb was off, and passion wholly unrestrained.

And then – despair, sorrow, repentance. All the savageries that have come out of the past to take possession of us are thrust aside. Reason is reinstated, and the centuries have their own again in the emotions that have justified the creation of man in God's own image. But it comes painfully home to you that the civilization which has possibilities such as this is a poor thing after all – horribly incomplete. If you could but gather together all the eloquent tongues of the world and put them on that death-strewn battle-field at the moment of reaction, when the finer senses thrill responsive to every appeal, what an invective against war would be the consequence. There would be a momentary indifference, I fear, as to the laws and customs of nations, as to tyranny and wrong in the abstract. Every other consideration would be swept aside in the one solemn appeal, "In the name of God let there be no more of this." You will be apt to forget, perhaps, that the long *cortège* of the victims of wrong and error never ends, that the consequences, could they be gathered together on the one field, would be more grim and sanguinary even than this. But for the moment this one picture is overpowering, and you are a peace party – without the parish politics. You will feel better – at any rate, more composed – when the field has been swept clear, when, to come at last to the chess-board allegory, the fallen pieces – Knight and Pawn – have been put into the box and the game is over. The pity that all that is best in man – the courage, patriotism, and duty you have so much admired – should have this for their immediate sequel! If the emotions that beset one in battle are so unique, so incomparable, so different from everything in every-day life, so, too, the reaction, the depression which comes with the immediate survey of the dead and dying, is the greater, the more universal. Ardour, hostility, revenge – all the poorer passions slink away in the presence of an overmastering pity, and man is again in some measure immortal. Every poor, dead, twisted, battered object on the grass – the mourned of some home, the centre of some one's hopes and heartburnings – is a reproach. What use to tell one then, that if anarchy and confusion are not to reign in the world, this sort of thing must be, and that for the soldier, whatever his individual convictions, there can be but one watchword, "In life and death, in right or wrong, first, last, and always – my country"? No, the moment and the mood are not for philosophy – only for heavenly compassion and sympathy, which is the marrow of life. Soldier and civilian, all, I am convinced, think alike then, though caste and training and tradition may help them in some degree to disguise their true sentiments. For the soldier must not be let ponder upon these things – he must sing his song of triumph while elsewhere they bury his dead, just as they play a lively quick-step on the return from a soldier's funeral. Now and again in the very heart of this unutterable sadness you hear an oath or a blasphemy that, by contrast with the solemnity of the surroundings, appals you. In the presence of those dead faces, some white and waxen, some blue and plethoric, it jars upon you, appals you, hurts you like the cut of a knife. If it were earnest, either the careless exclamation of the moment or the love of coarse expletive, it would be just pure brutality. Happily it is nothing of the kind – only the mask with which men uncultured but powerfully wrought seek to conceal their emotions. It is the weakness of most men – above all, the untutored man – that, like the Indian, they would be stoics when they should be humans. Lacking the Indian's power of self-command, they go to the brute extreme to hide the poor fact that they are just human beings with human emotions. They cannot well cry, so they swear; it would be unmanly to pray, so they blaspheme; but a discerning Providence, be sure, appreciates the situation, and the recording angel, that was kind to the frailties of Uncle Toby, has, in the inexhaustible wells of his pity, yet a few more tears. If Tommy hides his emotions under the coarser mask, his officer has recourse to something almost equally "thin" in caste and convention.

It is with a strong feeling of resentment that I have at times heard the Boers described as posturing on the battle-field. They have been heartless at times, and it is remembered to them, but never so heartless, so modern, and so artificial as that. When our poor dead fellows at Nicholson's Nek had been gathered together, so that the identification papers might be taken from their tunics, many of the Boers, who a little bit before had been concerned only to kill them, gathered about the open grave, and sang mournfully one of their old Dutch hymns. "A purely theatrical display," said some in whom the race hostilities rankled. "It was done to impress the English with the deep religious feeling of the men against whom they are fighting." I am not a great believer in the genuineness of some of the Boer professions, because their attitude and their actions are much in conflict, but those who credit the ignorant, unlettered farmers of the veldt with such a strange mixture of diplomacy and hypocrisy had themselves no actual experience of the sights and sounds of a battlefield immediately after the fight, or they must have realized the difficulties that beset an actor in such surroundings. Nero fiddling over burning Rome is just a simple-minded, whole-hearted musician as compared with those who can play the mountebank over even an enemy's dead. Theatrical it may have sounded to those who have not yet tested by the severe battle standard the suddenness of the variations in the long range of human emotion. Amidst the soul-subduing effects of the after battle no man can be theatrical. Then will the most heartless trickster who ever trod life's stage drop the character, and get something near his real self, whatever its value. The greatest artist who ever faced the footlights is no longer an actor in such a setting – only an overstrung, over-awed, repentant human being. The dead, set faces, the unclosed eyes, the shrunken fingers, the arms tortured and stiffened in death to such a mute, pathetic attitude of supplication – all these would be an eternal reproach. The thin distinction between Boer and Briton disappears, and the one sorrow is sufficient to embrace them all. If it be so with the enemy's dead, what of our attitude to our own? There are so many whom you may have met and known, whom you saw last in robust health, and whom you will meet no more. If familiarity breed indifference at all in such a scene, it is an emotion of slow growth, for the chances are that your sixth battle-field will mean many more severed friendships than your first. And yet men can loot in such a scene. Yes, that is so, but not immediately, and very often, I think, they are egged on by a false bravado – the desire I have already mentioned to exhibit themselves to the world as men divested of every weakness. I remember on Wagon Hill coming upon a dead and terribly mutilated Boer lying upon a beautiful sporting rifle, just such a souvenir as one would wish to have of a great fight, but not for a whole arsenal could I have lifted that torn body to get it. It was there for hours, until some Tommy, more callous than his fellows, dragged the man away, wiped the rifle clean, and admired his prize. Blink at the fact as one may, loot is inseparable from battle, and must not be judged by the moral codes of peace. Some are for spoil pure and simple; some want only a souvenir; nearly all – if they have the nerve for sudden and startling opportunities – loot in some way. The litter of the battle-field is the unclaimed property for which, as a rule, its owners have no further use. To rob the dead seemed to me at first the meanest act in the whole range of human capacity, but that feeling blunted after a time, and if one did not actually fall himself, he became very tolerant of the frailties of others. It was a latitude that reached even such sordid things as cash and valuables.

There was one other aspect of the battle-field that seemed to me always more or less revolting – the bringing in of the dead. Those with skill and thought and delicacy are so fully occupied then in attending to the wounded – the men who may yet be saved – that they have no concern for those who are lost for ever. There was something revolting in the calm, deliberate system followed in the collection of the dead. The Cape boys are on the field with their wagons, moving here and there, picking up the bodies, and packing them, not as the decencies of peace would suggest, side by side, and shrouded, but just stacking them roughly in piles, as one sees railway-sleepers in a truck. The black man is picking up the white, and bringing him to his grave, though it is so often the other way. Other black men are digging graves, grumbling and sweating over their work in the glare of the tropical noon, casting now and then an apprehensive look at the gradually-extending line of bodies, lest it mean more digging. The officers are, perhaps, rolled in a blanket, and placed apart, though social distinctions seem poor and hollow just then.

It seems odd to you at first that men who have marched and messed and laughed and campaigned side by side with these should have marched away to their lines, to eat, drink, and sleep, leaving their dead upon the field, and usage in this respect never seemed to divest it wholly of an element of gruesome heartlessness. But then, as I have said before, the quick-step follows hard upon the dead march, the soldier has not time to mourn and measure out his affection for the dead in the solemn splendour of obsequies. The weeping is for the women and children; the rest for the black boys and the burial parties. Sometimes, indeed, a well-loved leader, who has been at once a father and a commander, is not left there to the double darkness of death and night, but is taken up reverently, placed on a stretcher, and brought in by the regiment. That is always a moving sight. A corps may have passed you, hurrying home; the men, with the loosened discipline that follows upon some great service in battle, talking freely, some even thus early laughing over its incidents, some, perhaps, boasting cheaply, all eager to forget the spectacle they have left behind them; all with the air of men returning rather from a picnic than a tragedy. Then, close upon its heels, a contrast. A regiment marching with downcast eyes and slow pace, and half-way down the line a pair of muddy ammunition boots showing from the end of a stretcher, carried on the shoulders of four men. They are bringing in their dead. That, however, is a sight rarely seen, and more frequently there was nothing but the listlessness of after battle, the reaction which, even when one is but a watcher, seems for a day or two after a fight to drain away the nervous power, and leave him limp and apathetic. The volunteers, who had not been hardened by drill and usage, and whose losses were usually lighter than in the line regiment, showed more of that reverence for the dead which is the universal and sacred privilege of private life. It was all a sentiment, of course, one's feeling on these points, but it seemed a breach of comradeship to leave those who had fought beside one lying there so lonely on the hillsides.

> "His cot was right-hand cot to mine,
> Said Files upon parade;
> He's sleeping out and far to-night,
> The colour-sergeant said."

The popular idea of battle to-day, encouraged and strengthened always by the published descriptions of the fight, is a nice series of chess-board moves, check and counter-check, spread out like a map to the view of the spectator. It may have been so in short-range days, when troops approached each other closely, and the charge with bayonet or lance was the vital stage of combat – the final rout of the vanquished side – the last move that turned defeat into confusion and slaughter. It is not so now. At least, I never found it so, and the fights before and during the siege of Ladysmith were fairly typical. The complete system of intelligence and espionage that the Dutch had established made it essential that the general's plans should be known to as few men as possible. The chess-board part of the great war game, it seemed to me, was all played, or at least developed, afterwards – the more so, perhaps, in that with a mobile enemy like the Boer it is impossible to calculate very far ahead. If he holds, or is supposed to hold a position – plans for its assault and outflanking may be carefully made, but when they are put into execution the Boer, as a rule, is not there. The first development of the plan opens necessarily at so great a distance, that where our slow-moving infantry went out to meet the most agile and alert mounted infantry in the world, our move might be well developed ere we discovered that the whole situation on the other side had changed. There was one fight, at least, where the plan of action seemed clear to me, and that was before the siege, when we went out to Tinta Inyoni to push back a second time, as we had once already pushed them back at Elands Laagte, the Free State commandoes who threatened to cut in between us and the column which, with a dazed leader at its head and an active and exasperated enemy in its rear, was struggling through rain and mire on the long retreat from Dundee. There the plan was at least apparent – Lucas Meyer had pushed his rallied burghers in between, and thrust forward to the last point where the conglomerate of hills gave the Boer fighter the kind of cover he so dearly loves. They halted, hesitating before coming out into the open country, developing, Zulu-like, one of the long arms which eventually encompassed Ladysmith and pierced so far into the heart of the land below. It was to prevent them thrusting forward early enough to harass General Yule's weary soldiers that we went out to push them back. That was all clear enough to the civilian onlooker. We pushed them back, and every move on our side made on the open veldt was manifest and explicable. Of the Boers we saw next to nothing. A rout of black-coated galloping horsemen from a kopje when our shell fire became too hot, disappearing quickly in the smoke of the burning veldt where our shells had set it on fire – that was all. The hills, but for the din, looked smiling and peaceful enough; there were no hostile riflemen visible anywhere, but we heard from them always.

Lombard's Kop was quite another affair. We went out wondering in the early morning, speculating as to the chance of its being a demonstration or really a battle. We faced up to fight them at a position stronger and much nearer home than Tinta Inyoni. We went to the assault boldly, were met with equal determination, and faltered, fell, and came back again, pelted the whole way by the shell fire of an exulting foe. To us it all seemed a medley and a confusion; a repetition of those earlier fights where we had gone up valiantly, taken that which we could never hold, and came back again. This time, though we came back downhearted, broken in spirit, morose, savage, disappointed, we had spent the day, it seemed to us, in a series of disjointed, objectless, suicidal assaults on a well-posted and powerful enemy. Never at any time was there a plan apparent – never once a move that the average onlooker could follow. It looked for all the world the plain tactics of Donnybrook Fair, "wherever you see a head, hit it" – except that heads are seldom seen in a Boer fighting line, and shoulders even less rarely. Artillery halted under rifle fire to drive out the enemy, who were following us too fast, and as their gun-horses began to drop, they, too, pushed out of range, and so piece by piece we came back again, savage and disappointed. We had pushed no assault home, yet had gone sufficiently far forward to pay some of the penalties of failure and defeat. Correspondents trying to shape that tangled, tumultuous skein into something like a plan of action, so that they might send their waiting despatch-riders off with an intelligible account of the progress of the battle, asked each other as they met on the veldt what it all meant – what had we attempted, and how were we succeeding. "We are retreating, that's what it is," said a South African as he galloped in from an outlook which the near presence of an artillery battery firing and retreating suddenly had made no longer tenable.

"You should know better, sir, than to make such a remark as that within hearing of the soldiers," flamed out an indignant English correspondent, whose white military moustache and tall soldierly figure always led to his being mistaken for a general at least. "I know much better than that," retorted the Afrikander, "but you asked me a question, and I have answered it as far as my ability to gauge the situation goes. If you doubt the truth of what I say, go up into the firing line and have a look for yourself." It was just an illustration of the mood of the moment, when every one was savage and out of temper with every one else, when confusion was the only other emotion. Next an intelligence officer rode up, asking excitedly, "Where are the Boers?" It seemed a foolish question for an intelligence man, considering that their shells had been dropping all round us, but intelligible in that, for one who had not been present in the earlier hours, it was even yet impossible to locate the enemy. Next a mounted officer with, "Have you seen the –th anywhere? By Jove, I've lost my regiment." It was not a joke either on his part or mine – very far from it. With troops strewn about the veldt, the brown khaki lost in the brown rock and long grass, it was altogether possible.

It was late that night when we began to pick up the moves in the mysterious game of which we had been the witnesses. There had been a plan after all – you will have read the cabled account of it, how an outflanking movement had been attempted, the troops going out secretly in the darkness; how the secret had been made known, the column surprised, slaughtered, captured at Nicholson's Nek. It all seemed so concise and clear and unfortunate to you. You grasped it in a minute, yet we, who had been a day watching the greater part of the game, and knew nothing of the Nicholson's Nek affair, left the field dispirited and confused, knowing only that we had gone out and come in again; had seen little, but heard and felt a lot; that there had been fighting and loss; and that long after we were home, and fed, and sleeping off the sickening sense of disappointment, the ambulance lanterns would be flitting thought the darkness over the veldt; that tired surgeons and dressers would be picking up the wounded – who so rarely called for help – and bringing them to the gathering point, where the smell of chloroform was wafted down on the wings of the night wind.

Again, in the fight at Besters, it all seemed to us a mystery, a misery, an exasperation. We had tried to do something; had done it, in part; had pushed the enemy from kopjes which we left vacant, yet they galled us with their fire long before we were out of range again. It may have been different in the open of the western plains, where the long outlook gave some comprehensiveness to the prospect; with us, where the eternal kopjes shut off half the game, it was rarely otherwise than a mystery.

I speak, of course, of the onlooker only. There was ever the man who held all the threads of the tangled skein on his fingers, and pulled each in turn – the man with a responsibility so great that in the actual battle – the only place where that sense of responsibility can be wholly realized – one was awed by the possibilities of his every action. The movement of that one piece – the pulling of the one string – may bring darkness and wailing to a hundred homes. Were a leader turned from his purpose by such a spectacle, if he stopped a moment to think of all the possibilities, if he had not been drilled by hard experience into something more of concern for the end than for the means and consequences, he would, it seemed to me, falter in the face of such a dread responsibility, and, faltering, fail. For, as I have said already, you must see men in their death agony round about you to know what it means to send others, it may be fruitlessly, to the same fate. It is one of the reasons why a Kitchener succeeds, and a humanitarian fails. The one with his steeled nerves and sternly-disciplined heart sees only the great end – victory. The God-like humanity of the other – so good a thing in peace – responds to the pitiful cry of the dying, and the death which made him falter comes tenfold thick with failure and retreat.

You will not wonder, then, that the chronicles of battle disagree. In our camp there was always argument when the thing was over and we exchanged impressions. It was hard to convince a man at all obstinate that events were not exactly as he saw them, because one cannot easily be disloyal to his own eyesight and his own intelligence when he has been present at a thing so unforgettable as war. There never was a battle, I believe, fully and faithfully described, even where history has been turning over its incidents for half a century. And as it cannot be described, neither can it be illustrated. The camera at its best shows too little; the pencil – at its worst – too much. Pictures that give the smoke spirting form the enemy's riflepits are convenient and excusable, since they help those absent to locate the position. But in actual fight one sees no rifle-smoke. We are hitting at a shadow, it seems – except that the shadow, while immune, has a faculty for hitting back. Even in the worst confusion one knows that the double report or echo means rifles firing towards him, the volume of sound being thus really doubled; while a shuddering sound that seems to ripple through the air and die away in the distance marks the course of our shells in their flight towards the enemy. Even upon geographical names there will be disagreement. The Dutch have given one set, the English another; while the original owners, the Kaffirs, multiply the confusion by duplicating the name of a mountain just as it may, seen from either side, present different peculiarities.

It has always seemed to me that our two chief successes in

Natal – the assaults upon Talana Hill and Elands Laagte – were really our costliest ventures. At Dundee we undoubtedly met some of the Johannesburg and Pretoria rabble – poor shots as a rule, who, keeping low behind the rocks for their own protection, as a natural consequence fired high, and most of their bullets went over the heads of the British assaulting columns. It perhaps gave a false value to the bayonet. Men who believed in Britain's traditional arm said, "Well, in spite of long-range rifles and magazines, it is the bayonet still" – and we had to learn that lesson afterwards, both on the Tugela and elsewhere, at terrible cost. I fancy the ultimate conviction will be that, except for rushing a position already shattered almost to inaction by heavy artillery and rifle fire, the bayonet is a weapon only for desperate enterprises and night attacks. At night and against the Boers it is invaluable. Those night attacks seem to appeal to the primitive man in us, and rouse perceptions and emotions that are rarely stimulated by daylight movements, however imposing. There is a savage charm – a romance – in the stealthy night march, which one can feel always, but cannot explain. Were it not for the great difficulty of holding even the best-drilled men together at night we should undoubtedly have made many another sortie under cover of darkness, for it is all in favour of the bayonet. But the risk is tremendous. Men find such a difficulty in keeping touch of each other, and one blunderer can cut a column in two and have the two halves by mischance at each other's throats a few minutes afterwards. The leader who affects night movements must always be prepared for calamities, and so it is that they are rarely tried save in sore emergency, and are the more greatly appreciated when successful. Could we have sent out, as on the Cossack posts, colonials with some bushcraft, and each with a Kaffir at his elbow, even the Boers might have been harassed to death almost by continual sorties, but there were not enough men of the stamp to be implicitly trusted, and poor Tommy's capacity for losing himself at night is abnormal.

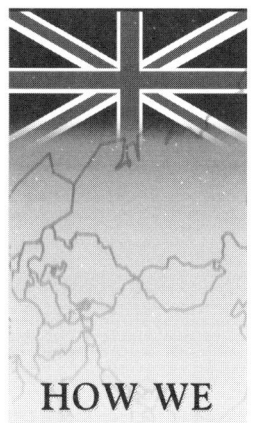

HOW WE KEPT THE FLAG FLYING

CHAPTER 21

A TIME OF STAGNATION

Another disappointment – Reduced rations – A distant view – The Boer trek – Camps re-established – Signs of disaster – An exhausted garrison.

SEVEN days had gone since the roar of General Buller's cannon, mellowed by distance, first came to us from the Tugela. Seven days of eager expectation and anxious waiting. On January 23, in spite of the diplomatic assurance that relief was "within measurable distance," it sounded and looked no nearer. The pessimistic were losing heart and declaring their conviction that we had no men on the north bank of the river, and that the Boer could just as philosophically face British shell fire at 8000 and 9000 yards as the British in Ladysmith had for more than three months stood Boer cannon fire at the same distance. Meanwhile the artisans at the barrack store kept up the supply of little white crosses for graves. There were twenty of them drying in the sun as I passed one day, and they would all be needed within hours. That was one of the hardest, most disappointing phases of the siege – the calm, cold-blooded preparation for the death of those who at the moment were alive, full of hope for the future, of fond concern for loved ones upon whom they had looked their last. Our loss from shell in Ladysmith was no so great as formerly, partly because a larger proportion of their big ones failed to burst on concussion. One of these was, however, responsible, in an unlooked-for way, for the death of two of our brave bluejackets. The shell had come into the possession of a clergyman, who, wishing to keep it as a trophy of the siege, arranged with these two men to draw the charge. While they were at work it exploded, killing one instantly, and so mutilating the other that his recovery was hopeless. Such a mishap was inevitable, for men with no experience in the work, and without the bronze tools required for it, had been drawing the explosives from shells for weeks, and the only wonder was that disaster had not come sooner. The accident took place near the ordnance stores, and showed how quick the Boer gunners were in noting the fact and drawing shrewd inferences. Knowing that the smoke of the explosion had not come from a shell fired by them, they were justified in assuming that some accident had occurred at the ordnance depôt, and that the smoke fixed the locality of the magazines. During that and the following days they dropped shell after shell on the spot, their expedition in picking up the range, and accuracy in keeping it, being both admirable. A big Australian gum tree growing there suffered a good deal, three shells striking it.

On the eighth day the firing from the Tugela was the heaviest we had yet heard. It was an almost continuous roar. Occasionally I timed it at almost thirty rounds per minute, and it went on for nearly six hours without a break. When the lyddite shells burst nearly twenty miles off the effect was unique. Save that the flash of the explosion was always visible through the hazy distance, it looked for some two seconds as though a brown stone house had suddenly sprung up on the crest of the mountain, so solid and dense was the body of earth thrown up. Seeing this terrific bombardment continue with more or less intensity for over a week, we could not but realize that the enemy were holding their position valiantly, and against heavy odds in artillery. Three months ago we would as soon have expected the red-legged partridges out in the veldt to hold their ground against that fire. If they could face it for a week, why not for a month? Thus the more timorous argued, and with our past experiences we could not but admit that familiarity, even with shell fire, bred, if not contempt, at least a large measure of indifference. On the 24th the last of our maize went through the mill, which meant that at most there was only six or seven days' supply in hand. Even the strong face of Colonel Ward, the chief of commissariat, ordnance, and transport, had lines of anxiety more clearly marked, though personally he was free of all reproach. No department had done such wonders with limited means – none of our army chiefs came out of Ladysmith with a better record than Colonel Ward. The cheerful courage with which many of our officers faced the situation amazed me. I talked with a surgeon who had the whole of his day occupied with patients, though himself worn down and in bad health. Inability to eat tinned meat had reduced him to maize-meal porridge three times a day since Christmas.

Upon the heels of that week of bombardment followed a succession of anxious, indefinite days, and there was a certainty of the month of January running out, not only without affording us succour, but without giving us any definite idea as to the state of affairs down on the Tugela. Never before had rumour been so busy or so contradictory, and what we could see of the Boers' movements rather complicated the situation than helped to a solution. For example, after the heavy shelling of the 24th, we saw late that afternoon what we assumed to be the Boer army in full retreat. Nothing could be more convincing. There were hundreds of wagons, heavily convoyed, thousands of cattle being driven – it was the great trek without a doubt moving back over the veldt towards Van Reenan's Pass.

That the enemy had been shelled out of the heights overlooking Potgieter's Drift seemed too great a certainty for argument.

On this memorable Wednesday, when a cannon fire – the heaviest, perhaps, that had been recorded for years in modern warfare – fell upon N'Taba N"Yama mountain (Spion Kop), we saw the lyddite shells, or what we assumed from the reddish hue of the smoke and the great volume of the explosion to be our lyddite shells, bursting first on that point of the mountain marked by the figure 1. Then it spread gradually along the whole extent of the mountain facing the Tugela river, across

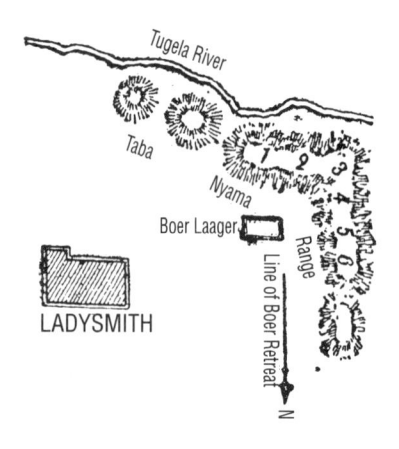

which our troops had to come, and reaching the point marked 3, the angle of the mountain followed it up as far as 6. Thus the whole extent of the range had been searched and scorched with our artillery fire, and when just before sundown we saw the Boers retreating on the line marked in the rough plan, the reasonable conclusion was that they had been shelled out and were retiring northward on their base, to take up, perhaps, a new position on the Biggarsberg, their next stepping-stone towards the border. It all seemed so clear and convincing that every one was in the best of spirits, and it looked only a question of hours when a clear road of communication would be open between Ladysmith and our friends on N'Taba N'Yama. On Thursday morning, the light being unsuitable for heliograph communication, we heard from Kaffir deserters from the Boer camp that the British had carried N'Taba N'Yama by assault at five o'clock on Wednesday afternoon, and were in possession of the whole mountain. The exodus, as we could see it in the distance, looked indeed like the hurried retreat of a beaten army. There were wagons, Cape carts, and every conceivable kind of conveyance, all hurrying in one direction. What troubled us, and caused the confusion which reigned for days afterwards in Ladysmith, was that on Thursday and Friday the Boers appeared to be trekking back again to their old positions, and the laager was re-established. If Sir George White and his Staff knew anything definite as to the situation, they were mute on the point. No intelligence was posted in the town, though it was rumoured that the news was satisfactory. All Thursday the guns were silent. On Friday we saw two huge explosions at the point on the range marked 6, and it looked as though redoubts there had been blown up.

The unsatisfactory point was the return of the Boer wagons, though by Saturday, the 27th, the explanation of even that puzzle was ready in the assertion that armistice had followed the fight, and that the Boer wagons trekking backward and forward were taking away their dead and wounded. There was a further rumour that Lord Dundonald – with a flying column – had made a circuit and established himself in a commanding position near Van Reenan's Pass, thus cutting off the enemy's retreat by that most convenient of roads to the Free State. It was repeated over and over again with quite remarkable persistency, yet never from a source that could be regarded as at all trustworthy. With ever-dwindling supplies, ever-increasing hospitals, and with the graves at Intombi numbering over three hundred, not to mention the space that was being so rapidly filled in the town cemetery, it was not difficult to realize that in the latter days of January the beleaguered garrison of Ladysmith was racked by many doubts and anxieties. Morning after morning the war correspondents, with horses saddled and packed for a journey, mustered at daylight at Observation Hill, and searched the veldt with their field-glasses in the hope of some active development. The Boers behind us on Surprise and Telegraph Hill got wind of the muster of onlookers, and dropped shrapnel and rifle-bullets over the brow, so that it became necessary for each to get his own shelter-stone, and even then the possibilities of a cross-fire were always a bit distracting. One morning Mr. Pearse (of the *Daily News*) had calmly taken up his position on the side of a rock which left him open to the shrapnel. On his attention being drawn to the fact, he remarked that he didn't mind their artillery, but was careful about the rifles. They had already hit his particular rock three times that morning, and the bullet-marks were there to show it. It was all long-range sniping, it had been going on continuously at this point for three months, and both sides were clever at it.

On Sunday, January 28, came the full explanation of the puzzle that we distant onlookers had sought to unravel – a heart-sickening solution to those residents of Ladysmith who had been so long living chiefly on hope. We knew how valiantly Brigadier-General Woodgate had led his troops to the storming of Spion Kop, which shot up like a tower beside the longer mountain, and heard with amazed unbelief that the position so dearly bought had again fallen into the hands of the enemy. Would blunders never end upon the Tugela? Would British officers never learn that they were fighting, not simple rustics, but men of matchless resource and cunning – men with a natural gift for tactics, ever ready, as at Amajuba or Tugela heights, to take advantage of a strategical mistake. We learned, too, how heavy had been the loss on both sides in that fierce four days' fighting on the river ridges, and it was but a partial consolation to know that seven of the Dutch guns had been put out of action.

The first and furthest of the three doors which gave us outlet had been temporarily opened just sufficient to let us see the liberty beyond ere it was slammed-to again. The Boer still held the keys. We could not blind our eyes to the fact that it all counted for delay – and delay in Ladysmith meant death. Though the Staff said little, there were signs significant enough to eyes ever watchful for signals of either hope or despair. We had an issue of fresh bread. It had been baked for the relief column, but was not required. Nearly a fortnight ago each of our Mounted Riflemen had been supplied with 20 lbs. of mealie meal – an emergency ration for man and horse – which they were to carry slung in bags across their saddles. The explanation of course was that they might be required to move out hurriedly to co-operate with the relief column. The forage and rations were called in again – a sufficient proof that for the present the idea of a sortie in any form had been abandoned. The increase in rations, which we once regarded as the most satisfactory proof of speedy succour, did not last long. Every one was back on half supplies, and the disappointment was borne manfully. We had got to the last stocks, the hard biscuit and tinned beef, which, with some coarse and mouldy mealie meal, stood between us and starvation. Of the ten or twelve thousand men who marched in here three months before, all physically as fit as athletes, for they had been specially trained for the campaign, there were not, I should say, a thousand able to do a five miles' march, so that the possibility of co-operation with the relief forces was speedily becoming a thing of the past. The men were for the most part gaunt and gloomy, worn down by want of proper and sufficient provisions and the ceaseless manning of the rifle ridges. There was no need for the Boers to lavish life in desperate ventures. While they held the drifts on the Tugela they had us in the net safe enough, and their two best generals for investment purposes were Enteric and Dysentery. Our second failure on the Tugela, after having absolute possession of part of the ridge, again showed how utterly astray were all preconceived notions as to

Boer methods of warfare. Again the Dutchman had fought splendidly and successfully in a night attack. After all, why should he not do so? Our artillery was admittedly superior to his, therefore he was better served by conditions which limited the fighting to the use of the rifle, and I am inclined to think that his great mobility and natural training fit him to carry out night movements more stealthily and effectually than British troops can do it.

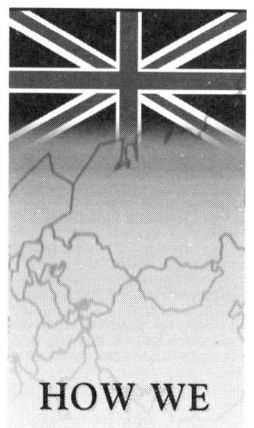

HOW WE KEPT THE FLAG FLYING

CHAPTER 22

THE HORSE-MEAT ERA

Eating horse-meat – A black depression – The rush for rations – An expected assault – Bracing up the town – A faltering foe.

RUMOUR continued for many days to flatter us one hour and depress us the next. The hard fact presented was that save for an occasional shot, shelling in the distance had practically ceased, though the Boers, judging from the movements of their wagons, still held the right of way, and practically the mountain. Even the elements combined against speedy succour, for a heavy wind sprang up – in this land where winds are extremely rare – and it was all against the use of lyddite, the fumes of which were blown away before they had time to do any mischief. Heavy rains, too, were a block to all movements, and made the lot of our poor fellows on the rifle ridges less enviable than ever. Never has the South African expression "Gone in" applied more aptly to a large body of men than to the Ladysmith garrison in these last trying days of January. Horses were being slaughtered daily, with the object of saving as much forage as possible for the gun-horses, which in case of emergency might be our first need, either in forcing a way out, or preventing the enemy in coming in. First 300 were shot, the best of them being made into Bovril – or rather "Chevril" – for the use of hospital patients, while mule-meat was being served out as an ordinary ration. All through the siege the mules, who could pick a scanty living from the few tough tufts of herbage remaining on the hills, kept in much better condition than the horses. Graves for dead horses and dead men were ever yawning wide. There were seventeen waiting as I passed the cemetery one day, and in this deadly environment it was little wonder that the ominous words "Who next?" knocked dolefully at the soul. Every pound of provisions in the town had been taken over by the military authorities, who made a house-to-house search, so that every one might share equally in the poor food available. The strain could not continue much longer – the breaking stage was almost reached. It was only a question of a few days, and then – surrender? No; that word was never mentioned. Those who had still the strength left for the dash might try to cut their way out, leaving the sick, wounded, and starving to the mercy of the enemy – though that would be a sad ending to the dangers and the hardships that the garrison of Ladysmith had so heroically borne. Bread of all kinds had disappeared, and we were living mainly on army biscuits, broken up in tea or coffee, when either could be got. The biscuit was of brown meal, nourishing, no doubt, but hard as a brick, and to tackle it was to face the problem of assimilating inorganic matter.

One thing that impressed me strongly all through the siege was that even with shell so largely used against us, amputations were singularly rare in the hospitals, and the great majority of those were undertaken by the regular army surgeons, amongst whom are operators wonderfully skilled. The ordinary surgeons who came in with the volunteers resorted to amputation only as a last resource, and with the help of the Rontgen rays their success in saving limbs, which at first sight seemed hopelessly shattered, was a triumph for the profession.

By the first day of February we were in the full stress of the siege. Men were given the choice of a full pound of horseflesh to their three biscuits a day, or half-a-pound of tinned beef, and gradually the majority in favour of the lighter diet became a minority, as we gave up our prejudices and were driven by hunger to the heavier ration. Indeed, we had been eating horse and mule flesh, deftly disguised as ragoût of beef, a week or so before we knew it. It sounded much better than ragoût of ammunition donkey. As the materials for the ragoût were exhausted, it came to us in no false guise, but just as plain horse. The cavalry, of which at the outset of the siege we had several crack regiments were gradually disappearing, the men, armed with rifle and bayonet instead of lance, sword, and carbine, being drafted into the infantry regiments to man the trenches, while the horses that were not reduced utterly to bone and sinew were passed on to the commissariat. Others, too poor for killing yet too valuable to kill, were turned out tethered in pairs and left to forage for themselves – so that stray horses were all over the town and tangled up with tent-ropes. The idea in coupling them was, no doubt, to prevent them straying far, but it was as unnecessary as cruel. All these big walers, even if they fell into the hands of the Boers, could be identified and claimed again, for, apart from the Government brand, there was nothing like them in the Dutch States. As it was, they twisted their couplings in trees and stones, and were found literally starving to death, while it was by no means rare to find a live horse coupled to one either dead or crippled by shell fire.

The same depression that followed upon General Buller's first failure to carry the Boer position across the Tugela hung like a black cloud over the town, and, judging by the preparations, there was every expectation of another Boer assault on Ladysmith. Under cover of darkness new redoubts were built, and the front lined with wire entanglements – preparations which two months before would have been laughed at as absurd precautions on the part of an over-anxious commander. For had we not then quite satisfied ourselves that, whatever the enemy might attempt, he would never nerve himself to an actual attack on the town? It was one of many delusions lovingly nursed this last ten years, to be cast away at last. The climax in stagnation was reached when men had no other aspiration but to lie down all day – no other desire than to be left to their own moody reflections. It was the dangerous stage – upon which fever and death quickly followed, for fever then meant in most cases death. No one had the vitality to fight the disease. Those who were wise crawled, while they had still strength left, to the outer ridges for a breath of air not yet tainted by contact with the town. Twenty horses a day were being killed and made into soup for the soldiers, while the bones were stewed down into a jelly, and clarified with isinglass for use in the hospitals. Necessity is the mother of invention, and, as pots large enough for the occasion were not obtainable, they adopted instead the iron earth trucks used in railway building. The fires were lighted between the railway metals, and when the contents of each truck had been thoroughly boiled, it was shunted off to make way for another.

The strictest supervision was exercised in the serving out of the daily rations. Every applicant presented himself at a barrier, and having produced his order, passed on through a gangway, guarded on either side by barbed wire, to the four depôts, where each in turn received his little packet of meat, biscuit, sugar, and tea – the supplies of sugar and tea being rarely sufficient for more than one meal. Here there was a daily jumble of the three races, European, Kaffir, and Indian, hustling and clamouring for supplies. Few of us ever expected to be reduced to such shifts for the bare necessaries of life, and the barbed-wire entanglements would seem to indicate that the military authorities looked forward as a possibility to the day when they might have to guard against the rush of a starving people inside the town, as well as the rush of an enemy from the outside. There was no longer even the cheering sound of a gun in the distance, while the enemy, becoming brisk again with their bombardment, were busy building further redoubts and rifle breastworks on all sides, as though determined to keep their grip of Ladysmith to the last.

One sign that cheered us somewhat, as indicating a limit to Boer artillery resources, was the appearance in the town of a number of the old-fashioned spherical bombs – such as might have been fired from those old Russian cannon, stamped with the double-headed eagles, which flank the entrance to the Victoria Barracks, Melbourne. Most of the Boer guns were of the newest and best, for they had the world for their ordnance market, and bought the best that every nation could supply. Those of the better type had presumably been sent to the Tugela to take the place of others disabled by British shell fire, and anything served to make a noise, and keep the Ladysmith garrison quiet with a show of power. There were rumours of another attack on the town, such rumours as the enemy themselves sent in, probably with the hope that they might be accepted, and the garrison remained strictly on the defensive. The industry with which the enemy ran their search-lights every night to illuminate the approaches to their gun positions, and the persistent fire of star shells for the same purpose, indicated rather apprehension of being attacked than premeditated assault from their side.

One day our Kaffir boy, who had been out grass-cutting, came back agitated. "Zip! zip! zip!" he said, imitating the whiz of the bullet, and pointing to a hole in his old felt hat where a Mauser had gone through. Aleck Macpherson, one of our camp, and a clever South African bushman, had been tantalized for days by some wild duck placidly floating on a clay-pan midway between the Boer and British lines. He crept out one day, bagged three of them, and got away safely. Next day there was a still larger flock on the clay-pan, and our sportsman again determined to take the risks. He had no sooner fired, and so betrayed his position in the long grass, than a perfect storm of Mauser bullets fell round him, and he had to leave his birds, and run the gauntlet for home. With their usual quick observation, the Boers had noticed Aleck's daring raid on the first day, and put a picket in a clump of wild peach trees to wait for him. The duck were excellent, such a change to the strong, musky horse-flesh – but the birds were not disturbed again. It was almost worth the risk, though, to venture a little away from the hundred and one smells of the town out to the open veldt, where the fragrant mimosa was just blossoming. In the coolness of the dusk a soft breath of wind often brought the scent of it even into the town – and it was divine. There were late lilies too, whose flaming red chalices shone like spots of fire on the hill-sides, and formed floral homes for swarms of golden-green beetles.

One found rather extravagant notions as to the effect of lyddite shell fire. I talked with an old English farmer from the Transvaal, whose disappointment with the effect of a week's bombardment was grotesque. "I 'eard as they could level mountains," he said. "Well, look at that theer one – not a crack in 'un – why, after they'd bin shellin' a week I expected we'd 'ave nothing' in the district but arable land." One man was arrested and sent to gaol, "for expressing in public opinions likely to create despondency." The crime was by no means confined to civilians though. An officer in some repute in the artillery declared that everything he had been taught to consider an axiom in connection with artillery work had been upset by his South African experiences. No wonder that the country is the grave of great reputations. The devotion to use and wont dies hard in the army. I saw a man who, in a country teeming with stinging insects, cropped his horse's tail short, and was then obliged to carry another horse's tail every time he rode out, so that he might switch away the flies, and prevent his poor, thin-skinned steed from being perpetually tortured.

One of the most anxious days spent in Ladysmith was Sunday, February 4. We knew that another great meeting of the Boers had taken place, such as that which preceded the determined attack on Wagon Hill, but were ignorant as to what it might portend. Every morning the ring of investment was tested on every side, and unpleasant work it was for the guides and scouts who undertook the duty. Nothing was left to doubt or conjecture. At every point it was necessary to prove the presence of the enemy by drawing their fire, and very ingenious were the devices brought into practice. A favourite plan was to ride up to within from 500 to 700 yards of a hill supposed to shelter the enemy's riflemen. Then the mounted men halted for a few seconds, and turned as if to ride home. That trick invariably drew the fire, if it were there to be drawn. The Boers, seeing their anticipated victims, whom they hoped to entice within short range, about to retire, as they thought, opened with every available rifle, and from the crackle our men, while galloping back to cover, were able to judge the enemy's strength at that particular point. On Sunday we knew that the Boers contemplated another night attack on Ladysmith, and had made very elaborate preparations to ensure its success. The warning came, strangely enough, from three points. General Buller heliographed us to be on the alert on Sunday; the War Office cabled a similar warning all the way from London; a Basuto chief sent in a messenger, and our own intelligence corroborated each. Every preparation was made to give the enemy the deadliest reception he had yet had from Ladysmith, and at dusk on Sunday evening every available man was in the rifle-pits or strengthening the outer pickets. They had hoped to surprise us by a trick characteristic of the Boer. Having gained possession of a great number of British uniforms, and practised British calls on British bugles, it was their intention to march boldly forward, representing themselves as portion of the relief column, and then with a sudden dash carry the trenches by surprise. The men were especially warned by a general order to be extremely cautious as to bugle calls either to "Retire" or "Cease firing". Further, our men were warned to ignore the white flag altogether, unless the Boers threw down their rifles and held both arms in the air. All our rifle positions were ingeniously strengthened, false redoubts being built some little distance out to confuse the attack if made in the dark. Between these sham sangars and the rifle-pits were barbed-wire entanglements, so curved that they presented apparent openings to an attack, but the enemy, rushing through these, would find themselves in the very worst of the maze. If Ladysmith were to be taken that night there would be a bitter toll for it. All night we waited, the men no longer despondent, but all keen and expectant. No attack came. News of our elaborate preparations had possibly reached them, as the intelligence of their movements reached us, and the responsibility was too great to face. Or it may have been that the bright starlit night was unfavourable.

There were thousands of the enemy all round us, for in the early morning they were seen hurrying away south, where a tremendous thunder of guns, beginning with the first dawn of day, told of another decisive movement. All day that muffled roar of artillery went on, awe-inspiring, unceasing – one salvo blending with another for hours at a stretch, until one would have thought that no ordinary flesh and blood could stand such a cannonade. This time there were no shells bursting on N'taba N'Yama, away to the right. The great volume of sound rolled up to us, not alone from the Tugela heights, but more incessantly, more vociferously, from a point to the right of it, believed to be Keat's Drift, where, on the previous day, it had been rumoured one of our brigades had crossed the river. Listening to that tremendous cannonade, one's mind was carried back again to the day when Oliver Davis – the original, by the bye, of Rider Haggard's hero, Alan Quartermain – riding in from the Ingogo with news that the Boers were bringing down a big gun, was laughed at for his absurd story. What a vast gap between the anticipated and actual! The very men who were not expected to get a gun beyond Laing's Nek were engaged in a great artillery duel in the heart of Natal with the finest siege guns that Britain could send afield. It was to the death this time – no one doubted that.

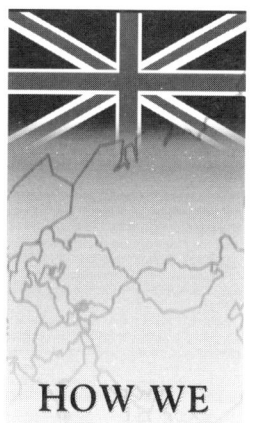

HOW WE KEPT THE FLAG FLYING

CHAPTER 23

THE SIEGE ROUTINE

*Tobacco famine – Commissariat trials – Cupboard love – Siege whist –
The hundred days – A cricket message – Usury in trade –
A contrast – Siege prices.*

IS there need to dwell at length upon these last, long-drawn-out, stagnant days of February – the last days in Ladysmith for most, the last on earth for far too many? The same two topics cropped up always with frightful iteration – "Is there any increase in the fever and dysentery?" "What rations shall we have to-morrow?" Men who had been accustomed to "do themselves well" in better days became tiresome on the subject of food, and in our camp we were compelled in self-defence to establish a system of fines against any one who between meals mentioned anything eatable – the fines being heaviest where a man was so inconsiderate as to refer to things which in ordinary life might be considered ordinary diet, but were now dishes for Lucullus. To mention something particularly choice which you intended to have on getting out was to provoke rage and execration. The temptation was great, though, when men took a really good appetite to table and brought away the greater part of it after the meal. Yet our wants were very modest. A little more sugar, a little more flour and we should have been quite happy. My own thoughts, I admit, centred largely upon a bottle of stout; yet with a stern resolution I locked the secret in my soul and was silent. None of us had realized before what an important bearing sugar had upon our lives and tempers – and I use the word strictly in the domestic and not the slang sense. Its scarcity was particularly hard upon the little ones, for it would have helped to make many a coarse meal palatable. It was the article we missed most. The adulteration of coffee was a flagrant thing, and under other circumstances would have provoked a prosecution. It was ingenious, certainly, to increase the bulk by mixing it with burned maize meal, but the roasters did their work indifferently, and the stuff had a skewbald look. The coffee seemed to shrink in very shame of plebeian company, while the mealies obtruded themselves unblushingly. The army biscuit, which we once resented, had become a luxury, for by soaking it in water first and then toasting it slightly, it was brought under the control of the poorest set of teeth, and, as you are perhaps aware, recruits are often rejected because their teeth are unfit to cope with the army biscuit in its native state.

The alternate days were bad days, when we dined lightly and were particularly appreciative of a pipe afterwards, for ordinary plug tobacco was then selling at £7 10s. per lb., and with the exhaustion of the rose-leaf crop a very useful blend was found in a mixture of peach leaves. Many experiments were made to discover, if not a substitute for tobacco, at least something that would eke out the supply, and nothing better was discovered than the peach leaves, that were just showing the first tinge of autumn yellow. Now and again at our worst we were cheered, though, by a pleasant discovery. It was noticed that none but the Indian coolies, whose stores clustered thickly at one end of the town, had tobacco or cigars for sale. There were hidden sources of supply, which these bland, innocent-looking merchants had not yet exhausted, so the provost-sergeant and his posse set themselves the difficult task of out-generaling a trading Oriental. The stores were ransacked, while the owners stood by and smiled, and called their own particular gods to witness that everything had been delivered up to their highnesses of the army. "Just slit that canvas ceiling up and shove your head through, corporal," said the provost. The corporal did so, and inside the canvas were heard words that might be a song of joy and triumph, mixed with a condemnation in army service terms of all the coloured races on earth. "Ten bags of rice and two bales of tobacco leaf," was the announcement. Every one cheered, and they brought an escort to see it safe down to the stores, where big Sergeant-major Dougharty ruled. A four-ounce ration of tobacco per man was announced next day. It looks a trifle, it was really an event. Correspondents draw rations from the military, and two of our four did not smoke, but their consciences, dulled by little use in Ladysmith, enabled them to fill in the requisition. I was deputed to draw the ration, and, without egotism, regarded it as a compliment to Australian character. "There may be a second ration, my boy," the sergeant-major said blithely. "In that case, mayn't I as well take it now, and not be bothering you a second time?" "You deserve it for your consideration to an over-worked and under-fed army service;" and I left with an armful of tobacco-leaf. It was a happy lot of men who sat round, while Mr. "Arty" Spring, a Natal farmer, and an expert in Boer tobacco, chopped up the leaf – chaffed it would be the better word – damped and sweated it, mixed in a little saltpetre, and then – well, it was good to smoke it, better even to be able to give one's friends a pipe.

At the worst there was always some pleasant surprise of that kind to temper the monotony and stagnation of waiting. One night some of our pickets ventured out to a mealie-field, and returned with their nose-bags filled with the green mealies, which are such a favourite vegetable through all South Africa.

On the second night there was a larger invasion, though the cultivation plot lay almost under the muzzle of Long Tom, and not a mealie cob was left in its sheath. Men had paid 3s. 6d. each for them in the public market, for with the scarcity of green food scurvy had made its appearance, and threatened to stand in with enteric and dysentery in decimating the garrison. The adventure in maize was just a godsend. On the third night, finding nothing for themselves, the volunteers thought of their horses, and before morning the green-stuff had been bundled and brought away. We could imagine how the Boers on the hill-top must have wondered when at sunrise they found that the mealie-field, which had so long been a vividly green ten-acre square under their eyes, had disappeared. Industry and enterprise in the cultivation of the soil had its reward in another corner of the valley. A man who in the early days of the siege had ploughed under shell fire now reaped his crop, and the military authorities, in recognition of his pluck, paid high prices. We had seen the completion of a harvest, the ploughing, the growth, and the reaping. It seemed a long time looking back, yet one needed some such standard fully to realize the measure of his own patience. Evidence of it came home to us on noting, too, that in the bomb-proof shelters we had built before Christmas, the roots of the trees had sent out suckers, and a young forest, white from the exclusion of sunlight, was springing up, while spiders spun their webs across the entrance. We had long since given up elaborate precautions, and were taking our chance.

But I have forgotten the bread – no, not quite forgotten it, for that will never be. It was served alternately with the biscuit, and as it was found that the coarse maize meal would not hold together in the baking, they hit upon the pleasant idea of mixing it with starch, for the laundry business had long since been abandoned.

It improved the dough, but not the bread. It caught us at our worst – in the non-resistant stage – and for a time, I feel sure, killed rather more men than the Boer cannon – though that is, after all, paying a rather poor compliment to the soldierly qualities of the bread. Even then committees of supply were able to meet the emergency. They used the bread either as thickening for soup, or, after putting it through a coffee-mill, made it into porridge. The least one could do, indeed, was to give a sorely-tried digestion some assistance. On thing we had in abundance – pepper. I never heard of people so lavish with pepper as our commissariat. They literally "threw it about," or, at least, we did. There was an inclination to throw things about when, on the arrival of the evening rations, one found pepper in the big packet and tea in the small one. We could have spared the pepper – the Boers gave us all we needed.

In this last fortnight of February we were living almost exclusively on horseflesh, and men who had sworn that they would starve ere they ate it slowly weakened in their resolves. One of our party, an old Scottish journalist and Natal correspondent, had, like his countrymen of the Gordons, expressed the strongest objections to horse in any form, but at last he said, "Tell me it's beef and send it in. I'm not inquisitive." At about that time we correspondents made the acquaintance of Mr. Olver, a fine old English farmer and Johannesburg miller, who was camped a mile or so outside the town. When we rode out in the cool of the early morning – for a ride was a pleasant and fairly safe thing before sunrise – our horses of one accord turned their heads towards Olver's camp. He had left his home in the Transvaal, bringing his stock and supplies with him, and had trekked into Natal fully equipped for the campaign. He had snow-white mealie meal; better still, he had milk; best of all, he had sugar, and we visited him unblushingly at breakfast-time. He was too hearty and hospitable to notice the coincidence or suspect us of cupboard love, yet many people, I fear, would have put some such nasty construction upon it. His friendship was equal to every test. It will be counted unto him for charity and to us for audacity. Sometime, when he had the carcase of a tender yearling in his pickle-tub, we were even persuaded to lunch with him. Dunn, who had some remnants of decency in him, occasionally martyred himself by staying at home, but always had his revenge in long lectures upon social observances, upon the strange thickness of hide characteristic of men who could wear out a welcome while pretending not to notice it, and such abstract questions. The rest of us were in better mood then to listen to a lecture. Whist was the one relief to the vast monotony and languor of the mid-meal periods. As the cards disappeared the packs were blended until, with the variety of the coloured backs and the dog-eared corners, an experienced and really observant player knew his opponent's hand almost as well as his own – rather better, perhaps, for upon the grimy face one might easily overlook the notice which converted the king of spades into the knave of diamonds. For a novice it saved the trouble of counting and thinking, and made whist a relaxation instead of a religious ceremony. Men needed to be entertained rather than instructed. The more recent variation of whist known as "bridge" was immensely popular in the volunteer camps. The town had its rare periods of brightness, usually when cannon were heard away to the southward, and I fear we were too selfish to remember always that if it meant Buller it meant battle also – and that away down there upon the river men were dying and bleeding because they sought by such heroism as the situation needed to rescue us. It is ever the same though. War at a distance is a magnificent thing – we realize its horrors only when they come right home to us. The things that really cheered us were the despondent observations of the Boer gunners, which occasionally, by the help of native runners, came home.

If any one of the besieged of Ladysmith were asked to name those days when the town was actually at its worst, he would pick the period between the hundredth and one hundred and twentieth days – roughly the last three weeks of investment. We had looked forward to the completion of the one hundred days as an epoch; speculated upon the double possibility of General Buller making that a day of advance, the Boers one of attack. The enemy were the first astir, and had kept such good count that all who might have otherwise overlooked the three-figure score had a hint of it when, a few minutes after midnight, they fired a half-dozen rounds from their big guns into the town – the only shots we had had after dark for a long time. It may have been intended as a triumphant salvo, in celebration of the fact that for a hundred days they had shut us in; we, on the other hand, might, if we pleased, regard it as a complimentary salute, in recognition of our having for one hundred days kept them out. But it might have meant, too, more than mere empty brag; so, in the expectation of something unusual astir, we turned out, with the moon shining brilliantly, and the Dutch search-lights sweeping the town from end to end. Little fear of either side attacking on such a night. Yet Kaffirs creeping through that night had come in contact with bell-wires, thus raising an alarm, and for a time there was promiscuous shooting at rocks, cactus plants, shadows, and things. It was one of the suspense periods, when men were sick in body and mind. For three days there had been heavy fire to the southward, followed, as usual, by a trying silence, broken at long intervals only by the roar of a single gun, easily recognizable now as the familiar note of the Dutch six-inch. During the day a smoky haze, such as we get in the south of Australia about Christmas time, hung over everything. The heights upon and around about which the stern drama of war was in progress were shut out altogether for a week, and our heliographs were useless. Still, where the eye failed the ear was a sure guide in distinguishing between Boer and British fire. Every gun had a double report – the firing, and the bursting of the charge: when the interval between the two was but a few seconds, we knew it for our own gun; when it was half-a-minute or more, we knew that the long period was covered by a Boer shell travelling away from us towards Buller's forces, and the sound of the bursting shell coming back again over the same ground. Twice before, when heavy cannon fire had been followed by deathly silence, it meant the partial failure of our advance on the Tugela – hence the depression and deep anxiety that came in with the hundred days. It was eased somewhat by Kaffir rumours that Buller was still bringing his siege train forward, and we heard that our friends were so fortifying the way as they came, that ground once made good could never be lost again, however many men Joubert and Botha might throw in between the two British columns. "We are making it as impregnable as the Rock of Gibraltar," one volunteer with the relief column wrote to his brother in Ladysmith. "I have a gang of a thousand boys clearing artillery tracks over the hill, and we shall all be on railway repairs the moment the way is clear." Thus was the pessimistic conclusion that no news meant bad news somewhat softened. The faces of our chiefs were watched as racing men watch the barometer on the eve of the Melbourne Cup. A smile from Sir George White or Sir Archibald Hunter put half the town in good heart, while gloom upon either face was the herald of despair. When Sir George patted a child on the head, and said, "You'll soon get some lollies," it was passed round as distinctly promising, and became part of the war news of the day.

On the one hundred and first day one of the enemy on Bulwan, who was evidently familiar with England's national game, called up the signallers at Cæsar's Camp, and flashed the curt message, "101 not out." The Manchesters were equal to the little pleasantry, and replied, "Ladysmith still batting." Our devotion to sport in the earlier days of the siege puzzled them as it has puzzled many other nations. "What is the use of shelling them?" said a weary Boer artilleryman. "They just go on playing cricket." It was the Armada and the game of bowls over again. All the cricket had gone, though, with the days when men of Ladysmith had still some heart and muscle left. It was a town full of unwholesome emotions rather than good manly animal British impulses towards sport and recreation, moody apprehensions which struggled for supremacy with patriotism and faith in our destiny. Broadly lined, the fears of the garrison had taken four different phases – first the fear of shell, next the fear of sickness, then the fear of starvation, while about the hundred days the fourth was beginning to shape itself vaguely in the fear of Pretoria. If disaster – otherwise starvation – were to be the end, we knew just how it would come. Some night when the supplies were no longer measured by days, but by hours, the gaunt decimated field column of Natal, the one-time flower of the Indian army, would be got together, and keeping to the open veldt as far as possible, would, after the destruction of its transport and commissariat train, crawl out after dark in the direction of Spion Kop, and try to cut its way through there in preference to a tame surrender. It was characteristic of this remarkable war, that men who were evidently anxious to kill each other, and rarely missed a chance when it offered, had always time and heart for the flippant badinage of every-day life. "How do you like horse-meat?" heliographed our friends the enemy from Bulwan. "Fine," was the answer; "when the horses are finished we're going to eat Boer." Be sure that the old Dopper Dutchman, the receptacle for the sullen racial hatred of two hundred years, had no hand in this. Light humour was not his forte. He was out on the veldt with a single purpose – homicide. Let it not be assumed that even the youngest or most enlightened of the Dutch spare their guns to exercise their humour on the heliographs. No sooner had we acknowledged their cricket message than Long Tom opened on our naval 12-pounder at Cæsar's Hill, and his first shot just missed the gun-trail, and threw about half-a-ton of earth over the shell-backs. "They've put on a new bowler," remarked the gunnery lieutenant.

There was much in the conduct of the people of Ladysmith during these days of death and deprivation worthy of unstinted praise; a good deal, too, that made one blush at times for the Anglo-Saxon race. The system of irregular private sales by auction, brought into practice after the corporation weekly markets had been stopped by the authorities, was a scandal – a disgrace to humanity. Measure, if you can, the soul of a man who, when sick children were crying for food, sick soldiers dying for want of nourishment, and eating blanc-mange made from starch, sweetened with Winslow's soothing syrup, had the hardihood to offer at public auction the luxuries that might have been these poor fellows' salvation. There were infants wanting jam to make their maize-meal porridge wholesome, yet some bright ornaments of the town were selling their spare supplies at exorbitant prices, so that those to whom money was not a consideration might buy and the poorer ones starve. Most of them had some sense of shame, if not reformation, left, since they put their goods on the market under a false name. The huckstering spirit came out in all its undisguised ugliness. Not even a Chinese or a coolie could have more greedily taken advantage of the misfortunes of his fellow-men. Some of these fellows would, I believe, have seen the whole garrison in its grave rather than have given up the right of sale over a single dozen of their hoarded eggs. It was one of the infamies of the siege. The remarkable thing was, that a few of these men, far from having a sense of shame over their transactions, boasted of them – and, I doubt not, are boasting still of the high prices obtained.

In fine contrast was the attitude taken by men who were storekeepers and merchants, and, therefore, in some measure justified in selling in the dearest market. It was their business to trade, and they traded in a spirit worthy of their manhood. There was David Sparkes, a merchant of the town, who declined to raise his prices a single farthing because of the siege. But Mr. Sparkes, was something more than a storekeeper; he was a brave and able officer of Carbineers, whose pluck in the field and kindly concern for his men were a model for all officers to follow. And there was Stanley Sutton, of Maritzburg, as keen a man of business ordinarily as you will find in South

Africa. He was an army contractor – sometimes with good reason called army robbers – and one of the fortunate few who had a fair stack of goods in hand. As long as anything remained he supplied it to the soldiers at ordinary canteen prices, and Tommy Atkins had no more resourceful or better friend in Ladysmith. And there was a woman, too, who, when the provost-sergeant went round and seized supplies, had managed to hide away a large stock of luxuries. This was wrong, very wrong; but there are thrifty housewives with the storing instincts of the squirrel, and this woman might have now the undying admiration of the hucksters had she followed up her success in a business-like fashion. But she fell away from grace altogether, and her last stage was worse than the first. For instead of putting her goods on the market, and making record prices to brag about, she smuggled them out of doors in her old wife's basket, and gave them away to other women who had little ones suffering. Some called her a fool, and some gloried in her folly, and said that she had got more for her goods than even a millionaire could pay. And the poor old soul, with her small ambition, was, I have little doubt, well content.

The last public sale of any kind was held on February 13. The pity is that, for the credit of the town, they were not stopped two months earlier. And though it smacks of usury, the prices at that market are as a curiosity of trade worth quoting:– 1 lb. tin of Jamieson's jam, 23s.; 1 1/2 lb. tin of jam, 31s.; small tin, local make (with slight traces of sugar), 25s.; jar of stewed peaches, 25s.; 1/6 lb. of plug tobacco, 15s.; 1/4 lb. do., 26s.; 1/4 lb. of cut Boer tobacco, 43s.; 3/4 lb. of rolled leaf, 35s.; 70 Three Castles cigarettes, 11s.; packet of Old Gold cigarettes, 17s. 6d.; 50 common cigars, £9 10s.; 100 La Union cigars, £18 10s.; vegetable marrows, 25s. each; turnips and carrots, 8s. 6d per bunch; mealies (green maize), 3s. 8d. per cob; eggs, 40s. to 45s. per dozen; tomatoes, 2s. 6d. each. At some of the earlier markets the more striking sales were:– packet of Old Gold cigarettes, 25s. 6d.; 1/4 lb. of plug tobacco, £2 5s.; 1/4 lb. of Navy Cut tobacco, 60s.; 3/4 lb. of sugar, 10s.; grapes 13s. 6d. per lb.; potatoes. 7s. 9d. per lb.; brandy, £7 per bottle; whisky, any brand, £6 per bottle; rum, £4 10s. per bottle; port wine, £3 per bottle; champagne, £3 10s. per bottle These last were comparatively early prices, for after Christmas it was impossible, except upon a doctor's certificate, checked by official inquiry, to get spirits at any price, and then only with an admonition from the P.M.O. to dole it out to the patient as though it were liquid gold. If the prices seem prohibitive to an ordinary buyer, what must they have looked to the soldier, who ordinarily gets the best brands of Scotch whisky from his canteen (free of duty, carriage, and middleman's profits) at 24s. per dozen? One such case, bought by a young officer early in the siege, brought perhaps the largest profit recorded even in the liquor trade. The poor owner was killed in action, leaving a young widow, for whose benefit the case of whisky was raffled by the commissariat, and it brought £120. A London war correspondent won the first prize – six bottles – and that night every friend he had in town called to pay his respects. The winner went into hospital a few days later, suffering from sunstroke, but there was no significance whatever in the sequence of events.

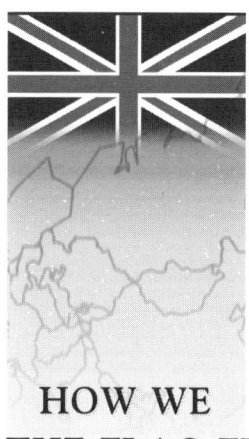

HOW WE KEPT THE FLAG FLYING

CHAPTER 24

A TIME OF ANXIETY

*Bird-seed porridge – The garrison meat bill – Preparing a welcome –
The Cossack post – A black night – The bridge builders –
Methodical Dutch gunnery.*

WHILE relief came a long step nearer famine came with even longer strides, and at least one of the military messes were crushing bird seed in a coffee-mill, and using the meal for porridge. Some of the Indian troops, familiar with Oriental methods in cookery, sought to make the mealie meal palatable by making it into chupatties. All the recognized authorities on cookery begin the recipe, I believe, with "Lard the pan with a piece of butter as large as a walnut." There was no butter, however, and no fat, and when the salad oil was finished, the dough had an obstinate way of sticking, so that pan and fire between them claimed more than their fair share of the pancake. Colza and castor oil were out of the question, so the high-class cookery collapsed, and we got back to the primitive methods of the Australian bush. I called one morning at the Leicester camp, and found the officers at breakfast. Each had a tin platter, a spoon, and a small helping of maize-meal porridge, and they asked me to join them with the air of men who were inviting one to a fried sole and sweetbreads. At the worst, style was never abandoned, and even minced horse was carried off with an air. "Kidded 'emselves they was living 'igh," the battalion cooks put it, and this was really one of the fine points of the British army in straits. They never grumbled. They could even joke over their troubles. "Nothing takes the starch out of a man," said a sergeant-major, "like taking starch in" – an allusion to the mixture of starch and maize meal in the bread. At that time, with black, white, and yellow, young and old, there were 17,000 souls drawing rations in Ladysmith.

In speaking of that period it is almost impossible to avoid dwelling much on rations. The actualities of life were food and its character – the possibilities, relief. Our meat was tough, even nauseating, yet the meat bill would have shocked even an Australian householder today. It took forty horses a day to supply the garrison with soup and joints, and each of these well-trained gun or cavalry chargers was worth £80 to the British army, so that our horse-meat bill ran into £3200 per day. Happy, indeed, was the forager who could once in a way capture a horse tongue as a break to the monotony of musk-brown meat. When all other fruit disappeared, we used to keep a sharp look-out for the m'forma, a white berry about as large as a strawberry, and with something of the same flavour. It grows on a low shrub on the tops of the stony kopjes, but the gatherers were many and the laurel-leaved bushes very few.

In the midst of the scarcity came an unpleasant discovery, which led instantly to a further cutting down of rations. Owing to bad soldering, some of the tins of beef and biscuit had become mouldy, and but for the supplies brought by the Indian troops we should have reached the stress of the siege much earlier. When they were landed in Durban the local commissariat laughed and said, "Why bring this stuff all the way from India? It was a waste of time and waste of transport. We have abundance here, and will only have the trouble of re-supplying the Indian regiments." Yet that bit of forethought on the part of the Indian contingent just about saved Ladysmith from disaster, as the pressed forage from Rawal Pindi helped to keep at least a few horses alive. To add to our troubles, maize milled during the siege had been stored away too soon, had heated, and was useless. There is nowhere so much general inspection as in the British army, nowhere so little by really expert men, so the thieves of the world continue to thrive in supplying it; but it was pleasant to learn from the commissariat authorities that Australian supplies were invariably up to the standard, and that in the case of the Queensland meat-preserving companies, they can accept consignments with confidence as being both in weight and quality all that they profess to be, which is not the case with the meats more attractively put up in other parts of the globe. In drink there was no variety whatever – just boiled sewage, otherwise Klip river water – and one smiled a bit sadly at times in remembering those early rumours that the Boers intended to poison the streams. It was so entirely unnecessary in the case of this stream, which the most virulent chemical could hardly have made more poisonous than it was. In South Africa the impression even yet prevails that when General Warren made his disastrous short cut by Spion Kop he at least succeeded in getting a convoy of wagons with food into Ladysmith. This is, of course, a mistake. Not even a barrowful of food passed through until the siege was raised.

The siege-worn soldiers, though quite unfitted for fatigue, were never idle. At points where it was thought likely the enemy might upon some dark night creep forward barefoot or upon hands and knees – broken bottles were thickly spread upon the grass after dark. At other points old tins were strewn on the veldt, so that men could not come forward without making a clatter. Every device that the town could afford, either to check a stealthy enemy or give notice of his approach, was tried. Before the fight at Cæsar's Hill we had trusted too much to the reputed unwillingness of the Boer either to attack at night or rush a fortified position at any time, but after that we made no mistakes. The barbed-wire entanglements were a perfect death-trap, fronting our positions. The man who imagined that the gaps in them were left by a stupid enemy for his convenience was likely to make the greatest and last mistake of his life, loops being cunningly let in at points where, owing to the contour of the ground, they were not visible from the enemy's lines. It was all very cunning and complete, and the garrison, in spite of its prostration, often prayed that the enemy might come on. There was a late moon just then, and until it rose the hours of darkness were long, and our Cossack posts were pushed right up to the Dutch sangars on every side, so that we should have early information of any movement in force. One night it looked as though the assault would be made under circumstances peculiarly favourable to the garrison. Our pickets had crept close up under the brow of Bulwan to raid a mealie-field. It was just after midnight, with the moon shining brilliantly, when all of a sudden from every redoubt, sangar, and shelter on the mountain poured out a stream of men. The dark figures came thronging like bees from a hive, until there must have been 2000 creeping quietly down the side of the mountain. Our pickets withdrew under shadow of the thorn bushes, and sent a messenger in haste to warn the Manchesters on Cæsar's Hill. But the lookout was perfect. The Manchesters, with their night-glasses, had noted every movement of the enemy, and sent a warning to the pickets, so that their messengers met half-way. They were seen from many other points, and the vigilance, if not the valour, of our men was satisfactorily tested. The enemy came on for a time confidently enough, and the strengthened outposts were getting ready to give them the volley which should be at once a welcome and a warning, when as suddenly as it had developed the threatened attack melted away. There had been all the preparation, but no assault. It may have been that they found crossing the open flat in the moonlight a more serious sacrifice than their leaders had the right to ask of them – anyhow, they faltered, stopped, and went back. Twice within a few weeks they had mustered heavily to assault the town, and twice at the crucial moment their courage had failed them. The second failure was their last serious threat against Ladysmith.

I always admired the work done by the Cossack posts, especially towards the close of the siege, when the tension was greatest, and the necessity for keeping touch of the enemy at night of the first importance. One experience is typical of the whole. The work was done by picked men, and would have been still better done by Kaffirs could they have been trusted to push the investigation far enough forward. This they will do only when stiffened by the companionship of a white man. Prompted by curiosity rather than a desire for adventure, we went out once with a Cossack patrol. He had been told on leaving camp that the sentries had been warned of his coming, but narrowly missed a shot from one of our own men. It was at a point where the river rushed noisily through a rocky gorge, and the roar of the water drowned the voice of the sentry, so that he challenged twice without being heard. Fortunately the Kaffir heard the click of the bolt as a cartridge was pushed from the magazine into the breech preparatory to the last challenge. Passing through the outer line of sentinels the Cossack post crept up close to the Boer trenches – all wearing rubber shoes so that there was no sound on the rocks – and sat there in the darkness listening intently for any sound that might indicate the movement of a large body of the enemy. That was the only thing in which the Cossack posts were interested. They were warned not to use their rifles except in a last extremity, and to avoid raising an alarm unless there was good reason for it. To untrained ears the ordinary night sounds of the veldt would have been confusing – perhaps at times alarming – but the Kaffir boys showed remarkable discrimination, and one marvelled at their readiness in identifying noises which to us had no particular meaning. Some slight sound out of the darkness ahead, and the Kaffir declared it a horse moving amongst the rocks, wandering at liberty, not being led. A faint gleam of light, gone in an instant like the flicker of a glow-worm in the dusk, was a Dutchman lighting his pipe. A rustle in the grass told of a prowling meer-cat hunting for a brooding partridge on her nest. Another slight patter amongst the rocks was a pair of reed buck coming down to water. Finally the Kaffir raised his hand, and whispered "Maboon" (Mabunu), the native name for the Boer. A couple of men, wearing heavy boots, judging from the clatter, and not the noiseless veldt-schoen, came down to the river-side, dipped some water, and stood for a while talking by the water's edge. The murmur of their voices came indistinctly through the night, and a laugh which followed was particularly clear. They had no idea that a Rooinek picket was sitting there in the gloom of the further bank, less than fifty yards away, or there would have been less laughing and more shooting. After a while they went away up the ridge again, and their voices faded away in the distance; nothing then for an hour or two but the far-away whinny of a horse or the cry of a bird that sounded like a wild goose flying overhead. At the first sign of the dawn the Cossack post fell quietly back upon its own lines, challenged by an alert sentry as soon as they came within earshot. This was the favourable experience of a fine calm night, but when it rained and thundered and the lightning lit up the veldt at intervals as no artificial search-light could have done it, Cossack post was not a duty for which many men hungered.

I had one experience of the veldt at night which quite satisfied me as to the difficulties of moving men to any point under unfavourable circumstances. I was riding a little way out after dark with some medicines for a friend, who had been suddenly seized with malarial fever, the legacy left to most men who have spent a few years in the miasmic country of Northern Rhodesia. A heavy thunderstorm came on just as I had got clear of the town, and although knowing the paths well, one had need to be careful, since they cut close round the heads of several steep dongas or ravines, where one step too far meant a fall of twenty or thirty feet. It was impossible to ride, so, leading the horse, and feeling the way with a long stick, I took a wide curve to clear the dongas, and of course overdid it. The flashes of lightning were so vivid and so bright that they almost blinded one for the instant, and there was no chance to pick up any familiar landmark ere the night wrapped everything again in an impenetrable blackness. It was impossible to leave the valley without knowing it, and the scope for wandering at large without striking something familiar was not great, yet for an hour I was as hopelessly lost as though in the middle of some unknown expanse of veldt. Finally I had that indefinite sense of being within a few yards of something without quite knowing what, and with the next flash of lightning found that I had wandered into the horse lines of one of the cavalry regiments, and had passed some distance between two lines of horses tethered heel to heel, not more than ten yards apart, without knowing it, and without letting the horse guards know it either. I could, I believe, have cut every horse away without risk of discovery, but that meant nothing. A sentry is just mortal like other men, and the chance of an enemy finding his way by design into these horse lines on such a night was most remote. I did it only through trying to reach another point quite a mile away. Just then, as the rain ceased, the Bulwan search-light began to play, and this fixed point, coupled with the knowledge that I could only have blundered into one cavalry camp in that part of the valley, gave me the hint as to the right direction. I came out of the horse lines without a challenge, knocked up against a Kaffir, who was herding cattle, even in that terrific storm, and with a good deal of trouble, for he knew little English, and I less Zulu, managed to get some further information, though I was satisfied for a long time that this chance child of the night wished to direct me to the Gordons' camp instead of the spot I wanted. Even then, with the storm over, I overshot the place, and would have been hopelessly fogged once more, only that I chanced to look over my shoulder just as the Dutch search-light in its sweep rested for an instant on the iron roof of the hut for which I was searching – the only building in the locality. The experience quite satisfied me that though an enemy might pierce our lines unseen on such a night, the chance of hitting the exact point aimed at was so remote that such shrewd leaders as the Boers were the last men in the world to attempt it. Later, when we were being threatened with attack, and my friends were apprehensive that such nights as this would be chosen for it, I went to bed in full confidence that there would be no other alarm than a false one before daybreak, and so it proved. Sometimes the sentry, when placed upon his post, got turning round, and lost all sense of direction. There was one such instance early in the siege. This man had unconsciously changed his front, and when the relief came out he was so sure that it was the enemy that he challenged once, and then fired.

The Boers never spared themselves either on the Tugela or about Ladysmith in works necessary for resistance or assault. Their energy found a new outlet in the building of a stone bridge or weir just round the southern shoulder of the Bulwan, where both the river and railway find a way out of the valley through a narrow gorge. It was this same convenient cleft in the ridges that gave us a clear view of the distant crest of Weenan's Hill, and enabled us to communicate with the relief column. All sorts of rumours were quickly afoot as to the intentions of the enemy, and the popular impression, the prevalent fear in Ladysmith, was that, in despair of getting us out immediately, either with gun or rifle, they were trying to drown us out by damming back the waters of the Klip river and converting the valley into a lake. The thing was feasible. One had only to study the position from the high points around the town, to realize that the facilities for forming a large artificial lake were exceptional. A single weir of no great length would effect the purpose, and, indeed, Ladysmith during heavy floods is more or less of a lake, and the residents take to the hills for safety, as rabbits in the Mallee make for the pine ridges when the Murray sends its flood of melted snow out through the backwaters into the wilderness. That was the original mistake with Ladysmith. It should have been a lake, not a town. It appeared to me, however, that if the Boers really meant to drown us out they had started work rather late in the day. Even an army with all its resources in free labour cannot hold back a lake of five miles in diameter and fifty feet deep with a Partington mop. It needs masonry of the most substantial kind, and watching the Boers at work from the summit of Cæsar's Hill, it seemed to me that they were bridge builders only, not weir builders. They had even then begun to see that Buller's persistency might win its way in the end, spite of every discomfiture, and what more likely than that those far-seeing Dutchmen, who leave so little to chance, were just making their own line of retreat secure. The Klip river, fed by the storms of the distant Drachenbergs, comes down occasionally in floods sudden and severe. It was quite a common experience to go to bed at night with the river low, and, without a drop of rain falling in the valley, to find it in heavy flood in the morning. The Boers, be sure, had noted this, and considered all the consequences of finding the drifts impassable when finally forced from the Tugela, and with the only bridge in the locality under our protection. We discovered that from one point on Cæsar's Hill we could look down upon the bridge builders through the cleft in the ridge, so a naval 12-pounder was got up there. As soon as work started next morning, we pitched a shell on to them, and the bridge builders went flying to shelter like a rock of frightened partridges. The following night we took one of the 4.7's to the same position, and thereafter work was casual, though the manner in which they persisted with it showed that they set some store on the undertaking. At first they were angry at the interruption – very angry – and for a while their Long Tom devoted himself entirely to the shelling of Cæsar's Hill, without, however, doing very much damage. We, on the other hand, were apparently sulkily silent. The fact was that we had no ammunition to waste, and, having got the range, we said in our silence, "When you've built your bridge, just send a convoy over it, and give us a chance." We wanted some better target than fatigue parties, and only gave them a shell when a fair number of them were at work. Thus the game of check and counter-check went on. So much of modern war is purely waste work, the measurement of move by move, much of it unseen by the looker-on, until all of a sudden one side develops the mastery in tactics, and a battle has been won ere yet a shot is fired.

One day word came from Lord Roberts that he had entered the Free State with a large force of artillery, cavalry, and mounted infantry, and he hoped that the operations of the few succeeding days would greatly ease the strain on Ladysmith. The Boers heard of it, too, and two nights later big, handsome Lucas Meyer, with a body of Free Staters, cut away for the Drachenberg passes. We heard all night the whistle of the trains that took them on to Harrismith. There was a co-incident activity amongst the Boer gunners, the bombardment grew somewhat heavier, and we fancied we recognized the note of guns that we had not heard for some time past, and which had, no doubt, been resisting Buller's advance on the Tugela. It was an extraordinary example of Dutch tenacity, that they should thus have been able to detach men and guns from their river fighting line and yet hold the ever-increasing relief column in check. There was a workmanlike method about their bombardment just then, quite unlike the attitude of men who believed that their time was limited – a tradesmanlike regularity about their working hours, such as might have been expected from men "on a stiddy job." At about ten o'clock every morning we could see them stroll over the plateau of Bulwan from their tents under its shoulder. Earlier in the siege they were careful, and the routine was always the same. After their gunmuzzle appeared above the redoubt, the gun's crew passed out to a bomb-proof chamber on the left of it. Then one man walked round the front of the redoubt under the muzzle, and within five seconds the gun was fired. But when they realized that we were saving our ammunition and could no longer answer, they stood in line upon the crest of the redoubt to watch the effect of their fire, and they had the range of every prominent building so nicely that they pitched their shells where they pleased – first, three or four rounds through the roofs of the long railway goods-sheds, that sent the chevril boilers swarming out like ants from a hillock; then a long swing of a mile to the left, and they were plump into the Gordons' camp. Afterwards we found the results for that gun all nicely tabulated, and showing a record of over 3000 rounds – for it was the identical gun which had first opened on us from Pepworth's Hill. The result of those 3000 rounds, as far as we could calculate it, was seventy men killed; the general result of siege, apart from men buried on the battle-fields, was nearly five hundred graves in the cemetery at Intombi camp – which in years to come will be a sad memorial of the siege – and something less than that number of graves added to the town cemetery in the bend of the Klip river, where some of the pioneers of Ladysmith sleep side by side with its latest victims.

We had but scant information as to the great game outside in these days, but the anniversary of Majuba was at hand, and we always had faith that the day would not be allowed to pass without startling developments from either or both sides. The runners were less successful than formerly. Many of them, checked at every point, came back with their letters, and the price rose to £15 per trip. One runner had almost forced his way through from the Tugela with some 600 letters for the garrison, when he was fired on, and twice wounded, losing his packet of letters. It was generally our experience in Ladysmith to find the rumoured good news of one day entirely counteracted by the official announcements of the next day. The reverse was experienced first on February 17, when a single paragraph in the orders of the day spread dismay through the beleaguered town. Owing to the difficulty of mounting guns on the captured kopjes, General Buller, we are told, had abandoned the idea of pressing the attack on the left, while his force was even yet insufficient to force a way, without terrible loss, through hills heavily defended by the Dutch artillery. Accordingly, in the night the whole force had been withdrawn from the neighbourhood of Krantz Kloof, and had retired, with some slight loss from the fire of the Boer 100-pounders. It looked like another case of breaking the bad news gently – our experience of retirements and retreats had been always so disheartening. To our surprise, next morning opened with an amazing thunder of guns, first, and with long intervals, the long and heavy roll of the Dutch 6 in. guns, then in the afternoon the lower, more constant rumble that could only mean British field batteries in action – the invariable prelude to storming a position. Later still, at sunset, our furthest pickets sent in word that they could hear even the low, deadly rattle of rifles, which always means so much to those who have once heard and noted its effects. Some great movement was afoot. We knew it, and were not surprised when late that night came a flash-light message across the hills telling us that the British had stormed and captured a position of great tactical value known to us as Bloy's Hill, and relief was at length within measurable distance, though there might still be a heavy toll in blood and suffering before that narrow gap was bridged by our brown-coated columns. The confusion of names made it difficult at times to follow Buller's movements exactly. There were generally two sets of Kaffir names for every mountain, the natives to northward christening it from some peculiarity when viewed from that direction, while an entirely different conformation gave it quite another name from southward. The early Dutch settlers in Natal had given their own names to particular peaks – Spion Kop, for example – while the English settlers, who came after them, exercised the same right, and, to crown all, the military authorities had made confusion worse confounded by adding Gun Hill, Hussar Ridge, and Lancer Ridge to landmarks already much overnamed. Thus there will always be confusion as to the exact order of events on the Tugela. Even in Ladysmith half the garrison spoke of the battle of Tinta Inyoni, while the other half called it Rietfontein.

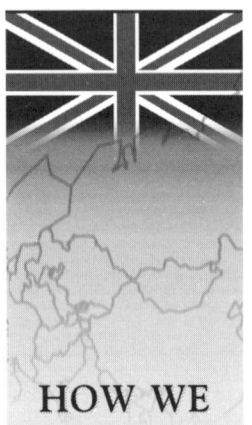

HOW WE
KEPT THE FLAG FLYING

CHAPTER 25

NEARING THE END

*A brave young surgeon – The rinkalse – Sir George White and the garrison
– Guns on the Tugela – "All going well" – Quarter rations –
Correspondents' luck.*

FOR a few days it seemed that though the mental and bodily stress of the garrison was at its worst, the sickness flattered us. The morning procession to the hospital, the number of ambulance wagons collecting the patients, seemed fewer, and any decrease in sickness meant an increase in cheerfulness, and the capacity for further waiting. But it was only a lull. The wave of sickness rolled back upon us again, and was worse than ever. Poor Buntine, over-worked and worn down, used to come to us of an evening, and sit with his head in his hands for a while, too tired almost to talk. All day he was at work, house to house, hospital to hospital, never letting a patient see the dark side of anything, holding up to his duty magnificently, though physically quite unfit for it. If the fighting side of the British army had brave men in Ladysmith, the medical profession had heroes. Hornabrook, the South

Australian, had done his best – done it too thoroughly, and with too little regard for his own troubles. The neglected wound in the side gave him trouble, and just as he had passed that danger safely, a sunstroke laid him low again, and for a time he was delirious. It was sufficient surely, but not the full measure, for no sooner had he survived this than an attack of enteric laid him low again. I went to see him in hospital, where Buntine – whose record in fever cases was unequalled – had made him as comfortable as the over-crowding would permit. The square, determined face, which in this case was so true an index of character, was sadly shrunken, but his eye was bright, his pluck unshaken, and with a smile he said, "Hurry up that relief; I'm waiting for a big bottle of champagne." As the sick were taken out of town to Intombi, a greater number of the convalescents crept back again, glad to escape from that haven of refuge, and sickness, and death. Poor fellows, they added little to the gaiety of the garrison. Most of them were just living skeletons, with a sallow, unhealthy, parchment-like skin stretched over them, and their semi-vacant clothes hanging in limp folds or flapping in the wind. Most of the convalescent were in the convent, or the private but vacant dwellings on the northern ridge, where, if fully exposed to shell, they had at least fresh air.

It was a favourite mustering point with the townspeople, too, since it gave a far view southward in the direction relief must come. But officers were none too pleased when the populace gathered on their verandahs, and they came out occasionally to protest. "I wish you gentlemen wouldn't stand exposed like that; you draw fire." One day three of the correspondents were lying in the shade of a stone building, when a large rinkalse, or spitting-snake, glided across from the rocks to the verandah. We began a bombardment, missing the snake, but hitting the house with every round. The door opened suddenly, a surprised face looked out, and a voice began: "I say, don't you know – what the deuce is all ———." Slam! He had seen the snake with a foot of its neck arched, and the cobra-like sacs below the head puffed out to eject the poison. His curiosity as to the row was satisfied.

One day we were undecided as to whether we should take the convent or the next building for our noonday lounge, but as the Dutch gunners had been paying the convent much attention, we decided against it. Half-an-hour later, Father Ford – a man whom nature intended for a soldier, and his parents made a priest – was reading on the verandah, one eye on the book, the other lifting at intervals to a set telescope and Long Tom. As he glanced up he saw the gun-muzzle raised – a tiny black disc above the sandbags of the redoubt. "Come out quickly," he shouted to the naval officer writing in the room behind. "It's coming right at us." They ran down the steps to the shelter of the bluestone foundations. The shell tore a hole in the brick wall, burst in the room where the naval officer sat writing twenty seconds before, and splintered things in the usual way. This illustrated the keenness with which the gun was watched, even at 8200 yards.

Men wore mostly boots in these days. Officers and men alike wore the heavy, thick-soled ammunition boots; all had lost their calves, and thought it little good in advertising for them. The close-folding, universal putties betrayed only too faithfully the outline of the shrunken shanks, which, in turn, threw into greater contrast the imposing magnitude of the boot below. Where was all the style and superb finish of the British army now? Gone, and the greatest exquisite in the service troubled his head not a bit about it. Deeds, not dress, were glory then. It was the day of action, not of appearances. I saw one Tommy halt at the town tip and pick up an old boot, examine it, then, taking off his own, the sole of which was held to the upper by string – the derelict of the dust-heap was obviously the better of the two – he put it on, and went his way satisfied. Yet critics outside were asking why the garrison was so inactive, why we did not dash out upon the rear of the enemy, link hands with Buller, and so facilitate the relief. But we were past the power of working out our own salvation, save by patient waiting. The mission of this town and garrison, quite as much as in the spring of the previous year, was to hold itself out a buffer to the Boer advance, and an impediment to concentration and supply upon the Tugela, since everything they needed must be untrucked at Sunday river, and taken a wide circuit in wagons over the veldt. Through all the haze of doubt and difficulties we were beginning to see now with retrospective eye the development of a far-seeing plan – which at one time seemed to be only an inexplicable and unsoldierly inaction. Not even the youngest and most inexperienced civilian amongst us really believed then that he knew more than the General. Sir George White had not taken us into his confidence, but we had had all the assistance of the tacticians and generals of the street corners and the shady mimosa trees, who had brought tactics and the whole art of war down to the irreducible minimum. The man who began all his observations with the words, "If I were the General," abandoned war as a topic, and talked only of victuals.

The volume of sound from the Tugela all at once grew denser. It had come to us first in occasional bursts – a far-off titanic drum-tap, beating sometimes the reveille, sometimes the last post. Now it was a steady, ceaseless din. All the energies of the relief party, all its resources in artillery fire, were surely being gathered in that great bombardment. In the early morning we woke and listened; it still came through. We hardly knew what we wished for most, its continuance or its cessation. The last must necessarily be the prelude to relief, but the silence of the cannon had so often meant failure and further waiting. Even the sound was deceptive, and varied with the atmospheric conditions. On the second day it seemed nearer, clearer; on the third more distant and irregular. And with every variation in the sound our spirits rose and sank, true as the barometer to the storm. The news from the river was sparse and uncertain, for the Boers had exhausted ingenuity in their endeavours to trap the native runners, and along the river, the route now invariably chosen, the Kaffir paths were watched, and the traps multiplied. The bell wires had been doubled – one placed close to the ground, the next at just about the height of a man's head, so that the runner, in keeping a sharp look-out for the one was almost certain to strike the other, when an electric bell on one of the kopjes brought the Boer guards swarming down like soldier wasps from their mud houses in the syringa trees. The Kaffir matched cunning with cunning, and was equal to every emergency. From the time they were put through our outer line of pickets and flitted away silently like shadows into the night up to the nearest native kraal, they carried their despatches; after that and until they were handed over to General Buller's Staff the runner rarely handled them. A Kaffir girl, who day by day passed the Boer camps, calabash on head, on the way to a spring, took the despatches in the empty vessel and planted them by the spring side. Another girl carried them from the spring to the next kraal; to-day they were in the calabash, to-morrow in the mealie-jar, which the Kaffir women poise so gracefully on their heads. The runner might be stopped and searched a dozen times – he had no papers on him, was only a vagabond native following his sister to the kraal. The plan was expensive, since so many had to be paid for their labour; but it was effective – that was the main point. I shall never cease to admire those Kaffirs, their quiet daring, their audacity, their fine bush-craft, their sterling honesty, and their matchless physique.

The news that the runners brought and the heliograph flashed was generally cheery, though the relief contented themselves with a curt "All going well," or "Progress satisfactory." They would not encourage hopes that once again might become only delusions. The biggest, the best news we had was perfect as a prophecy, but as a fact some weeks ahead of the event. "Lord Roberts has entered Bloemfontein, and been received with open arms." There appeared to be verification of it, too, in the news that Lucas Meyer and a large Free State force had been entrained for Harrismith. The meer-cat was having its tail pinched, and was turning round to see about it. Then came the intelligence that Cronje was surrounded with his army, and must inevitably be captured or destroyed. Everything was shaping well for a great Majuba Day celebration, an anniversary which every one felt would be fraught with consequences to Boer and Briton, reducing to insignificance all that had made the day one of celebration for the Dutch. There had been a Majuba – that no English could ever forget. Once a year the old wound in the breasts of the English was made to rankle even in the very strongholds of the African English – we felt sure now that there would be a Majuba obliteration, a Majuba revenge. Everything pointed to it. And still the cannon fire went on in the distance, but on the fourth morning it seemed fainter and further away. For ninety-six hours its echoes had rolled unceasingly, imposingly amongst the hills. From Cæsar's Hill, where whole batteries of field and stalking-glasses were turned south, we saw in the far distance stray squads of brown-coated men upon the kopjes that could only be British soldiers. In the stillness of the night some believed that they could hear the faint crackle of rifle fire, though that might be but a strained expectation playing tricks with the reality. The heliograph sat upon a nearer hill, and blinked at us with a brighter eye, and General Buller still said, "All going well."

Then the blow fell. The garrison was on quarter rations. Only a few knew that the discovery that maize hurriedly milled and stored during the siege, in such a manner that it heated and became useless, was the main reason for this last economy. Every failure on the Tugela had been followed by reduced rations in Ladysmith. It came so promptly again upon the cessation of fire that we could draw but one conclusion. That was Ladysmith's best and worst day. To me personally it was the saddest forenoon of all. Two of my friends, Dunn and Greenwood, had gone down with fever and dysentery, and the cruelty of their luck was only manifest later on. To have endured it for months, and then to miss the grand climax – that was the bitterest trick surely that Fate ever played upon a mortal. That forenoon I begged for brandy and corn-flour and tinned milk for the invalids, and while the suave Baboo at the stores measured it out in ounces, the medical chief said, "You must look upon it as liquid gold. Make it go as far as possible." Later I took an ambulance out to Olver's to bring in Greenwood, not knowing then the sequel to that ninety-six hours of ceaseless shell. It had come in another brief message from General Buller, "I believe the enemy is in full retreat. My cavalry are in pursuit." It was just as well, for in riding out I had the luck to see that which very few in Ladysmith saw, and coming suddenly, hard upon the heels of disappointment, sickness, and despair, the *dénouement* was the more dramatic.

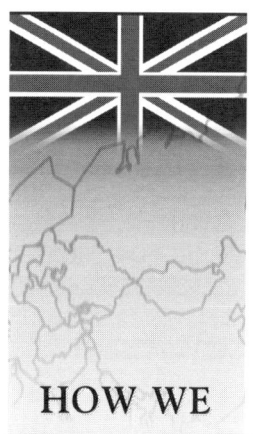

HOW WE KEPT THE FLAG FLYING

CHAPTER 26

THE END OF THE SIEGE

The great trek – How I saw it – A silver snake – A remarkable retreat – Shelling Long Tom – Fine artillery work – Buller's cavalry in sight – The rush to meet them – "Thank God we kept the flag flying" – The fighting chiefs – The fate of the flag.

THE relief of Ladysmith came at last with dramatic suddenness. Different men saw it in different aspects, with different eyes. To all of us, though, it stands the personal experience of a lifetime, something that next to the battle scenes we shall never forget. We were at our worst, as I have told already, hoping much, believing much, expecting something, but not anticipating that one short day would see in quick succession despair, the dawn of hope, and the glory of realization. I was standing in Olver's hut, and the open window gave a far view across the town over our ring of entrenchments, over the encompassing lines of the enemy, away in the direction of the Zululand borders, where a gently rising green hill made an abrupt horizon. It is a characteristic of Natal, indeed of all South Africa, that on some days the hills seem very near, on others vague and distant, an atmospheric effect that cannot easily be overlooked. On that day the hill was very near, and suddenly it seemed to me that there was something in the prospect which had not been there before.

Under the strong and somewhat strange sunshine which so often precedes a tropical thunderstorm in the highlands of Natal, it seemed as though a long silver snake were stretched against the green background in ever-extending curves, that had a look of motion in them. As yet only half-curious, half-expectant, I took up a pair of field-glasses, and set them to the long focus. The silver snake of the distance was a line of white-tilted wagons suspiciously uniform in build and cover for Boer transport, but still unmistakably wagons. I could see the tilts sway against the skyline as they dipped over the ridge, but at the foot fresh wagons were continually coming into view – the train was endless. "Look," I said to young Olver, "look there! What do you make of it?" "It's a trek," he said excitedly, "a great trek. They're retreating, they're going at last." Then closer home, right in at the northern shoulder of Lombard's Kop, we saw something less reassuring – a huge laager of wagons visible to us from our high outlook, but just hidden from view of the town by the Boers' rifle ridge, and covering, it appeared, acres. They seemed to be forming a square, just as they were accustomed to form it in older days to throw back the impetuous charges of the Basuto and Zulu warriors. It looked more like fight than flight. It might mean that the Boers were concentrating suddenly for a last great assault on the town, though it was difficult to see how they could reap anything of the fruits of victory even if they gained one, for had they forsaken their works upon the Tugela, Buller's cavalry would be quickly on their heels. Coupled with the silence of cannon to the southward, it meant something of import. "Let us get up to Maiden Castle," I said, a high peak overlooking the veldt on the opposite side, as well as the route over which the enemy's transport usually travelled.

We hurried to the summit, and there was a wonderful sight,

The End of the Siege

the great trek we had so long anticipated. The enemy were in full retreat. For five miles another train of wagons, longer, more dense, more jumbled than the first, for there were blocks and long halts in the line, stretched across, and just as the ice-birds are snow-white on one side of the ship and sky-blue on the other, so the flying enemy on one side of Ladysmith were all black; on the other, as I have said, a glistening white. The realization of the long-expected was so sudden, the suppressed excitement so great, that we could not keep the glasses steady without resting them on a rock. It was the great trek – not wagons only, but riders – galloping black-coated horsemen moving forward in groups of twenty, fifty, a hundred, a continuous living stream of more or less density coming into view round the corner of End Hill, sweeping away in a long curve, and disappearing northward behind Telegraph Hill, in the direction of their railway base. These galloping horsemen were not an escort for the transport train. They went their own way, and went fast. In any other army it would have been the evidence not merely of defeat but demoralization. But we knew the Boer way. When they moved it was anyhow as to disposition, but rapidly and effectively; that is why pursuit is such a hopeless thing. The one thing, the great thing, was that they were going. It was the flight, not of a commando or a column, but an army. Give them their due, too, they were doing it well. Their retreat was as masterly a thing as their desperate clinging to the hills of the Tugela. But, then, the Dutch are born transport riders. They have been at it all their lives, and the best organized military transport in the world cannot keep pace with them. He must fly light who goes in pursuit of the flying Boer.

Down at the foot of the hill a little picket of the Highlanders sat in a stone fort all unconscious of the great event beyond. We shouted and pointed, so they came up to us, and then – well, there were strathspeys upon the hill-top. "Look yonder; look yonder, mon; ain't they rinnin'! Aye, it's a pity we canna get at them." That was the general feeling. They had locked us in, mocked us, starved us, battered us for months, and, instead of thanking God for our deliverance, we were eager only to get at them. It was the opportunity of a campaign. Could we but have rushed out our field batteries and mounted troops, we could have decimated their transport trains; but our field batteries, the darling of the R.A., had become slow-going siege trains, our cavalry and mounted infantry were unhorsed. We had eaten them into immobility. The sight was exasperating, maddening. And, as though knowing it, they cut in tauntingly close, nearer than they had ever dared to come in the early days of the siege, when the big walers were still fit for a gallop. Our gunners on the top of Cæsar's Hill were sorely tried. They swung round their long-range naval 12-pounders, and a shell pitched at the greatest possible elevation went screaming high over our heads. It was short, miserably short. They tried again and again, but the nearest shell was still some hundreds of yards on this side, and the Boer horsemen, laughing at our impotence no doubt, galloped on, for a great thunderstorm was gathering, and would soon burst. There was always such a storm on our great days.

We were curious as to Bulwan. The one thing that would have consoled us for the escape of the enemy was the capture of that gun, and how Ladysmith would have prized it as a trophy in the years to come! It had all been arranged by the gunners of the *Powerful*. The moment that the relief was assured they were to open on that redoubt with all their available ammunition, and, if possible, prevent the gun from being dismounted. It had fired a single shot early in the forenoon, and was afterwards silent. At that moment something black, like a huge letter A, appeared above the redoubt. We knew in an instant that it was the tripod, to lift the gun from its pit. The Powerfuls saw it too. There was that ear-splitting crash from the Lady Anne redoubt behind Convent Ridge, another roar from the crest of Cæsar's Hill, and both the 4.7's were in action. They picked up the range splendidly. The first shell burst upon the mountain side, close to the summit; at the second the red earth flew from the front of the redoubt. When the smoke of the third shell, which seemed to burst right on the redoubt, had cleared away, the tripod had disappeared, and we exulted. It was not the time for stoicism and deportment. We yelled, for we had still our voices unimpaired; we danced as well as our physical exhaustion would permit; we conducted ourselves as school-boys do on slight incentive, but as staid men are only expected to do under such and overmastering emotion as war. We shook hands with the Highlanders, were filled with a great sense of satisfaction, and turned to look at the flying Boers, for the tripod over Long Tom was raised no more while the daylight lasted. There was a redoubt on End Hill, and we could see through the glass the figures of men moving about it, but whether there was a gun in it just then was a problem. In the niche between Wagon Hill and Cæsar's we had lurking a howitzer, and it opened fire on something it could not see. That, to the uninitiated, is the marvel of howitzer fire. The muzzle looks up the steep hill in front of it. The gun-layers can see nothing beyond a couple of little flags aligned from the crest above, yet how wonderfully they shot. I think it was the third shell that tore a great hole in the right-hand corner of the redoubt, the fifth that made a similar gap further to the left. Through both rents the sky-line showed behind; the gaps looked large enough to drive a team of oxen through. It may have been – possibly was – useless as to results, for I doubt if there was a gun in position just then, but all the same, it was a magnificent display of marksmanship. It showed, at least, how fortunate were the Staats Artillery in that all our operations had been hampered by the miserable want of ammunition. If we could only have done it earlier! There was nothing more to see just there and then. The heavens had opened, the hail was beating upon us, and, happy and saturated, we went down through the storm to tell the glad news to our fellow-correspondents, who, with a temperature at 103°, were fretting and fuming only that in having stood up all through the siege, they should have gone down on this latest and greatest day, and so missed the climax. They longed for one look, at least, at those Dutchmen flying across the veldt and pelted by the hailstorm, a duty of which we would have been so savagely glad to relieve them.

I had just got a change of clothes, and we were sitting down to our last dinner of horseflesh, when there was a rush of feet, a shouting in the streets outside, and through the tumult came the one clear cry, "Buller's cavalry are in sight; they are coming across the flats." Waiting neither for horses nor horse-meat we ran, joining the stream of excited people, who were making for the nearest river drift, in quick intuition that there the incoming column must cross. There was a little flat beyond the river; further on a little ridge, and down the side of this came a brown column of trotting horsemen. They had come through the gap by Umbulwana; had cut across by Intombi Camp, and were almost in the town. The setting sun shone full upon the hill, for the storm had passed, and though they were only brown horsemen like our own, we knew they were not our own – for they had horses, and the full kit of men who had been in action and bivouac, and even those of ours who had horses had not trotted for many a day. It was the relief column – every one knew that.

Then followed a wonderful scene. One could not be in Ladysmith long without having realized that it was a strangely composite community, but never was the fact brought so vividly home to me as then. All the colours and all the nations of earth seemed blended together in a confused throng, all its tongues raised in one exultant din. It was worth having lived and suffered through the siege for that supreme hour. In the rush to the river were the red fezes of the Malays, for once roused from their Oriental stoicism. Mixed up with them were the parti-coloured turbans of the coolies and dhoolie-bearers, their scant white clothing flapping in the wind over their spindle shanks, bare from the knees. The Zulus and Kaffirs were delirious. They leaped in the air, and sang and shouted, their white teeth and white eyeballs gleaming. The hospitals had

First sight of the Deliverers

poured out their sick and wounded; all rushed to join in the pæan of welcome. There were soldiers with white and shrunken faces; men wounded in the legs, who shuffled slowly down the road. One poor young infantry officer had stopped at a deep street channel – he had not strength to step over it. I lifted him to the other side, but it was no trouble, he was light as a child. Two other officers drove down in a pony trap, and the ghastliness of their faces impressed one, even in that time of wild excitement. They were, in plain and painful truth, living skeletons. An old Kaffir woman tottered along the footpath, the tears streaming down her face. "Listen to her; listen to her," said a Natal farmer. "That's good; isn't it?" I could listen, but not understand, so he interpreted. The words the Kaffir woman spoke were really the sentiment of that time of triumph. "The English can conquer everything but death; why can't they conquer death?" They had conquered it, in defying it to its worst, in lavishing their brave lives upon the slopes, where to go was but to meet death. Had there been terror of death there had never been conquest.

The riders from the Tugela came down the slopes to the river, and the horsemen from the town had already gathered about them. The men of the relief column emptied their pockets and haversacks, and every man of ours who rode beside them smoked a cigarette or a cigar. They had pushed on and on when they found the Dutch had left the last of their trenches, had got touch with the enemy in many places, had fired upon them, and got not a single shot in reply. Why not go right in? There were two rival corps in the column – the Imperial Light Horse and the Carbineers – and it was appropriate that regiments which had comrades in the garrison should be first in. They had raced for precedence at first, but thought better of it as they reached the ridge above Intombi Camp, and saw before them in the sunset the iron roofs of Ladysmith. Then they formed up their detachments side by side, and so came in together, with Dundonald – descendant of an old Scottish fighting family –

and Major Mackenzie, one of the bravest of the citizen soldiers of Natal, leading the way – good types of the newer, greater empire which this war had irrevocably solidified. They swung into the main street, marching through a living avenue of cheering men and women, whom they had placed under a lifelong obligation, while the little ones were hoisted on shoulders for a look at the long-looked-for relief column. And in the halflight of moon and twilight Sir George White and his Staff galloped round the corner, and the leaders shook hands.

Then the long-pent-up excitement and enthusiasm burst forth in a very tumult of joy, and none who were privileged to see and hear it will ever forget. Men were no longer ashamed of their emotions. They cheered and laughed and even cried, for there was a catch in the voice and tears streaming down many a face, and women, more deeply moved, caught up their little ones and kissed them, and thanked God for their preservation and deliverance. Surely it was the greatest sight, that little gathering of mud-stained, battle-worn riflemen, that the eye of man ever looked upon. So we, who were so deeply concerned, thought it. They had fought by day, slept under rain and storm at night, and not a man of them but had his full reward. And the old Kaffir woman, jostled on the outskirts of the crowd, still mumbled, "The English can conquer everything but death."

Cheers for the relief column, cheers for Buller, but loudest, longest, and most heartfelt, cheers for Sir George White. There was something of filial affection in the ovation that the garrison gave its General. Long before there had been impatience, sometimes irritation, born of the feeling that it was not right for ten thousand of the pick of Britain's soldiers to sit down there and endure insult and aggression. All that had long since died away, and, repentant that they had, in their ignorance, wronged this grand old soldier, they made it up to him now in the fulness of their hearts, in their hour of succour and exultation. They gathered about him, caught his bridle-rein and stirrup-leathers, hung around his horse, and cheered until the flying rear-guard of the Boer army must have heard them over the ridges. All mark of the superior race, the caste between exotic and aboriginal, was swept away; they mingled together – black, brown, and yellow, European, Ethiopian, Eurasian – in one exulting throng, and all cheering their General. The bowed back of the old fighter straightened, his sunken cheeks flushed, and his eyes shone. He had borne disappointment after disappointment – a responsibility the weight of which few could share, and this, too, was his reward. More than once he tried to speak and failed. Fifty years of soldiering and the subjugation of the weaker man were not equal to that great occasion. Finally he found his voice, and beginning almost inaudibly thanked them for the loyal way they had, civilian and soldier alike, co-operated with him in the defence of the town. Then he struck the keynote that went straight to the hearts of all his people, and roused them to an indescribable enthusiasm. "Thank God we kept the flag flying." Such words, spoken with an intensity of solemn feeling, were as a match to the mine of human emotion, and what a roar rose in the night air, while the Zulus, knowing not that something fit to be immortal had been said, but inflamed by the infectious joy of the multitude, sprang into the air again, and shouted the war-cry that some few there had heard many a year ago, when Cetewayo's impis swept down upon them. "It cut me to the heart," the General went on, "to reduce your rations as I did." Then his voice faltered and failed him, and it seemed for a moment that he would break down altogether. The sympathetic crowd filled in the break, helped him over the crisis with another roar of delight long drawn out, and with the promptness of the soldier he pulled himself together, and mastered his deep feeling. A smile came over his face, and he saved the situation with a laughing, "I promise you, though, that I'll never do it again." The people laughed and cheered, and gradually melted away. Ladysmith was relieved.

A word of our three fighting chiefs as I saw them in this their hour of triumph will not be amiss. As for Sir George White,

Natal had left its mark upon him as upon so many more. After the storm of enthusiasm attending that long-looked-for relief came reaction. Soldier and civilian alike realized that four months of siege, shell, and starvation had left them for the most part nerveless, strengthless, and utterly undone. For most of those who clung to the insanitary trenches, through daylight and darkness, in storm and sunshine, the war was over – in effect, that fine fighting force was as completely out of action for the time as though Ladysmith had really fallen. It was a pitiable thing that so many went down in the last few days of the siege, some even on the last day. The Headquarters Staff were, however, singularly fortunate, very few of them going through hospital. They had had more than their share in the anxiety and the responsibility of the position, for they alone at times knew how really bad was the outlook upon the Tugela. They were spared, however, the long, harassing days and nights in the trenches, which played such havoc with our combatant officers and linesmen. Sir George White himself had just been able to see the realization of the hopes for which he had planned, when he had to strike his flag to the all-conquering fever – not enteric in this case, but a purely local, unclassed and unidentifiable type, born of siege anxieties, camp stenches, and "short commons." You have seen many portraits of Sir George White, but not one in the least like the grey-faced, worn officer. The General of the studio looks tall, straight, fresh, and springy, but the General of the siege was at least ten years older than any of his pictures – a stooped, patient, almost pathetic figure, stalking, cane in hand, through the streets of Ladysmith. When I first saw Sir George White, in the flush of the double victories of Dundee and Elands Laagte, he seemed to me even then an anxious man, quite unlike the trim, taut soldier of the illustrated papers, and that impression of him was intensified through each successive week of the long-strung ordeal.

I have told of the dark spirit of disaffection which at times dwelt in the besieged town, when men, overwrought with the uncertainty of the situation and repeated disappointments, complained bitterly of the inaction of their leaders. To have omitted any mention of it would have been just, perhaps, to the men upon whom the responsibility rested, but that disaffection was still an aspect of the siege, and to have ignored it would have meant telling less than the whole truth. It was sufficient that it was suppressed while the Dutch were at the door. The real test of merit lies, however, not in the hastily-formed and petulant impressions of the moment, but in the cool after-survey of the man and the situation made with the fullest knowledge of the facts. There was a time when people in Ladysmith almost pitied Sir George White, and looked forward hopefully to the advent of a stronger man; but long ere the situation had reached its solution, that feeling had changed to one of unbounded admiration and trust. The things that had seemed so grossly and palpably wrong to the general of the street corners all turned out so right and well-considered. So it is that in spite of the rigour of the time, Sir George White is better loved and more admired by the people of Ladysmith to-day than at any period of the siege, and every taunt directed against him has recoiled upon those who made it. He has been cheered and fêted outside, but none bade him good-bye with such genuine emotion as his besieged garrison, and not a man or woman there but will ever have a kind wish for the General, and an affectionate remembrance of the tall soldier who in plain khaki moved so quietly amongst us.

Ian Hamilton, I am free to confess, always caught and held my fancy more than any man in Ladysmith, as the very beau-ideal of a soldier. One may be prejudiced in a man's favour by personal charm, a personal acquaintance, but as I had never spoken to General Hamilton it cannot be that. It was chiefly Cæsar's Hill, where he held command during that desperate seventeen hours of fighting. Spare, tall, quiet, smiling as ever, he caught the eye of the people because he had even more medal badges than his chief. They were attracted by the smile, which was that of a woman – we by the quiet, masterful manner of the born soldier, who fights without making a fuss over it, and only begins to impress you afterwards, when you look back in cold blood, and pick up one by one the half-blotted recollections of the combat. The difference between the calm, constant, ever-reliable commander, and the national hero, lies often in one little but picturesque opportunity. Some men miss the dramatic point in action; some are found out – others are not discovered; many, like poor Penn Symons, who sleeps in the lee of the little church at Dundee, are discovered too late, when they have fallen victims to a system which has taught men to attempt all that they never should and never could do in South Africa – a system that has made men of all ranks in the British army figure during the campaign in the mixed capacity of soldiers, demi-gods, and fools.

As in the case of Sir George White, the camera, it seems to me, has never given you the real Sir Archibald Hunter. It makes his face longer and thinner than the one we knew in Ladysmith, but it has succeeded to perfection in conveying that lackadaisical droop of the fair moustache, which always makes "General Archie" look so much more of the beau than the Bayard, but, all the same, ever a fine thoroughbred figure of a man, whether you met him in the ball-room or battle-field. Truth to tell, I believe there is nothing at all of the lady-killer about him. The only woman he is said to worship is a grey-haired old lady up in an Ayrshire village. Like many of the Kitchener "crowd", who affect the Spartan ways of their chief, he has been too much absorbed in war to think of women. Well, he came out springy, and fit as a prize-fighter.

And what of the flag – the flag that Sir George White in the fulness of his heart thanked God had been kept flying over Ladysmith so long? It flew no longer. That night the officers gathered about the flag-pole, and then in a burst of enthusiasm, and urged by a common impulse, they pulled it down and tore it into shreds, and each pinned a little fragment of it in his buttonhole. These bits of the Union Jack will be heirlooms in English families a hundred years hence, but somehow it seemed to me that it should not have been destroyed, however worthy the motives that led to its partition. When "Long Cecil," the Kimberley gun, was given to Mr. Rhodes, he with exquisite taste said, "The place for that gun is over the grave of the man who made it. Let it be his monument." So it seemed to me that the right place for that flag was in the home of Sir George White in County Antrim, Ireland. Surely no man had a better claim to it.

For some in Ladysmith that night there was reaction and lassitude, from all a deep thankfulness for many things, but most of all, it seemed to me, because they had been able at last to show their General that they knew his worth. "I'm glad of that, I'm glad of that," men said over and over again, and the women naïvely admitted, "I kept up through it all; I never cried until they cheered Sir George White. Oh, I liked that." And sick men, realizing once again that they were invalids, crept back to bed, well content that they had disobeyed the doctor and risked their lives. And scanty dinners cooled at vacant tables, and the cook, who had done his best for the great occasion, was heartbroken in the knowledge that there were greater men than he in Ladysmith. That night, too, we gathered in the Relief Column camp, and the men, who had given away their rations to others more hungry than themselves, told us of the long fights upon the Tugela. And we, poor, inhospitable hosts, having nothing to offer them but our gratitude, they rolled themselves wearily at last in their greatcoats and went supperless to sleep. But they were entirely happy. They had "jumped" the situation and come in. Every half-hour there was the crash of our naval guns, and a shell went shrieking overhead. The night-glasses showed dimly the flicker of lights on Umbulwana, and we knew that the Dutch were trying to take away their gun. The bursting of the shells made a great flame of light upon the mountain-top, and we hoped that an occasional shot might hamper their work.

From the other side of the town the Dutch mortars threw out star shells, which lit up the veldt between the rival positions. They were not easy in their minds, and feared lest we should come out and harass them. Our far-out patrols on that side heard all night the whistle and puff of trains as they were loaded and sent away northward, and early on the first morning of March I went to sleep with the words of that old Kaffir woman still ringing in my ears, *"The English can conquer everything but death – everything but death!"*

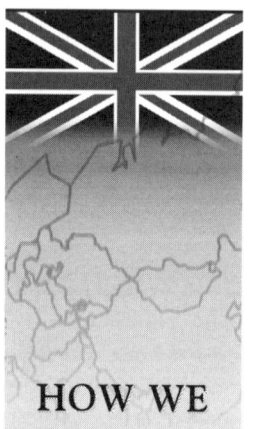

HOW WE KEPT THE FLAG FLYING

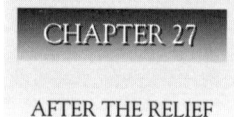

CHAPTER 27

AFTER THE RELIEF

*A dead Boer – The toys of Umbulwana – Harassing the rearguard –
A deserted camp – Mistaken for Boers – A sailor's welcome.*

HE evacuation by the Boers both of their positions on the Tugela and around Ladysmith was as creditable as their investment of the town and their stern defence of the hills upon and in front of which General Buller lost so many brave men. No British force of equal magnitude could have got away in the same time, and taken their guns with them, but then the Dutch are born transport riders. They have trekked and trekked all their lives, as many of them will no doubt trek again at the close of this war further into the heart of the African continent. In positions to which they had clung to the last they left everything but their guns. On the morning after the volunteers entered Ladysmith, our first thought was to determine whether the coveted Long Tom, which had done us so much damage from the crest of Bulwan, had really been taken away, and at the first break of day Alick Macpherson, one of the local guides, led a party of men up its steep sides. We crossed without a challenge the mimosa flats, upon which to venture any time this last four months meant death. Not a Boer was to be seen upon the summit – the position had been hurriedly and completely evacuated. Within fifty yards of the Dutch gun-pit, and on the Ladysmith side of the mountain, lay a gruesome relic of hostile occupation in the body of a swart Boer, who must have been dead quite three weeks or a month, yet, partly sheltered by a thorn bush, had lain there unburied, without his comrades on the top being aware of it. His bandolier, stocked with bullet clips, was still over his shoulder, his rusted rifle lay beside him. The black-bearded cheeks were already drying under the hot African sun, the body shrinking deeper into the grass plumes. It gave proof, if any were needed, how rarely the enemy ventured down that side of the mountain, though the continued silence of our big guns should have told them of the scarcity of ammunition. Yet another victim of war we picked up on the mountain side. Close to where one of our 4.7 shells had exploded on the previous evening, when we vainly sought to prevent the enemy getting their big gun away, was a little locust bird, yet alive, but with both its legs and one wing shattered. A splinter of shell had struck the tiny thing, which is not bigger than a quail, and it was probably the last victim of the Ladysmith investment. Nearing the top of that hill, upon which our eyes had so long been covetously turned, eagerness to be first overwhelmed every other consideration, and there was a unanimous rush for the redoubt. It was empty: our night bombardment had been futile; the gun – for which Ladysmith would have given much as a relic of war – was gone, and everything else had apparently been left. In the magazines were 250 rounds of shell, which a few days later we destroyed. The cases of Mauser ammunition must have reached tons in weight. Even their search-light remained, though the engine was missing. The redoubt was less formidable than it looked in the distance. The top wall of earth was eleven feet thick on the crown, enlarging towards the base. It was heavily faced with rough stone, upon which was the mark of many of our naval shells. The 40-pounders had evidently not been heavy enough to do it great damage. Their camps were just as they had been evacuated, the tents – mostly our tents, and many of them comfortably furnished – still standing. In one building there was a batch of freshly-baked bread – circumstances over which the bakers had no control compelled them to leave in a hurry. In the storehouses were many bags of rusks, the biscuit the Boer loves with his coffee. In another corner were stacks of biltong, freshly made. There were both variety and plenty in the Boer stores on Bulwan, and they had lived luxuriously while we starved on our maize meal and horse-meat. There were boxes of fresh butter nicely printed, and newly arrived from the Transvaal. Soon our men had bivouacked, and in the fresh air of early morning we breakfasted bounteously at the expense of the enemy. The rusks, soaked in coffee, were especially a delicacy. At one of the tents a young calf was fastened. "The cow can't be far off," said our farmer guide; "I'll collar her." Just then she came up over the brow, and he found he had the best right to her. It was one of his own dairy herd. With all their skill in transport, I cannot even now think that the Boers got their guns away safely, for there were marks at one point of an overturned wagon. It had rained heavily all night, making wagon work difficult, and it may be that the Boers buried the gun, as they did many of those upon the Tugela heights.

One of the life regrets to every one who had suffered investment in Ladysmith was that we were unable to take a more active part in harassing the enemy in their flight. It was a tantalizing sight, that long train of trekking wagons moving slowly over the veldt, and had our cavalry, mounted infantry, and field artillery been horsed as they were when the enemy first sat down in front of Ladysmith, we might have sallied out, turned the retreat into a rout, and captured their whole baggage train; but gun-horses and chargers had alike been eaten, and the scarecrow troops were unfit to march five miles had their lives

The meeting of Generals Buller and White.

depended on it. Next day we did make an attempt to follow up and harry their rear-guard, but it was a lame and impotent affair. We shelled them from a few of the hills near the stations, saw the last of their transport trains leaving, saw and heard the explosions which told of railway bridges blown up behind them, and then, as we had so often done before, toiled back into Ladysmith, though the Gordons, for the first time for many a long day, marched with their pipers playing at the head of the column. And in their front rank stepped Kenny M'Leod, who, on the slope of Elands Laagte, rivalled the Findlater feat at Dargai in piping the Highlanders on after he had fallen wounded. It was Kenny's bad luck to have imitated, and not originated, the feat. On the way in one passed many empty military saddles stacked by the roadside. There had been no casualties worth mention, but at every furlong horses had given out, and the saddles were being picked up by the baggage train, while the ambulances were full of men who had fallen from mere exhaustion. The troops as they rested were feeding upon the green corn cobs taken from mealie-fields planted by Dutch sympathizers, who had been left unmolested on the farms, and many of whom had added to their inferior farming plant the better implements of their English neighbours. The national impulse to loot at any and every opportunity will in the end have proved their ruin, and cost many of them their farms.

As we rode up the Newcastle road, down which our troops had retired before the enemy four months before, we were surprised to see under the steep rear of Surprise Hill a Boer camp of about one hundred tents. It was the most western arc in their ring of investment, the nearest point to their base and line of retreat, so that there was no reason why it should have been left standing. The white tents nestling in the mimosa had a live look, so we manœuvred to cut them off, but these cautious tactics were unnecessary. Like Bulwan, it had been evacuated on the previous day, leaving everything but the gun standing. There again was disorder. Great quantities of new saddlery, clothing, and boots lay upon the grass, and Tommy in his rags never had a greater justification for loot, and has rarely taken such full advantage of it. Scores of them were soon busy picking out new suits of khaki, and transferring their corps badges. Others ransacked the tents, and there was something very like a riot when one man unearthed from a box a bottle of old Dop brandy. As one man his comrades rushed him. In the midst of the *mêlée*, a thought seemed to strike a shrewd-faced Cockney. He disengaged himself from the tangle, ran to the same tent, and brought forth four other bottles of brandy. Next to spirits, tobacco was the great prize, and there was abundance of it. The enemy had lacked nothing round Ladysmith, though we had often heard that they were greatly dissatisfied with their supplies. The framework of one of our mountain guns taken by the enemy at Nicholson's Nek lay in this captured camp.

I forgot to mention that an inspection of the Long Tom redoubt on Bulwan revealed a circumstance which caused general surprise. The gun-table, with results of the shooting all carefully tabulated, was hanging in the redoubt. It showed, beyond doubt, that this very gun was the same which had first opened on us from Pepworth's Hill in the first days of the siege, and that of the 11,000 rounds of shell fired into the town, some 3000 had come from this one muzzle. We had assumed that the life of the first gun had been long since exhausted, yet here were the tabulated figures for the shooting from Pepworth and Reid's Hill, as the enemy described it, and the date of the transfer to Bulwan clearly marked. It may not have been actual proof, but it was strong presumptive evidence of identification. Thus a heavier butcher's bill than even the seventy lives we had calculated must be allotted the gun, and in missing it we had lost a greater historical trophy than we at the time realized. Nothing that Ladysmith can show the tourist in the future – not even its grim fever record – would have been so great a curiosity as Long Tom.

On every side, the morning after the relief, we pushed out

scouting parties, and everywhere, save towards their railway base, we had lost touch of the enemy – the retirement had been most complete. One party of Guides, under Major Henderson, pushed southward, on and on, until, in the rising sun, the Tugela river shone beneath them, and in the clear morning the bivouac fires of the army of relief rose through the still atmosphere. Suddenly bang came a 40-pounder shell, almost into them, and as they scattered for shelter three others hustled after it. They were being fired upon by their own comrades in mistake for Boers. Greathead, one of the Guides, galloped forward with his hand up, but the naval gunners who had loosed off at them so suddenly were scarcely apologetic. "Why didn't you keep both hands up?" an officer said brusquely. "You may consider yourselves lucky you weren't shot." Even with the knowledge that a couple of hundred rifles in front are bearing on you, and needing only a touch of the trigger finger to bring certain death, it is not easy to gallop over the broken veldt holding both arms in the air. A sailor, who often does strange things in the saddle, might have done it, but to an ordinary South African rider it was difficult.

The early visit to the deserted Boer camps yielded much that was of interest to the Intelligence Department – especially the official papers, which, when I left, were still being translated. One of them contained the names of the men forming the different commandoes, and will be invaluable as evidence against the Natal rebels, who may seek to show later that they took no part in the fighting. Another was a sort of circular letter from General Joubert to the field-cornets, and dated from the head laager at Elands Laagte. It complained bitterly of the continuous desertions from their ranks, and threatened that unless a stop were put to it the field-cornets would be held personally liable, and dealt with under martial law.

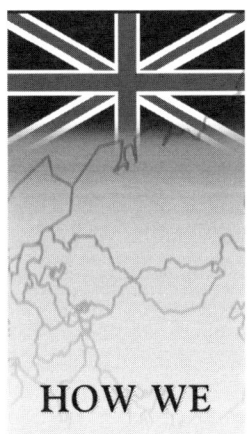

HOW WE KEPT THE FLAG FLYING

CHAPTER 28

ON TUGELA HEIGHTS

*In the Dutch trenches – The Union Jack – Boer gun positions –
Where lyddite fell – A natural citadel – Gunner and priest – A brave pair –
An Englishman's experience – Good-bye to Ladysmith.*

LEAVING Ladysmith to recuperate in a more genial climate – for during the four months' siege I had lost three stone and a half in weight – I took the earliest opportunity of riding through the deserted camps from which the enemy had so lately been driven. Everywhere on the Tugela, as in their camps about Ladysmith, was the confusion and sacrifice of hurried flight. One might have spent days there, and read in the camp litter the whole story of occupation and evacuation. The too hurriedly buried dead, with their knees and hands in many cases protruding from the thin covering of red earth. A rough strip of hessian bagging, pinned down with stones, seemed to cover up something of value in one of the sangars. Again it was only the dead – some of them wrapped in the gaudily-coloured blanket which appeal alike to the artistic taste of the Boer and Zulu, and which was particularly manifest in the gaudy lining of their waterproof coats. One could locate the wounds of these dead Boers without laying a hand upon them, for the last drops of the life fluid as they well from the wound do not blacken so quickly with exposure to the air as in the first flow, but long after death remain a pale, bright scarlet, so that the position of the wound is nearly always indicated. Many of the faces were swarthy almost as Kaffirs. I saw no women amongst these Boer dead, and think that reports as to women having fought in the trenches are exaggerated. In following the Boer wagon roads I came to many branching paths, which were smooth and hard, but not recently trodden. At the point of departure from the main trail there was always a notice-board, with the following intimation in Dutch:- "Voorboden ter gang volgen der spoor. Aus u blif." The lead-pencil copy of the inscription was afterwards blotted by rain, and may not be quite exact, but a rough translation of it would be, "It is forbidden to go down this path. If you please." I assumed that the track had been mined in anticipation of the British carrying the position, and that Dutchmen were thus warned of the danger. I did not push the investigation further, and it may be that one day some farmer, ploughing the veldt, will discover a Boer mine with the point of his ploughshare. The composite character of the Boer camps was betrayed in the address labels, which had come with provisions from Pretoria. In the first camp I visited the labels were all addressed, "Italian Brigade, Colenso," and it is understood that a good deal of their mining work, such as the blowing up of bridges and railway culverts, was done by Italians. German camps were more numerous. "Come the four corners of the world in arms, and we shall shock them," is a quotation that very often occurred to one in traversing the deserted camps of the enemy. Not that the allied nations apparently benefited greatly in trade by the association. The provision tins and boxes invariably bore an English label, and, as a rule, were of the best. What struck me as an amusing incongruity in one camp was a tin with a flaring

Union Jack on the side of it, the conspicuous brand of some English confectionery. I fastened it in the fork of a mimosa tree – a visible emblem of the survival of the fittest. The empty cigarette boxes were all of the Derby winner brand, with the picture of a racehorse for a label. In most of the foreign camps empty wine bottles were plentiful, and we, who had travelled all night over the veldt, sleeping in the open for a few hours at midnight while the oxen were outspanned, were impressed with the precipitancy of the flight, which had left, in one case, a couple of bottles of St. Julien claret, with the seals intact. We used them, and some of the Dutch rusks, for an early breakfast on Colenso heights, where twenty-four hours earlier the article most liberally supplied was lyddite.

In amongst some tall grey cactus, and confronted by a heavy wall, masked in front by a thatching of coarse grass, I found the first of their gun positions. The gun had been taken away, and was evidently a quick-firer, of about 3 in. calibre. It had never been clearly located by our gunners, for the shell-marks were not more numerous there than on other entrenched portions of the heights, though the ground in rear of the gun position was literally strewn with brass cartridge-shells, branded "Berndorf, 1896." Close by was a pit, that had been occupied by a gun of the same bore, but of greater range, for the brass cartridge-cases were almost twice as long as the others – about 15 in. completing, with the shell attached, a cartridge nearly 2 ft. 6 in. long – the disproportion between length and thickness striking one as something unique in modern artillery ammunition. "L 41" was the only mark upon the shells. This position had clearly been vacated in a hurry, for there were many cases of ammunition still intact, while other cases – all painted in dull drab, our own army colour for guns and ammunition wagons – had been opened, and only a few shells used. They were all packed in neat layers, each shell resting on a grooved rack. In like manner I found the station of one of the machine guns, the "Pom-pom" of which all our men in South Africa have so great a dread. At close quarters its sprinklings of bursting shells wreak great havoc, as no two ever pitch in exactly the same spot; but around Ladysmith, though it was so constantly in action, the distance was always too great to do much damage. There they kept it chiefly for our Kaffir grass-cutters. At Colenso they had pushed this particular gun well forward on the exposed brow of a hill, and it was protected by a heavy stone redoubt. No gun station that I examined on Colenso heights bore so many marks of bombardment. Our shells had burst on it and round about it, so that the whole area was ploughed deep red. Lying close to the walls were the bases of a score or so of our 4.7 shells. In rear of it were portions of blood-stained clothing cut from wounded men, and there were blood-marks, too, upon blankets and bagging. The Boer gunners had not come out of that sangar unscathed, and no doubt it had in turn wrought havoc amongst our men, for it commanded the level, open flat between the river and the foot-hills across which our stormers came to the attack. In the rear of the gun there were cart-loads of the little brass cartridge-cases, mixed up with the straw envelopes in which they had been packed, but no unused ammunition remained. At the larger of the three gun stations I have mentioned there had been many miss-fires, for there were scores of shells lying about where the dent of the striker on the cap had not been followed by an explosion.

What impressed me above all else in my hurried morning ride over the just vacated Boer trenches on the Tugela heights was the amazing strength of the position. The mind had room for no other conception – details were blotted out and forgotten. During those long days of waiting, we in Ladysmith had at times been intolerant of the slow progress made for our relief. We were too closely concerned in the issue, too greatly overwrought by the gloom of the surroundings and the uncertainty of the future, to be generous or even just, but in face of the actual position all feelings save that of unbounded admiration for the perseverance of the General and the valour of the troops who had carried that position against the finest sharpshooters in the world were swept away. The besieged had failed utterly to realize the magnitude of the task. No wonder that one of the foreign *attachés* had declared that no less than one hundred thousand men could carry the position; that another considered it a task for an army corps; while the American *attaché* asked quaintly, "Is there no way to get round it, General?" The only path round it – that by Potgieter's Drift – had been tried by General Warren long before, and ended in the black disaster on Spion Kop. In the end we had to face it, and trust to British infantry to find their way where it seemed impossible for men to go and live. How shall I describe that position? I know of no familiar landmarks in Australia that exactly illustrate it. Beyond the river for nearly twenty miles towards Maritzburg one sees the Boer sangars seaming the low, smooth ridges, but that was not their country, and they were easily driven out of it as soon as we had mustered a force at all commensurate to the undertaking. Following up that line of retreat from the southern side, we approach the Tugela over bare undulating flats, with not a scrap of natural cover anywhere. Right opposite the few white-washed mud houses, now rent and roofless, which form the hamlet of Colenso, the conical hills rise abruptly from the river bank. There, right in the centre of the position, is the famous Fort Wylie – a hill seamed from crest to base with gun galleries and rifle trenches. From this central clump the hills retire slightly on either hand, so that a half-mile, sometimes a mile, of flat lies between the river and the high ground. Here was another deadly space to cover, even after the crossing of the broad river, flowing yellow and deep between its low, shelterless banks, had been successfully accomplished. Then, worst of all, the rugged, rocky ascent literally seamed across with walls and trenches. If rifle trenches only, the earthworks were always masked with dry grass, and visible at but a short distance as you approached them. At other points the stone walls stood up grimly, and with no pretence of concealment. An incredible amount of work had been put into these entrenchments and fortifications. The whole ten-mile front of the range was crossed with them, and with the enemy using smokeless powder for all but their heavier guns, it was impossible for our men to say which of the trenches were occupied.

The wagon tracks wriggle down the front of these steep slopes to the drift to ease the descent, and in the alternate curves the trenches were thickest, each body of riflemen enfilading the fire of the lower trench. A simple diagram illustrates the idea.

It can be conceived that nothing could come up a road so defended, and live to boast of the feat.

Knowing its strength, men would not attempt it, and extra precautions taken were no doubt due to the fact that it was a sunken road for the most part, and viewed from a distance looked like offering some shelter to an assaulting column – the last shelter they would have needed in this world save the layer of turf above them. The bottoms of the trenches were carpeted with dry grass, and the earth benches upon which the riflemen rested their elbows were also grassed. In many of the trenches a rude shelter had been made with a sheet of corrugated iron. I might dwell upon the difficulties of that tremendous position for hours, and yet fail to impress you with its immeasurable strength. Short of an unscalable wall, it was naturally the strongest fighting line in all Natal, a country, in its western and northern parts especially, simply teeming with ideal battlegrounds for the force whose duty it is to hold and to defend.

Writing only of those things I have myself seen, I can say little of that long-continued fight upon the Tugela river, and without its vivid colour the story of the siege of Ladysmith can never be complete. There was one incident, however, in the shadow of Monte Cristo that morning which I shall not soon forget, as showing that the grimmest scenes of war – and there is nothing more grimly solemn than a battle-field on the day after a fight – cannot quite obliterate Tommy Atkins' sense of humour. The stretcher-bearers had brought in a Boer, wounded in the right side with a bayonet thrust. Our men had gone up a steep slope, sheltered momentarily by a railway cutting in its side, and galled all the way by a withering fire of rifles. The historic red and white roses of York and Lancaster, and the shamrock of the gallant Enniskillings, went up that hill together, and the blood-mist was in the eyes of our men as they reached the summit,

> "When the red rose was redder than itself,
> And York's white rose as red as Lancaster's."

They spared few of the Dutchmen who still clung valorously to the trenches. As this particular Boer was being tended, a Cockney soldier passing had a look at him. "Why, I've seen 'im before – that's my mark on him. Is he bad, sir?" "Yes, pretty bad," the dresser said. "Well, I did it as gently as I could," said the apologetic Cockney. "Fact, it wasn't so much the shovin' of it hin as the drorin' of it hout that 'urt 'im. Then I give 'm a drink out o' my canteen when I was done with 'm. I think it was a bit o' luck for 'im to ha' met me, don't you?"

Considering that seventy British guns of all calibres had so long hurled their iron death upon those hills, and that a great part of it was the lyddite – upon the deadliness of which so much has been said and written – the Boer graves in the glades behind were not so numerous as one would have expected. If these operations can be taken as a fair example of the destructiveness of lyddite, the power of that explosive has been exaggerated. The Boers say that they can overcome its stifling fumes by a drink of vinegar, and whether that be so or not, I think the anticipations formed from the effects of lyddite upon the closely-packed and exposed masses of the Khalifa's spearmen have not at all been realized with the more tactful Boer. Our field artillery has been described as inaffective, and out of date, but bearing in mind the difficulties of getting batteries into range against the long-reaching Boer siege guns, our field batteries have, through all the hard fighting in Natal, done wonderful work. That they have been disastrously trapped at times was an almost inevitable consequence of the fact that, by comparison with slower-moving field guns of the enemy, they dared too much. Had their guns gone into the open as frequently in the teeth of our 4.7 guns as we did, when fully exposed to their heavier metal, the result would have been disastrous to the self-esteem of the Staats Artillery. Whether in taking a position or changing it cleverly under fire, the British field batteries have to my mind done wonders, and never shall I forget the coolness of their movements, or the destructiveness of their fire, as shown in the fight on Cæsar's Hill a few days after the New Year. The precision of their shrapnel then and on every other occasion where they have had a fair chance has been remarkable, and I feel sure to-day that the Boers have a much greater dread of the shrapnel than of the lauded lyddite. There was one incident of the artillery duel that day which has not been told in its proper place. While a battery was in action one of the gunners was wounded, and a reserve number went forward to take his place. The new man had finished his detail, and crouched with his left arm supporting his head and the elbow resting on his bent knee. The next shell from Long Tom struck the poor fellow just where the knee and elbow met, smashing both joints to a pulp. Hurled across the gun bleeding, dying it seemed, the indomitable gunner, looking to his startled comrades, said, "Lift me off the trail, boys, and get on with your work." A hurried amputation was necessary, and he was being taken to the hospital, with Father Ford, the chaplain of the

Imperial Light Horse, sitting in the ambulance beside him, when suddenly the tourniquet burst, and the poor fellow's lifeblood was pouring from him in spirts which promised a speedy death from loss of blood. Father Ford caught up the ends of the severed arteries between his finger's-end, and held them thus for an hour, until the hospital was reached. Even then it looked so hopeless with a double amputation that the surgeons only glanced at him at first, shook their heads, and passed on to men who had yet got a chance for life. Just then the poor gunner opened his eyes, and gasped, "Hurry up, doctor, please; she's beginning to hurt a bit." "I'll give him a chance," said the surgeon impulsively; "he deserves it." So the operator went to work, the resourceful priest still holding the severed arteries, and to-day that gunner, though having only one leg and one arm left, is alive and well. Only one man in a hundred is blessed with such a constitution as would have stood the strain of a double amputation. Poor fellow, let us hope that the path through life in future may be made easy for the one leg to travel.

For a country blighted and blasted by the passage and presence of hostile forces, the condition of the farmhouses passed between Ladysmith and the Tugela was strangely contradictory. Some were as peaceful and perfect as though the sounds of strife had never echoed amongst the hills. At many of the farms cocks were crowing cheerily in the morning, the cattle gathering by the milking kraals, smoke rising homelike from the chimneys, and the mealie-fields ripening all around. These were the homes of the Dutch farmers who have settled thickly on that side of Natal, and who knows but in many of them there was mourning for a father or a son who had gone with Louis Botha to the Tugela and had not come back. That blood was thicker than water, patriotism greater than policy, with many of these Dutch farmers, was shown by the number who retired with their flying countrymen, leaving their homes vacant, just as their English neighbours did before them, and thus admitting their complicity in the rebellion. Many of the better class of

English farms were used by the Dutch as hospitals, and the fumes of anaesthetics still clung about the rooms, in some of which we found wounded men who could not safely be moved, but will be well cared for in our hospitals. Other farmhouses vacated by their English owners had been wrecked and ruined, though in many cases where Englishmen decided to stay on their lands they found the enemy unexpectedly generous, and considering their loose organization, very obedient to the orders of their commandants. I met two young Englishmen, brothers, who had determined to stay at home and take their chances, and the treatment accorded them was almost quixotic in its generosity. They were at first offered the alternative of joining the Boer commandoes or going south to their own countrymen, but expressed an equally strong aversion to either fighting against their country or leaving their homes. They were therefore allowed to stay on their farm, with a warning that if found outside its boundaries they would be shot. Most of their cattle were taken, a span of oxen being left them, however, to put in their crops. "As long as the Ladysmith garrison holds out," explained one of the field-cornets, "we do not look upon this part of Natal as conquered territory. Therefore if any of our men molest you, tell them you have General Botha's permission to remain, and will complain to him of any misconduct." That threat was always sufficient. Even the most blustering of the Boers shrank into silence, as though under a discipline as severe as that of some of the continental armies. By and by the want of meat became to these two Englishmen a hardship, so they went down, argued the thing out with the commandants, and thereafter were regularly supplied with good rations.

The saddest thing in leaving Ladysmith was the parting with good comrades, who, at the eleventh hour, had gone down with fever. Dunn and Greenwood, two of the correspondents, had the bad luck to be smitten with enteric on the very eve of relief. When I said good-bye to my self-sacrificing fellow-countryman, Hornabrook, in the volunteer hospital, he had been sadly reduced by illness. Going south to recuperate, I had the good fortune to find comfortable quarters in the suburb of Newlands, a long-settled and picturesque hamlet just outside Cape Town. Pitched right under the shadow of Table Mountain, and in rich soil, it is difficult to realize, but for the multi-coloured peoples who inhabit it, that one is not resting in some old-fashioned English village. There are magnificent avenues of oaks, tall and far-spreading, which must be over a century old, and beside our younger Australian gums are springing up, and in height, at least, challenging their supremacy. The fruit-shops teem with splendid grapes, melons, and peaches, and a pleasanter spot in which to rest and recruit, after the horrors of the Ladysmith siege, could not well be found in all Africa. The great mountain, with its towering crags, dominates everything, and underneath it are the close-packed orchards, vineyards, and gardens, the flamboyants of the further north vying in colour with the earliest of the chrysanthemums and the porcelain blue of the late water-lilies. But the English oaks are a never-ending source of wonder and admiration, and give some idea of what our own Australian gardens will be in the years to come.

THE END

Richard Clay & Sons, Limited, London & Bungay.